Men Who Batter Women

It is estimated that as many as 40 per cent of men may be violent towards their partners. But what sort of men use physical violence against women? Do they have any identifying characteristics? How do they rationalise their behaviour, and what is their self-concept?

Most existing published work concentrates on the victim. Drawing on over ten years of clinical work at the Men's Centre in London, Adam Jukes examines the *perpetrators* of the abuse and the root of battering in the male personality. He recognises but challenges models of clinical intervention with violent men, and looks at motivation and the social construction of gender, arguing is part of the continuum of contempt which both men and patriarchal society have for women. He also isolates certain tendencies in these men which lead to abuse: for example, to feel threatened men's behaviour contravenes their expectations, and to assur naturally right. Most importantly, he explores be used to treat men who batter women and

Containing a wealth material and case studies, *Men Who Batter Women* is an important study of what has been established as a major social problem.

Adam Edward Jukes is a psychotherapist and group psychoanalyst in private practise in London.

Men Who Batter Women

Adam Edward Jukes

London and New York

First published 1999
by Routledge
11 New Fetter Lane, London EC4P 4EE

Simultaneously published in the USA and Canada
by Routledge
29 West 35th Street, New York, NY 10001

Routledge is an imprint of the Taylor & Francis Group

Reprinted 2000

Typeset in Times by Routledge
Printed and bound in Great Britain by TJ International Ltd, Padstow, Cornwall

British Library Cataloguing in Publication Data
A catalogue record for this book is available from the British Library

Library of Congress Cataloguing in Publication Data
Jukes, Adam Edward.
        Men Who Batter Women / Adam Edward Jukes.
        Includes bibliographical references and index.
        1. Abusive men – Psychology. 2. Abusive men – Counselling of.
        3. Wife abuse – Psychological aspects. 4. Abused women – Psychology.
        I. Title.
        HV6626.J84   1999   98–38319
        362.82′92–dc21   CIP

ISBN 0–415–12942–7 (hbk)
ISBN 0–415–04099–X (pbk)

This book is dedicated to Melinda and Elli for whom I finished it, and to the memory of my mother who would have thanked me

Contents

viii   *Contents*

Preface

There are many reasons for writing a book about men who are violently abusive to women they live with and also those who are abusive without being violent. Perhaps the most important is that I hope it will help the many women who are victims of this appalling crime, either directly by changing the behaviour of their attackers, or indirectly by influencing the development of effective social policies which aim to tackle the problem; something current policies fail woefully to do. I have already written a book about the theoretical understanding of male abuse which I have reached after ten years of working with abusers (Jukes 1993a). This present volume is intended to be more of a cookbook of practice, of use to clinicians who work with abusive men. My experience is that most of these 'clinicians' are not so at all, but social workers, probation officers and counsellors who have not had deep psychodynamic training. The definition of abuse we use is formed from a mindset which integrates many different frameworks, including the feminist, the psychoanalytic, the political and the sociological. In part, as this is a book about the psychology of abusive men and their treatment, one of its aims is to persuade practitioners to adopt this mindset. For that reason I have not attempted (with one exceptional chapter) to write a deeply academic book but one which is accessible and useful in such work. As such it will also be idiosyncratic in places, and discursive in others.

In *Why Men Hate Women* (ibid.) I attempted to develop a paradigm for understanding the worldwide oppression of women and in doing so to connect what are, *de jure*, normally regarded as aberrant male behaviours, such as wife battering or child rape, with the everyday, ordinary, socially syntonic behaviour of men towards women. In that book I argued that the differences between the extremes are quantitative only, not qualitative, and that there is a seamless connection between individual men's rationalisations of abusive behaviour and the political ideology of sexism – so that a rape victim who was 'provocatively' dressed is connected to 'they secretly want and like it'. Rather unsurprisingly, that view has received a fair amount of criticism. In part this book is an attempt to address that by setting out what I believe to be the differences between men who inflict physical and sexual violence on women and those who do not. However, it will also cover developments in my thinking and practice since I wrote *Why Men Hate Women* and address some of the criticisms of that work which have come from men working in the tradition of humanistic psychology and, to a lesser extent, socialist feminists. These are mainly to do with the way in which I present men's suffering derived from gender demands, the status of feelings and female passivity as it is represented in *Why Men Hate Women*. That book was an explicit attempt to present a way of modelling men's motives for abusing females in all the ways in which we do it, from flashing, to rape and murder. It gave, and asked, little quarter in its presentation of a way of thinking about abusive masculinity which was designed not to give an inch to men's rationalisations for dominating and subduing women. It reflected a central tenet of the clinical approach to abusiveness: that it is not possible to give an abuser any degrees of freedom to negotiate his behaviour. The same principle has been applied in this work.

In my early days of working with abusers, I was very much influenced by what might be called a humanistic framework, centralising men's suffering, gender role demands, early trauma etc. I could recount many vignettes which would explain why my position has changed. I hope one will be sufficient. I remember vividly one young man who had been in treatment for about eight months of weekly groups. He was something of a favourite in the group. He seemed to have undergone a radical change. He had experienced what seemed like genuine guilt and remorse, worked very hard to understand his behaviour and learnt new skills to repair the damage he had done to his partner and his marriage. After one group which seemed to reinforce this movement he went home, found his wife and children had left him and he made a serious suicide attempt. His wife had left a note saying that although she had been glad that he no longer physically attacked her, she could no longer take the level of emotional abuse he had been inflicting on her. She was simply too afraid for her sanity to stay with him. He was at a loss to understand what she meant. It transpired that he had been in total denial of his abusiveness. He believed that having abjured physical abuse his work was done and no other form of behaviour need be problematised.

Experiences such as this led us, at the Centre, to a position which is a difficult one for a psychotherapist – put simply it is that 'you can never trust an abuser'. This is not to say that they are insincere (although they often are) but that the denial is simply too strong and insidious to assume that you are getting the truth. One simply has to assume the worst, however difficult this is. Positive counter transference may be a very good sign that you are colluding with the abuser's denial and his continuing victimisation of his partner.

Some of my concerns with what I think of as the humanistic method of framing male abusiveness could not be better illustrated than by the comment made in a public debate with one representative of this strand of thinking, who worked at a counselling centre for abusers, at a Forensic Psychotherapy conference at the University of Brunel. The speaker began his address by telling the audience that the most important thing about working with abusers was 'to know where you're coming from'. Perhaps he felt he was adding to the exactness of the language, or redefining the counter-transference, but I was forcefully reminded of Rosen's work *Psychobabble* (1977). Not that concern for the suffering of abusers is irrelevant, quite the contrary if any significant long-term change is to be effected. However, the primary task is to stop the abuse. Addressing what the abuser presents as its underlying causes would involve honouring his account beyond any degree of clinical reasonableness and may be dangerous for his victims.

Perhaps I should also add a few words about the status of clinical knowledge. This book is intended primarily to help practitioners who have not had psychodynamic training. However, it should be clear that in spite of almost one hundred years of psychotherapeutic practice it does not seem that we are any nearer being able to make clear the connection between any particular technique of therapeutic intervention and its effect. We have a lot of ideas about the parts of the mind which are involved in therapeutic processes and change. We also know a great deal, in the abstract, about what it is about human psychic functioning which we are attempting to change – at least those of us who locate ourselves within theories of object relations. In addition we have to hand a wide variety of therapeutic techniques and potential therapeutic relations to offer to patients. In the final analysis, however, what we offer is an art form, an act of creation, not a scientific enterprise. For these reasons, many of which will be elaborated, what follows is a personal statement of my work. I believe that what I do is effective in stopping men from abusing women and children. Precisely why it does this I am not sure, however rationally I am able to present what I do. This will not prevent me from attempting to articulate what it is that I think works in my clinical practice. A caveat is important here. Whenever I read clinical texts I am amazed at the clarity of the writers in their analysis of the patients' material. The sheer brilliance of some analytic insights is sufficient to remind me of my motivations for doing this work. This certainty, this clarity, however, seems to contrast with the confusion and doubt with which I struggle daily. It is easy, in the comfort of the relation with the word processor, to have brilliant insights that are never communicated to the patient and which are, I believe, selected to make a particular theoretical point but have little bearing on the therapeutic process as it actually occurred. Such selection can give the impression of certainty in a situation where the important process was the struggle to make sense rather than the sense that was made – where striving to know (and sometimes failing) was more important than knowing. I will attempt to avoid that here by giving sufficient details of a history to enable the reader to construct a different narrative and speculate creatively about how they might have handled the same material.

I wish to make clear that this is not a book about violence. I am not at all sure that the academic distinction which is sometimes made between aggression and violence is not potentially damaging to women. Archer (1994), for example, is correct in his criticism of the Conflict Tactics Scale (CTS) test which is often used to measure aggressive behaviour in relationships, his main critique being that the measure is a gender neutral one of aggressive behaviour, whereas it is quite clear that acts of aggression by women on men cannot be equated with similar acts by men on women, the latter being much more likely to result in serious physical and psychological damage. He argues that it is essential to differentiate between aggression, which is a behavioural definition and not concerned with consequences, and violence which is concerned with the consequences. Another distinction which academics and practitioners draw is between aggression and violence which is hostile and that which is instrumental. The former is defined as being inflicted with the intention to cause pain, the latter to achieve something else with the pain as a means to that end. As I will demonstrate with case material, this is hardly a meaningful distinction for the women who are on the receiving end of aggression, whether or not it meets the criterion of being violent. Additionally, it is crystal clear to me that all of the over 1,000 men with whom I have worked and who have physically attacked their female partners have mixed motives at the time of the attack. Instrumentality is clear. Even if they are not immediately able to articulate their objectives, it takes little work to elicit them later. However, in my opinion, in every case the desire to inflict pain and punishment was also present, as was satisfaction in so doing. That they resist this knowledge, as we shall see, is hardly surprising. It requires a major review of the self-concept to discover that the sadist is not 'him over there' but 'me over here'. Not all academic psychologists are so taken with the firm distinction between instrumental and hostile or sadistic aggression. Howells (in Archer and Browne 1989, p. 156) acknowledges the need for further research to discover the prevalence of mixed motive aggression. The treatment implications of accurate differential diagnosis are important so far as violence in general is concerned, but not in my opinion when we are treating batterers or wife abusers. As we shall see a further difficulty arises in suggestions for treatment of violent individuals who are diagnosed as instrumentally aggressive.

A major weakness of academic and indeed psychoanalytic psychology is that anger is often taken as the starting point of inquiry, it is seen as being the irreducible cause of aggressive behaviour. For example, Howells again 'research into...violence suggests that anger is a common antecedent' and he promotes the idea of anger arousal as being helpful in understanding violent acts. From this point of view an understanding of the determinants of anger and people's perceptions of them (triggers) can help in reducing aggressive behaviour. Actually it is not quite true that anger is a common antecedent of violence. What research reveals is that people commonly report anger as an antecedent and they may well have motives for so doing which are more existential than physiological. I would suggest, as you will see, that self-deception about one's motives for acting anti-socially is more commonplace than antecedent anger. Anger, from my understanding, which admittedly places the commonsense cart before the horse, is actually more of a way of rationalising anti-social or sadistic behaviour than a cause of it. The frustration/aggression hypothesis dies hard in academic psychology in spite of the fact that if one takes a large sample of wife batterers, they all (with the exception of a small two per cent), show ample evidence of a capacity for reacting creatively to frustration without violence or even overtly aggressive behaviour. This should not be taken to mean that frustration is not a significant factor in men's abuse of women. On the contrary, it is essential that we understand that it has a central role. However, my experience is that men, including non-abusers, are deeply frustrated most of the time, and that this is implicated in most violent criminality. Abusers' 'triggers' simply evoke this frustration and evoke responses which are out of all proportion to the provocation but are consonant with the intensity of the underlying frustration. Much of this book is an attempt to elaborate the origins of this frustration and to outline its treatment. Far too often, subjective accounts of violent behaviour are attempts to negotiate a non-deviant identity and manage the self-image and should not be taken at face value. People's accounts are more concerned with making a case and presenting themselves to the listener in a way which strives for coherence and narrative integrity. Such considerations raise interesting questions concerning not only the subjective experience of anger, but also the nature of its weak physiological components and, perhaps more importantly, its psychological origins.

Some of what I say here will cause distress to those men who are happy with traditionally organised family structures in which the man is dominant and who are either unaware of feminist thinking or dismissive of it. There are many men who believe that a return to such traditional structures would mitigate against the decline in modern marriage, a decline often attributed to feminist proselytising and successes during the past 30 years. I am reminded of a comment attributed to the well known analyst, family therapist Robin Skinner. He is reported to have said that American researchers were suppressing findings that families in which the man was dominant were more functional and happier than those in which women and men strived for egality. Their motives for so doing were, he is quoted as believing, that they were afraid of the feminist academic reaction and of accusations of sexism. My response to these researchers (although more likely to the journalist, misquotation being the nature of the beast) is that there is no doubt whatever in my mind that plantations ran much better when slavery was commonplace and the slaves were unprotesting rather than struggling against their subjection. In fact plantations could not have existed without slavery. I am sure South Africa was a much better place for the whites when the blacks knew their place. It sounds ridiculous, doesn't it, to compare women's place with that of oppressed blacks? In spite of this, I would hate to be thought a wolf in sheep's clothing. I have no doubt that the men in such marriages or relationships are happier. I am sure that the creature comforts provided by such an oppressive relationship, if indeed it is experienced as such by the woman, far outweigh any threats posed to the feeble or non-existent gender consciousness of the men themselves. I am only too well aware of the parts of me which would value highly such a relationship! Such a perspective also contains a model of relationships which is in itself oppressive – a model of non-conflicted relating as healthy. In fact, my experience is that nothing could be further from the truth. I believe that truly healthy relationships are characterised by a continuous cycle of disruption and reparation. Non-conflicted relationships are symptomatic of compliance and adaptation, the denial of separateness, individuality and desire.

Perhaps this is also the place to say something about the place of violence in abusive relationships. As will become clear, this seems to me to be simply the most easily defined and visible form of abuse. In work with abusers it is interpreted to them as the abuse they use when all other techniques for getting control of their partner fail. But why do men want to control their partners? All these methods are directed at the same goals: to get immediate satisfaction and to ensure future compliance. Apart from the treatment of abusiveness, the motivation for and the methods used to achieve and maintain power and control are the principal themes of this book. These other methods include verbal attacks, emotional abuse, humiliation and of course, threats of violence. Actual violence has a particularly important place in the repertoire of abuse. Instilling in the woman the fear of it is intended to ensure that its use is not necessary. However, this usually requires its use at some point in the relationship to impress that future threat is not empty. In order to maintain it, power must sometimes be used.

Adam Jukes
September 1998

Acknowledgements

This book has been in the making for nine years and as is usual at this stage of writing I become aware of all the people without whom it would not have been possible. Firstly, my thanks to the succession of editors at Routledge who have kept faith during those times when the manuscript on my desk became a persecutor. Thanks also to my researcher Shoshana Garfield, to whom I owe much of Chapter 2, and to the many friends with whom I discussed my ideas over the years. Particular gratitude is owed to Bernadette Wren of the Portman Clinic whose encouragement and wise reading of the draft did much to ensure its completion, and to Marie Maguire for her informed commentary and suggestions. The friendship and support of Christopher Scanlon and Michael Maher has been invaluable. My thanks also to Lionel Kreeger of the Institute of Group Analysis who, it could be said, has been the midwife for what follows. Although these and many others have some responsibility for the fact of its existence, the contents of this book are entirely my responsibility.

Finally, thanks go to all those men in these pages who gave their trust to me and from whom I have learned so much.

Portions of this book have appeared previously in the journal *Free Associations* (see Jukes 1993b, 1994). I would like to thank the editor, Bob Young, for permission to reproduce this material in the present volume.

1 Introduction

I had intended to subtitle this book 'Living in the bubble' to reflect what I see as a basic element of the personality structure of men who abuse women – or indeed of the many men who commit violent crimes against other people. Even now, after more than five years of working with the 'bubble' as an operational concept of significant clinical value, it becomes difficult to define in a way which encapsulates all its nuances. That it derives from women's understanding of chauvinism and the ideology of sexism and psychoanalytic thinking about narcissism and dissociation will become clear. I will begin this study with some simple examples which illustrate what it means to work with a man who is in a bubble. A great deal of the remainder of this book will be an attempt to elaborate and explain its origins and its praxis.

'She has no voice and cannot speak.' Anyone familiar with recent developments in psychoanalysis, particularly the French variety, will know what this means. For the uninitiated it refers to a complex set of discourses about the construction of femininity and masculinity and the way these are understood by the psychoanalytic community. As I understand it, the phrase itself, first used by the psychoanalyst Lacan, means that since women never enter the symbolic order begun by the little boy's initiation into the social world through his identification with the father (who is outside the child's relations to the mother) which takes him away from the 'imaginary' realm of the relation with the mother, she is in effect denied her entry into language. I am aware that it gives great pleasure to write in an obfuscating and esoteric way about the mist of gender, and for a man, even one publicly committed to the loosening of the categories, it is strangely reassuring to read Lacan's accounts of femininity. His text has the effect of bolstering my maleness, not undermining it. Could it be that he himself, in writing from within the categories, as a man, and in his attempt to reposition the masculine in psychoanalytic theory and practice, actually was more invested in reinforcing than subverting them?

Although it is not the central aim of this book, it is germane to its main theme to try to understand what is the significance of women's muteness for ordinary women in their relations with men. Let me give a few simple non-esoteric examples of how I believe it works in practice. These case studies have another purpose. They are intended to introduce the reader into the idea of what I call bubble perceptions, that for an abusive man there is only one reality and it is 'here, behind *my* eyes'.

The first concerns a man who attended, two years ago, a three day long workshop I conducted on the subjects of male aggression and sexuality. He had been in therapy with another man for about three years and during that time had been abusing his wife, mainly emotionally and verbally, but also on occasion, violently. She was very angry with him about his abusiveness and his therapy was having little effect on his behaviour. He began by saying that he was out of control when he acted abusively but we succeeded in confronting his denial to the point where he acknowledged that his behaviour was decisive and instrumental. Subsequently, on the first day, actually within a suspiciously short time, he managed to make public a decision to give up his abuse. The next day he reported how when he had informed his partner of his decision she had become very angry rather than grateful as he expected. Apparently she had said that it was typical of his lack of respect for her that he should spend one day with a powerful man and make such a decision when she had been saying the same things to him for years, fruitlessly. She had said that it simply underlined the seriousness of the problem that he should ignore her for so long and yet be so influenced by me.

Is it that she had no voice or that he could not listen? Is there any difference? Are women mute or men deaf? I could multiply this example a thousand-fold and each story would be the same: that the men I work with, and they are apparently no different from other men, do not listen to their partners. This deafness does not simply apply to the problems in the relationship identified by the woman, it applies to their politics, their sexuality, their careers, their everyday concerns – in fact seemingly to everything that goes on in women's heads.

The second example concerns me. It illustrates what I believe is an abiding concern to all men, that of the fear of woman's separateness. It occurred when I was travelling on an underground train from Heathrow airport to central London. It was a beautiful sunny day. In the carriage was a group of eight French women all aged around 35. The carriage was full of their luggage and they were clearly about to begin their holiday. A quick glance confirmed a thought that they were all married, or at least wearing wedding rings. Why did I look for this evidence? Was it my chauvinism, my need to confirm that they were safely possessed? Thinking about it at the time I realised it was because they were so happy. They talked non-stop in a very animated fashion, the conversation being picked up and handed on freely (in a way which I believe is impossible for men), with much laughter and physical contact. I speak only school French and was excluded from the conversation, if not from the wonderful energy and pleasure they shared with the whole carriage. I was thinking 'is this what it is like to have no voice?'. The happiness is important. It led me to thinking about their supposed muteness. Perhaps, I thought, nobody has told them that they have no voice. Also, the absence of men struck me as crucial. I had the feeling that I know many men have in such circumstances, that women share a secret language from which men are not simply excluded but simply cannot learn, that we are constitutionally incapable of learning. Of course it is our anatomy which excludes us, even when we are driven to desperate measures such as cross-dressing or masochism. The language is not a language of men, the symbolic of the social order or Law, it is a language *about* men, predicated on women's shared and intimate knowledge about us, the contradictions, the frailty, our bullying, our insecurities, our fractured selves. It saddened me, this awareness, not only because of my exclusion, and the knowledge that any attempt to include myself would lead to these women changing tongues (not simply from one language to another, but the switch to a tongue which they know is the only one men can communicate in), but also that they can never speak it with men. The presence of men makes women mute, silences their voice, forces the use of the secondary, ordered symbolic. I believe also that it is the voice of 'jouissance', a voice of joy and of openness, rhythm and flow. This is why I looked for the wedding rings, which they all wore. Their voices seemed to me to be the voices of the newly released prisoner, anticipating the denied pleasure to come, the desire acknowledged, the voice heard.

The question which is still with me is to what extent this is predicated on, actually needs the deaf man to exist. I have to believe this, if only because of my firm commitment to the social construction of gender. What this means is that I am committed to the notion that there is nothing innate, that the categories masculine and feminine are a forced division of dubious evolutionary status which now have the effect of bestowing legitimacy on forms of behaviour which might otherwise be highly questionable. I do not believe that there is an innate sense that we belong to either category.

Another case history illustrates everything that this book is about. In particular it illustrates how 'reaction formation', in this case compulsive helpfulness, can be used to defend against very violent and aggressive feelings and impulses. As usual the man functioned without any awareness at all of its underlying motivation. His true motives were neatly encapsulated and denied, but broke through with regular ferocity. The nature of the bubble is illustrated sharply here. It concerns a successful entrepreneur in his late thirties who was referred to me by a psychiatrist with whom he had sought a consultation. In recent months he had physically attacked his wife of ten years when they had been arguing. The argument had gone on most of the evening and he had eventually fallen asleep on the bed. He woke to find her leaning over him and shouting, apparently continuing the argument. He had grabbed her by the throat and, choking her, had pushed her upwards against the wall whilst lifting her by the neck. During our first consultation he informed me that this was his second marriage and that he had broken his first wife's cheekbone with a blow from his fist. His account was long and difficult to follow. It was clear that he and his present wife were tearing each other apart emotionally and that this was not his first attack on her. The relationship was the worst possible mixture of projective and introjective indentifications with all the boundary confusions one might expect. They had been in each other's company, virtually exclusively, for the whole of their relationship to the point where his various businesses were suffering financially from inadequate management and supervision. She had finally left him after this last attack and he came to me in a state of great confusion. His account was that if she were less aggressive and argumentative they could have a good relationship.

His background is quite disturbed. It involves a lot of loss of significant others during the first two years, including father and a second mother figure. Later his stepfather had him sent to boarding school with his mother's collusion because the stepfather could not tolerate his presence and consistently humiliated and rejected him. The patient hated his present relationship but was completely unable to end it, as apparently was she. He insisted he was in love with her in spite of everything. He described how when he had met her that she had been very depressed and he had taken it on himself to cure her. After a short time, during which she pursued him obsessively (this was typical of his denial during his early sessions), he fell in love with her and left his then live-in partner to be with her. As he put it, she became his 'project', his aim being to make her happy. He began to devote enormous amounts of time and energy to lifting her depression and raising her self-esteem. Apparently her depression lifted and she became increasingly involved in his business affairs, initially at her insistence, according to him. However, she failed to carry out her responsibilities and his businesses began to suffer. Seemingly, her depression made way for a great deal of undifferentiated anger and employees and colleagues began to experience difficulties with her. Their relationship deteriorated and they spent much of their time quarrelling, with him becoming increasingly violent and abusive. He acknowledged that he had become very disappointed when she had not become the happy person he wanted her to be. He was able to see that his expectations of her had changed substantially and that he had ceased to provide her with the degree or quality of support with which he had begun the relationship.

On the face of it he had a strong case for her being the cause of most of the problems in the relationship. The picture he painted was grim. She had upset most of his colleagues and employees, failed to present business accounts and consequently got him into legal trouble, constantly criticised him and generally blamed him for the sorry state of their relationship and her moods. He was obsessional in the detail with which he presented her shortcomings. His resentment of her failure to appreciate his efforts on her behalf and to provide him with the love he had never had was overwhelming. Surprisingly, he was completely unaware of this until I pointed it out. By this point in the relationship he was almost incapable of conversing with her without getting angry, and in very short order. He interpreted everything she did or said from the most negative perspective possible and was convinced she consciously wished to ruin him. It was very difficult for him to focus on his difficulties in the relationship, particularly his violent and abusive behaviour. Instead he constantly recounted her shortcomings and the catalogue of ways in which she failed him or hurt him. I cannot portray the intensity with which he did this. He was clearly very hurt and disappointed by her behaviour. When I asked him if he was as judgmental with her as he was about her in my presence, he smiled ruefully and agreed that was so. He then had no difficulty in seeing that even discounting his violence this might go a long way to explaining why she was so angry and 'aggressive'. His initial denial of any contribution to the problems in the relationship began to give way as I consistently and firmly challenged his preoccupation with her behaviour. I had already informed him of my working hypothesis and he had agreed to follow it in a spirit of experimentation. Put simply it is that since his partner was not present and we were powerless to change her, we should assume (ridiculous as it is) that he was 100 per cent responsible for any problems between them and try to understand how he was creating them. He seemed to rather enjoy the intellectual challenge this provided. For example, when he talked about how angry she seemed, I reminded him of *his* violence and asked him how often he was angry with her. It emerged that angry feelings were the only ones he expressed to her. She had never seen any of his anxiety (which was plentiful) or his sadness and grief which were profound. He had been incapable of thinking about why she might be the way she was, other than in pathological terms of her being sick or crazy (with which all his colleagues agreed). The fact is that since they began the relationship his agenda was the only one they had followed. She had fitted into his life completely. He had made no allowances for any of her desires except to be with him. He had sacrificed nothing. These ways of thinking about the past were a revelation to him. They opened his eyes to the narrowness of his perceptions and the fact that he actually knew very little about her because he had always assumed that she was an extension of him, wanted what he wanted, felt what he felt, believed what he believed etc. The only voice she had (and here we might ask questions of her which may be relevant) was the voice of her anger and frustration, a voice to which he was completely deaf.

The similarity with the first example may be clear – his inability to see the world through her eyes. Actually, this is a major developmental failure suffered by the vast majority of men I see. It is the failure to have developed the notion that other people have minds and mental states of their own – usually indicative of failure in early relationship with primary caregivers (Marrone 1998, p. 69). Helping men to develop this capacity is a major goal of treatment.

The next case history illustrates how this developmental lack, coupled with normal male chauvinism and abusive behaviour can place a woman in a situation where the only way she can be sane is to define herself as mad. The client is a middle aged accountant who will also appear later in a different context. Briefly, he had been abusing his partner in a variety of ways, most seriously by conducting a secret affair for many years. She had long suspected and finally found irrefutable proof with which she confronted him. He steadfastly maintained his denial and told her she was imagining things. She refused to desist and he began to violently abuse her. This went on for some months before he finally came to me. By that time she was feeling suicidal. He attended an anti-abuse programme and had not been abusive since he began. They had in fact spent a great deal of time discussing his behaviour and its painful consequences for her. He had felt genuine remorse and guilt about the suffering he had caused her. After about two months into the programme he told of having abused her again by banging a table and approaching her with violent intent. He had seen the fear in her face and stopped, apologised and informed her that he needed to take 'Time Out' (an anger management technique) to think about what he was doing. He had banged the table after she had become angry with him when another of a long running series of consequences of his affair had come to light and she became angry and confronted him. This happened frequently, as one might expect. The issue he wished to talk about in the group was his '...desire to move forward in the relationship and her constant need to look backward'. As he put it, he was struggling with coming to terms with his past abuse and his almost obsessive need to control her and he could not understand why she insisted on raking over his past misdeeds.

Sounds reasonable doesn't it? And he is the very epitome of reasonableness (see Seidler 1994). This is a perfect example of bubble behaviour, a combination of blind egotism, selfishness and narcissism where it is assumed that there is only one point from which to view reality and it is 'here, behind my eyes'. He has actually assumed the moral high ground in a way which is socially syntonic. We all know that it is good to want to move forward in relationships don't we? We all know that raking over unhappy experiences is bad and can have destructive consequences don't we? As he innocently asked 'If she really wanted the relationship to succeed why does she behave in this way? I'm doing everything I can to listen to her and not be controlling.' At various points in the narrative, other men in the group were nodding vigorously. Many of them had the same difficulty. Perhaps the reader can anticipate my analysis of this event. The most striking thing about it, and there are many, is his assumption that he knows not only what constitutes moving forward, but that he also knows the best way to do so. She, meanwhile, is misled, destructive, rather insensitive and stupid not to be able to see the sense in his analysis of the situation. Her way of proceeding, or being in the relationship, is not moving forward at all, but regressive. He does not think he is elevating himself into a superior position, implicitly showing contempt for her or discounting her feelings and thoughts or needs. He believes he is simply being reasonable and concerned for what is best for both of them. He fails to see why she does not agree with him. My comment on hearing all this was 'why is it that her insistence on talking about her pain and your abuse is not a way of moving forward? How come what you want is the only way to move forward and that you are the only one who knows what is needed for that?' The effect of this remark on this unusually laconic, passive man, was dramatic. His mouth dropped open. 'I'm astonished', he said, 'I simply had never thought of it in that way.' It was clear to me that his astonishment was genuine. It was as if another reality, whose existence he had never suspected, had been revealed to him. It was like a deaf person being given hearing for the first time. For a moment his cognitive bubble had been broken. He saw a reality at right angles to the one he had always assumed was the only one – HIS. However, one should not be deceived into believing that this insight would have shattering permanent consequences. Experiences of this sort are common with abusive men. As in analysis they have to happen many times and be worked through from different perspectives and situations before the penny finally drops and a permanent change occurs.

The next example comes from work with a man who is not in an anti-abuse programme but ongoing twice-weekly analytic therapy. It illustrates how men who would not ordinarily be defined as abusers also suffer from the same problems and that there is a connection between ordinary maleness and abusiveness. He is a professional in his late thirties married to a woman with two teenage daughters from a previous marriage. He has spent over two years complaining about his marriage and her behaviour. To say the least she has a Mediterranean personality compared with our rather repressed, inhibited and ironical Britishness. His difficulties in living with her were considerable. Over the years he had tired of what he saw as her tantrums. As far as I could tell, these 'tantrums' were inspired first by his fear of intimacy and general lack of loving warmth, and finally by his punishment of her because of his resentment at her emotional ability, the typical sort of system one sees in couples with problems. This particular example comes from a time when he had been in treatment for about two years. He started his session with a sigh as he sank onto the couch and began his routine catalogue of her recent misdeeds. Work with him was particularly difficult. He is a concrete thinker and obsessed with his partner's behaviour towards him. Although I am going to give a particular example, I want to make clear that the whole context of it, his relation to her and his way of thinking about them could as well be used to illustrate my point. He had returned late from work, that is at a time later than he had told her he would return. She had been very angry with him for not phoning and letting her know that he would not be there when they had agreed. In fact he had stopped off on his way home to carry out a job for a customer, and it had taken him nearly two hours. I should mention that he has a mobile phone. He was incensed by her behaviour. She had told him, 'your dinner's in the dog!!'. She had shouted and yelled about his thoughtlessness, his insensitivity and general lack of care for her. He was particularly angry that she did not understand that his work was of primary importance and paid the bills, put the food on the table etc., and that he hated doing it but had to. This is nonsense, he loves his work and would hate to have her life where she effectively sits at home all day waiting for him to come home. He is her life, and he would not, at that time, have had it any other way. He is highly paid, powerful, active and respected. 'Don't get me wrong' he said, 'I know that I should have phoned, but her behaviour is completely crazy and over the top.' Her 'hysteria' was a constant thread in his accounts of their life together.

I know that this is a rather gross example, as I am sure that anyone reading it will readily say that he was in the wrong (although right and wrong are not the point here and have no place in any relationship, a point I will address later). He himself could see that he had not behaved responsibly. What preoccupied him though was her 'hysterical' response to his behaviour. It emerged that when she confronted him, rather than apologising he had become defensive and aggressive, finally withdrawing into another room 'to avoid her persecution'. Actually his unconscious motive was to protect her from the desire to be violent which he felt at that moment. He had so far managed to restrain his physical abusiveness, although his verbal behaviour could be very aggressive and abusive. He had gone into a sulk and was still in it when he saw me. One could, and of course we did later, analyse his neglect of her. When I asked him why he had not simply apologised he replied that she had no right to treat him in that way, that if she had approached him 'more reasonably' it would never have blown up out of proportion. An important piece of information about this man is that he first came to me for treatment because of his rage with his partner and *his* frequent angry outbursts towards her.

You can see that he assumes many rights in the relationship. First he retains the right to define the reasonableness and appropriateness of behaviour (actually only hers) in the relationship. He never questions the appropriateness of his behaviour, he simply assumes that everything he does is okay. Overall he assumes the right to define reality, to say what is important and unimportant. He never questions that this is his fundamental right, as a man. One of his constant complaints about her was that she was always interfering with his right to work, or to pursue his interests which are many and varied. He felt very misunderstood and unjustly treated because, as he put it, 'I never interfere with what she wants to do, I always encourage her to see her friends or follow her interests but she wants to stop me from doing what I want'. I asked him how often he was encouraging of her when she suggested that they do something together which conflicted with his own interests. There was a long silence. Finally he said quietly, 'almost never'. From the discussion which followed he came to see that his encouragement was always for her to pursue the interests she had *outside the relationship*. He was unable to see how this was deeply rejecting of her, an attack on the relationship, and a source of real pain and anger. Basically he had no concept of partnership or relationship. She was emotionally more mature and had the capacity to include the concept of the 'couple' in her frame of reference. His was that of a child who was living with a maternal figure who should adapt to his needs and be prepared to be an object when he had no need of her. This is a common problem for men and the source of much abusive behaviour.

My next example illustrates how severe the dissociation of the bubble can be. It concerns a young man, married, aged 30, with a five year old stepdaughter. He had been in treatment for only two months and was regularly reporting the significant differences in his behaviour, particularly and worryingly his love for, and treatment of, his stepdaughter. His marriage was 'good for the first time in two years' and he had 'hardly abused at all'. I have written elsewhere of the honeymoon period and will do so again later. In spite of repeated challenges to his perception of the situation, in particular his own behaviour towards his wife and stepdaughter, he maintained that things were just as he reported them. I did not then nor do I now doubt his sincerity – he was convinced that he was telling the truth and indeed he was: his own. However, what I was being told simultaneously by his partner about his behaviour was so at odds that it is almost impossible to understand how they could be sharing the same space. Her account was that he had stopped abusing her for about two weeks after his first consultation but had then resumed his former treatment of her. Her daughter was crying at school and had told a teacher that she was afraid because 'daddy is always shouting at mummy'. I did not confront my client with this knowledge but continually and unsuccessfully challenged his perceptions by asking for details of his routine contact with his partner. Eventually I had to cease his treatment and inform his partner that I had done so. His denial was simply too intense and the risks to her safety and the physical integrity of her daughter, too great to continue to collude. So long as he remained in treatment she was encouraged to believe that he would change and my judgement was that this was unlikely without her being seriously damaged during the process.

My final example concerns Lou, a man of West Indian origin in his early forties. He is university educated as an electronics engineer. His story illustrates, I believe, the importance of previous clinical training and good diagnostic skills for those working with abusers. He presented in a state of great distress. He was living apart from his wife of three years with whom he has a two year old son. When Lou was born his parents had given him over to his maternal grandmother to raise. They had come to England looking for work in the great rush of immigration in the 1950s. When he was six they had sent for him and he had arrived in England to meet these two strangers. Meanwhile they had produced two children. He joined them and the five of them took up residence in one rented room in the centre of London. He describes his mother as being possessed of a fearsome temper (hardly surprising in the circumstances) and as frequently threatening him with a beating when his father got home, a promise his father usually carried out. Lou had married in his early twenties and in 14 years had two children. He had begun an affair and made his mistress pregnant. His wife became violent with him when he attempted to leave and gashed his forehead with a bottle causing a wound requiring six stitches. He moved in with his lover but was unable to tolerate it after six months. He told her he was going to leave and she attacked him without causing any physical damage. After moving out, but while his relationship was still ongoing, he met a social worker, also of West Indian origin, who already had four children, all in their late teens, from two previous marriages. It seemed they had much in common and although he was not in love with her asked her to marry him in the belief that he would grow to love her. They married and bought a house. Within six months he was finding the situation intolerable. He was working all hours to earn enough to support his three children and meet his responsibilities to his new family. He told how there was never food in the house, Betty never had a meal ready for him when he arrived, the children were always watching TV and he could not see what he wanted and the house was always full of strangers. Apparently his wife Betty was very sociable and popular and as he put it 'always had guests in the house'. The truth, which he admitted when pressed, was that there would be one or two of her colleagues or friends at home two or three evenings a week when he came home from work. In any case he acknowledged that her sociability was one of the qualities he had married her for, as he felt he had lived a very isolated and withdrawn life prior to meeting her. He raised his complaints with her and found her uncomprehending. Fairly soon after moving in he had taken to going up to their room alone on returning from work, with a second television, and effectively sulking. After 11 months they had a huge row during the course of which she 'attacked him' and told him to get out. He took her at her word and more. He went to stay with the mother of his third child. During the first night Betty turned up at his lover's home and caused fairly serious damage to the body of his car which was parked outside. He stayed with this girlfriend for two weeks during which time she became pregnant again. After those two weeks he moved back to the marital home in an attempt at reconciliation. Shortly afterwards they heard the news that his girlfriend was pregnant. According to him, his wife then became pregnant without his consent because she was so upset at his fathering a child with his girlfriend.

Unfortunately the difficulties continued, with him sulking more, becoming more withdrawn and finally moving out into what he described as a squalid studio flat. This long story emerged during his assessment. At that time he was still living apart from Betty. Other relevant information is that both his parents had died within the past two years and it was clear that he had failed to mourn them. When I asked him about why it was that all the women in his life 'attacked him' he smiled and said he did not know. He disclosed, however, that he had been a professional boxer for a few years after graduating from university. His immediate reason for seeing me was that a few weeks previously he had been drinking with his brother who had said, on hearing the story above, that he, the brother, would not put up with such treatment and would show her who was the boss. Lou had gone to the house in a semi-drunken state and attacked Betty. He was arrested but released without charge (Betty would not press charges) after a few hours. Why, I enquired, was he here? What did he want from me? It seemed clear from his account (whose object, as I will show later, is the negotiation of a non-deviant identity) that he felt innocent of any culpability in the events he described. At every step of the way, sometimes tearfully, he described his innocence and his strong sense of the injustice which was being inflicted on him. It seemed to me that what he was asking for was absolution from me, as if I were some kind of judge. His response was that he did not understand why, when he was such a good person who worked his fingers to the bone to meet his responsibilities, women got so angry with him and why he could not build a secure, stable relationship. His marriage was not yet over, he would like to save it but did not know where to begin.

I liked Lou from the first. He is a mild mannered, softly spoken man with an infectious sense of humour. What was so striking was his complete inability to modify his account with anything which might accommodate the stories of any of the women he has impregnated. His world view is utterly androcentric. He told of how he always bought flowers for his partners, was a 'listening ear', a kind of agony aunt, supplying understanding on tap, did housework, cooking, babysitting etc. To hear it, he had always been a saint, but his martyrdom was apparent also. Not that I doubted his veracity for a moment. My problem was to account for his difficulties in a way which accommodated this saintliness even in modified form. Once he entered an anti-abuse programme he showed his resistance to any attempt to modify his self-perception. Every confrontation earned a quick, although gently expressed riposte. He quickly drove the other group members to a state of frustrated exasperation, much to his bewilderment. When he was asked if his behaviour was the same with his partners he agreed. However, he failed to see not only what was wrong with it, but that even if there was something wrong, how that was relevant when he did so much to 'keep his women happy and look after his kids'. He was unable to focus on the fact that he had physically violated every woman he had lived with, and insisted that sexual infidelity was culturally syntonic for West Indians, 'all my friends are like that', he insisted. In fact he told how one of his closest friends had seven children with seven women and none of them closed the door in his face whatever hour of the day or night he turned up. This story, told with much smiling, clearly cheered him up but he denied he wanted that kind of life for himself. He insisted he did not want to repeat the same pattern for the rest of his life and wanted to try to save his marriage. He cried as he talked of feeling totally deprived of love and affection by all his partners and that they had always exploited his generosity leaving him depleted and unhappy. He was sick of 'giving and giving and giving' and getting nothing in return.

I realise that his story illustrates many of the dilemmas of post-modern men (and, clinically, the dilemmas of many depressive adults who have suffered an early and traumatic loss and develop all the defences we see so clearly in Lou), particularly the 'male suffering' so dear to that strand of that men's movement derived from the quick cure, feeling oriented 1970s. In the conclusions to this book I will address the issues concerning the struggles of men to cope with the demands of masculinity. My point in Lou's story is rather different at the moment, and it illustrates one of the most important issues in successfully working with abusive men, their inability to relate when their partners become angry. To the benefit of all the men in his programme, Lou came to see, with some shock, that his compulsive behaviour of pleasing women was actually an attempt to prevent them from becoming angry. He simply could not tolerate women's anger because it evoked in him the most frightening feelings of violence and hatred. When his attempts to control them with kindness failed he would act abusively and violently to prevent what he felt to be the attacks on him. All anger from a woman represented a massive threatening attack. He was able to learn that it is not possible to prevent anyone from becoming angry and to begin to learn how to deal with his problem in a different way.

The most striking thing about these examples is the seeming impossibility of men being able to suspend their subjectivity and position themselves as objects in relation to women's desire (see Frosh 1994, pp. 3–6). In simple terms what this means is that we are unable to recognise that women are people, equal to us, with their minds and mental states, needs, wants and desires that are as important to them as are ours to us. This is what I mean by 'living in the bubble'. Every abusive attack I have heard about occurs when women, either passively or actively express needs or wants or fail to demonstrate that they are positioned response-ably, waiting, expectant, to their male partner. It is not necessary that female desires be in conflict with men's desires. It is enough that they are expressed. Not being response-ably positioned, waiting expectantly for a male desire, or indeed anticipating it, is expressive of a woman's desire to be subject, agent of her own desire. This is enough to trigger abusive controlling behaviour from a man. The development of the capacity to be responsive to women's desires is one essential pre-condition of men's giving up abusive behaviour. It goes further than the necessity to position oneself in relation to women's desire. The need is to learn to position oneself as object to woman as subject. In large part this book is about men's failure to do this. In fact what I want to do here is to examine whether it is possible for a man to do so without losing what he feels is quintessentially male about himself. Apart from any difficulties this presents to men, given the nature of masculinity, it also presents difficulties insofar as it is seemingly very difficult for women to define their desires.

Family and marital therapy literature is full of examples of a particular desire of women. In the case of the pursuer wife and distancer husband, now almost a cliche, the woman's desire is to be the object of the man's desire and to establish intimacy. Women generally have two goals in a relationship, to be intimate and to avoid conflict. Actually, men have the same goals but prioritise conflict avoidance whereas the woman prioritises intimacy (Markman *et al.* 1994). Her increasingly frustrated and angry pursuit will often evoke the sort of violent, abusive response with which I work. I believe (like Benjamin's 'Does a woman want?', 1990, rather than Freud's 'What does a woman want?') we are entitled to ask whether her desire is desire at all; and if not, what does it represent? This is a difficult issue for me personally as well as a clinician working with abusers. Where can I position myself? I have acknowledged that as a man I am prone to the same sorts of behaviour as the men with whom I work. Frosh (op. cit.) wonders if he is posturing when he acknowledges 'the links between masculinity and abusiveness', and whether 'the act of acknowledgement functions to free men from the responsibility for actually becoming different'. Do I, by acknowledging my gender, therefore disclaim any responsibility for changing whilst implicating myself in the processes which create and maintain a masculinity which is predicated on domination?

In working with abusers these issues are real and alive. From what position do I confront and attempt to change male behaviour when it is impossible to strip myself of my gender and can only act from within it, a gender which I have defined as inherently abusive? Do I have to abuse, dominate, in order to initiate change in my clients? Given that I believe (see Jukes 1993b) it is impossible for them to relate from outside a sadomasochistic frame, is there a way in which I can function without being in the same frame? Can I be a male therapist who repudiates certain elements of masculinity without repudiating what is also creatively different about maleness and furthermore makes me what I am, a man? How is my masculinity important in the work I do with abusers? Does it make any difference, add to or subtract from my effectiveness? Frosh makes the point that in work of this kind 'an alignment is made from within a gendered position; gender is not external and is not escaped but is used as a fuel for what is said' (Frosh op. cit., p. 4). He does not question whether his masculinity has any relevance. My use of the word 'inherent' above may be slightly confusing set in a context where it is clear that I believe in the social construction of gender. One of the difficulties is that in addressing the reflexive nature of the gender issues in clinical work one has in a sense to address 'masculinity' and 'maleness' as if there is actually an essence which can be held still during the process of thinking abut it. Indeed, the existence of a category suggests something real, innate, essential. And in using the categories, actively employing them, does not one actually reinforce, even recommend the traditional normative conceptions rather than, as psychoanalysis should do, subvert them? The problem is that when I attempt to hold it still, it shifts, it changes shape. The closer I look the more cloudy, blurred, the categories 'male' and 'masculine' become. And yet I am convinced that there is 'a something' (albeit a socially constructed something), other than anatomy which differentiates the masculine, which makes it 'other' than feminine.

Perhaps I should go further. I am beginning to see that the important issue is not so much how we define or operationalise masculinity or femininity, but how we use these categories to impose boundaries on the development of human sexuality. The real fluidity (a real feminine word that) of gender, which defined the radicalism of early psychoanalysis, more diffuse, indefinable, unconscious, as opposed to everyday conceptions and indeed practices in a world divided along gender lines, in which the self is centrally and subjectively defined and experienced as gendered, should in my view lead us to problematise the politics of the praxis of gender which is heterosexuality. This book is not a dedicated attempt to elaborate this particular issue, rather it is to look at one area where I believe this difference is actually real and visible, in the abusive behaviour of men towards women, and what it is that causes and maintains this abuse. Where I actually position myself will I hope become clearer in the course of this work.

I hope I have succeeded in this short introduction, in giving the reader a flavour of the sorts of issues and men with whom I work and of the ways in which these issues are thought about. The plan of this book is relatively simple. Having, as it were, set the tone and raised the questions with the above case histories, the next task in Chapter 2 is to give some idea of the scale of the problem of men's abuse of women. In Chapter 3 I will give a short critical overview of how the problem of male violence has been understood. Chapters 4 and 5 will give men a more explicit voice. They will present the ways in which men who are abusive have attempted to account for their violent and damaging behaviour, how they subjectivise this apparently deviant part of themselves. In particular, Chapter 5 will look at the ways in which abusive men attempt to dissociate themselves from their abusiveness, and how clinicians often collude with them in this process. Chapters 6 and 7 articulate the theoretical basis of the approach of the Men's Centre before its practical elaboration in Chapter 8. Chapter 9 will address the particular contribution of groupwork to the treatment of abusers. In the light of some criticism of the model presented here, which I can anticipate from reactions to *Why Men Hate Women*, the conclusions will address the male project (as I called it at a public lecture at the Institute of Contemporary Arts in London, 16 February 1994) of men's emancipation from sexism and chauvinism and women's liberation from men's abuse. There I will also take up the issue of where heterosexuality goes from here.

As this is also a clinical text intended for my colleagues, both psychotherapists and facilitators working solely with abusers, it is necessary to provide a review of the relevant literature and add to that my own observations about the clinical issues in working with abusers. Effective intervention requires rigorous definition of the problem and its causes. Goodwill, kind hearts, empathic nodding and soft voices (in copious supply in some men's groups) are insufficient. I intend to experiment to some extent in this book. From one perspective, working with abusive men is actually rather simple. The way in which they present, the language, the manipulations, the defences, the emotions, the cognitive structures etc. all become very familiar after some years of experience. From within the feminist informed cognitive/analytic behavioural model employed at the Men's Centre, encouraging, initiating and monitoring change can become almost routine. This is actually encouraging for us and for the women who are routinely victimised by these men. However, the intellectual challenge of elaborating that model so that it not only provides us with better resources for changing men, but also provides a way of understanding the subjective accounts of men's abuse is a constant source of stimulation and excitement. We meet with such a diversity of character, of personality, of backgrounds, of narrative, that it is only natural that a curious clinician would want to develop a model which ties together, which integrates this variety of experience. Over the years I have noticed a wide range of phenomena in abusers which have stimulated me to write. At this stage I find that these phenomena and my writing about them can develop a quality of fragmentation, rather in the way that attempts to develop a typology of rapists have ended up almost with every rapist having his own category. I believe this fragmentation is illusory, at least clinically, that it is based on my ignorance, not on the nature of the phenomena.

What I propose to do is to present these different issues as I have encountered them and propose a way of understanding each. Finally I will attempt to pull them together, to see if there is a perspective, a vantage point which will relate them to each other. For example, what is the relationship between the rigidity of abusers, the chronic sulking of many of them, the 'bubble', the difficulty in coping with an angry woman, or other issues mentioned here? Risky as it feels at this stage, I regard this book as being like a voyage in uncharted seas with many unexpected islands. The intention is to draw a map of this territory and link those 'conscious' islands with the 'unconscious' terrain beneath.

In general, those works which are extant on the problem of male abuse fall into two distinct schools. The one is cognitive and behavioural. Programmes for intervention which are based on this understanding tend to be psycho-educational with a large amount of input from facilitators and structured responses from participants. The other is the psychoanalytic. These tend to view the problem from a genetic point of view and as a consequence the behaviour and cognition can become obscured to the detriment, even danger, of women as victims. There is a third approach, which is not clinical but political which sees abuse entirely as a learned behaviour deriving from learned values and belief systems about women and their inferiority. The aim of any intervention based on this paradigm is that of raising consciousness. Of course these approaches are not mutually exclusive and what follows will be an attempt to steer a middle course. In itself completing such a task is impossible, but I hope to be able to begin to show how these different approaches can supplement and enrich each other.

2 The problem outlined

The social context of abuse

Another difference between this book and *Why Men Hate Women* (Jukes 1993a) is that the first was largely a polemic, however soundly empirical it was. In it I repeated what some researchers in the field of family violence refer to as facts about abuse which develop as a result of the 'waffle factor'. This occurs when a fact is repeated so often that it is no longer challenged even though nobody can remember where it first emerged, but people are afraid, because of the politics of abuse, to question its validity. The figures are not necessarily incorrect; they simply are not checked. One factor which shapes the politics of abuse is the social policy implications of public statements by 'experts' in the field, a large proportion of whom are men who undoubtedly have their own unconscious axes to grind. If, for example, one published research that showed women are as violent as men this could adversely affect funding to women's refuges and provide an underpinning for individual and social rationalisations of violence towards women. Nowhere is this 'waffle' factor more evident than in statistics purporting to reflect the scale of men's violent abuse of women. I have been as culpable as others in spreading waffle. Of course any interest group or lobby wants it to be known that the problem about which it is concerned is serious. As a result I think we are inclined to take, rather uncritically, those statistics which achieve this end. However, we should not forget that all statistics lend themselves to differing interpretations and that it is impossible to eradicate bias in research methodology (notwithstanding Grounded Theory), even if simply because all research derives from extant discourses. After all, the bottom line is resources to mitigate suffering. Not that funding is the only contributory factor to 'waffle'. Activists also want to raise public awareness, and nothing achieves this more than shocking figures.

Here I want to present the facts as they are presently known, and separate them from the extrapolations, of which there are many. I also want to seriously examine the feminist assertion, which I took up in *Why Men Hate Women*, that there is no discernible pathology in batterers or indeed in any kind of abuser of women or children. These two issues are connected, because if the assumed, extrapolated scale of abuse is even remotely accurate we would have to acknowledge that as many as 40 per cent of male humans are sick (this is the percentage of men in some surveys who say they use or are prepared to use violence on their partner if she behaves in ways he considers inappropriate), which is tantamount to saying that maleness is a form of sickness. Or again one could quote the shocking findings of a recent survey in the Borough of Islington (a large London local government district) that *every* woman asked had experienced physical violence from a man. On such a scale the idea of pathology is nonsense. If so many do it then sickness is a norm. Pathology is not an absolute, it is a relative concept. This is especially true if we can connect physical forms of abuse with non-physical forms and demonstrate that they are instrumental behaviours rather than being due to loss of control. In effect, this is what I did in *Why Men Hate Women*, and with some success I hope.

So where do we begin to look at the figures? Let us begin rather parochially by looking at those which were distributed by the Zero Tolerance campaign initiated by the government in Edinburgh in 1994, on a model first developed in New Zealand. This campaign was a year long. Its aim was to raise awareness of male abuse of women and children in order to prevent and reduce this crime and it set out to achieve this mainly through advertising posters using ironic slogans and hard-hitting statistics. The following sample illustrates this:

- One in four children are sexually abused (Kelly *et al.* 1991);
- Ninety per cent of sexually abused children attempt to avoid or stop the abuse; most tell somebody and are disbelieved (ibid.);
- Almost one-third of women experience domestic violence in their lifetime (Mooney 1993);
- One in every 50 pregnant women experience physical violence from their partners;
- Two in every five women have been raped or sexually assaulted;
- More than one in five women are raped by their husband or partner (Mooney op. cit.);
- Domestic violence against women accounts for a quarter of all reported crime (statistics taken from the National Working Party on Domestic Violence by the Victim Support Scheme 1992);
- Domestic violence is more common than violence on the street, in the pub or in the workplace (ibid.);
- It is estimated that only 2 per cent of violent attacks on women are reported to the police (ibid.);
- Almost half of all homicides of women are killing by a partner or ex-partner (ibid.);
- One in two girls will experience some form of sexual abuse (from flashing to rape) before their eighteenth birthday, one-third before they are 12 (Kelly op. cit.);
- Over 95 per cent of adult abusers of children are male (ibid.);

- Eighty-two per cent of adult abusers are known to their victims and 19 per cent are relatives (ibid.);
- Only 5 per cent of...sexual abuses...are ever reported to a statutory agency and less than 1 per cent lead to prosecution (ibid.);
- Eighty-five per cent of rapists are men known to the victims (Home Office 1989);
- Sixty-one per cent of rapes are committed indoors, usually in the victim's home (ibid.);
- The acquittal rate in rape trials is 78 per cent (Scottish Office 1992);
- Seventy per cent of all women have experienced sexual harassment at some point in their lives;
- One in every 11 women are raped on a date, over one-third of them on the first date (Mooney op. cit.).

I will first of all restate that these figures are undeniably shocking, even appalling. Their overall effect is to end up damning men. The fact that a woman cannot tell which man will rape, hit or be mentally cruel to her leads to the sort of activist sloganising in which 'all men are rapists, batterers etc.' simply to help women protect themselves. Continued repetition of such figures induces a kind of shock fatigue. After years of working with men who batter and rape or abuse children I find myself struggling with a jaundiced view of mankind as a whole. I believe, also, that such statistics, whilst of value, probably induce denial in people, rather in the way that figures linking cancer with smoking can make smokers reach for a cigarette to calm their nerves.

How reliable are these statistics? Well, that depends where you place yourself in the discourse about abusiveness. However, that said, they are as reliable as you can get when allowances are made for all the difficulties in social science research design. The above sample is taken from a narrow range of sources, although much reliance is placed on Kelly's research at North London University for figures about the incidence of child sexual abuse. I have studied this research in detail and it is in keeping with Kelly's position in her other published work. She is committed to the notion of a continuum of sexual abuse, which is far from consensual even within pro-feminist academia. More legitimately she espouses the idea that it is not for men to define what constitutes abuse or to define the seriousness of abuse. For one woman, being flashed at may evoke fears of being killed, whereas for another it may be shocking but not traumatising. In fact the assumption of a linear connection between supposed trauma or a normative idea of trauma and the perception of trauma is of crucial importance, especially so in the treatment of abusers, as we shall see. What of other sources of data? What I will do is to present statistics from around the world which relate to different forms of violence between intimates, not simply that relating to men on women. The reason for this will become clear when we have to examine hypotheses about the causes of male to female violence.

The numbers and statistics are painfully clear: we live in a violent world, and most of that violence is perpetrated by men. Whether at home or in the street, in secret detention centres or on battlefields, men do most of the wounding and killing; the dying is more evenly distributed between the genders, but only when counting civilian war deaths. These rather depressing numbers are organised into two main sections: violence perpetrated by individuals and that executed by states and state agents, which are predominantly male.

Before continuing to list the counts of injury, physical and sexual assault, and death, it bears noting that comparisons across countries are methodologically difficult, as are comparisons of different studies, of even the same national origin. Each study has its own particular definition of the problem at hand and breaks information down differently. For instance, incest will only count in one study if the victim is 16 or under, while another accepts cases up to the age of 18. Methodology impacts results; rates of abuse are far higher for volunteer samples than are those obtained from random sampling. Interviews with room for free respondent input yield more accurate and higher results than questionnaires with rigidly defined answers, while interviewing in-depth in a safe environment procures higher, more accurate reported rates of abuse than does telephone calling. Comparing rates of crime internationally is subject to similar problems: the definitions of crimes vary; sampling at different stages of the judicial process varies; and effective record keeping and the scale of participation varies. Moreover, the definition and reporting of atrocities committed by a state against its population is mediated by international political delicacies. What many studies have in common is that they underestimate the real scope of the problem. To get a picture of world violence it is nevertheless useful to gingerly undertake such comparisons with these issues in mind in order to start brushing in the canvas, however broad the strokes (see Table 2.1).

At home, children and women are on the receiving end of the fist. Estimates of the prevalence of child physical abuse ranges from a high of 44.8 per cent amongst the middle class in India (Segal 1995) to a low of 15.2 per cent in Spain (de Paul *et al.* 1994). Women are with children far more often than are men and therefore have more opportunity than men to abuse children. Considering the stress and frequent frustrations of child rearing (especially for a single parent, usually the mother), they have more potentially angering interactions with children than do men. Men, however, do most of the hitting in straight percentages, and when adjusted for differentials in time spent with children in 'at-risk' situations, the percentage of male perpetrators of violence shoots up by a third.

Surprisingly, the youngest of our population, infants, are the most vulnerable to homicide. With the exception of Italy, the infanticide rates all over Europe and in Japan are higher, and up to six times higher, than the rate per thousand age population for adults (Briggs and Cutright 1994). And for

Table 2.1 Physical abuse

Country	Rate (%)	By gender of perpetrator (%)			By gender of victim (%)	
		Male	Female	Both	Male	Female
England	15.3	29	17	23	42*	24
USA	20.9–21**	56–76^	23^	–	19.5**	22.3**
India	44.8	–	–	–	–	–
Russia	28.9	–	–	–	–	–
Spain	15.2	–	–	–	13.7	16.7

Notes:
By population at large unless otherwise specified.
* In this study (Creighton and Russell 1995) of interviewed adults who had reported experiencing physical punishment (81.2 per cent n = 838) 42 per cent of the men were slapped with a shoe or belt as compared to 24 per cent of the women. This was not categorised as abusive if it did not happen frequently or constantly.
** Defined as sustaining an injury.
^ Controlled for by time of access; the figure of 56 per cent is not to say that 56 per cent of men physically abuse children.

this singular category of crime, it is overwhelmingly women who perpetrate infant murder (according to Home Office statistics, virtually only women kill children under one year of age in England and Wales).

The rates of sexual abuse are lower than those for physical abuse, but the proportion of male offenders is more heavily skewed (see Table 2.2). England has both the lowest and the highest estimated rates (16.2–46 per cent) for countries whose rates of sexual abuse are available, with up to 59 per cent of girls being abused sexually before reaching the age of consent (Creighton and Russell 1995; Baker and Duncan 1985). Men are approximately 82 per cent of the perpetrators in England; this percentage worsens in the United States, where it is estimated that well over 90 per cent of the perpetrators are male (Jason *et al.* 1982; 1986). Some women, then, do abuse. However, one study by Wolfers (1992) found that for 70 per cent of the female perpetrators in her sample, the abusive acts had been precipitated by a perpetrating male. This dynamic may be more likely when the woman is being abused by a mate (Stark and Flitcraft 1988b).

Domestic violence statistics yield similar proportions for the gender of the perpetrator, and in some countries are estimated at 100 per cent (So Kim 1994; Yoshima and Sorenson 1994). The scope of the issue is massive by any count available: in England rates estimate that 20 per cent to 33 per cent of women will be in violent relationships in the course of their lifetime; in the United States, 11.6 per cent to 35.5 per cent, while gays in the US face a rate of 38 per cent, and lesbians rates of 25 per cent to 48 per cent; and in Japan the rate is estimated at 57 per cent (this last number is bound to be an overestimate due to non-random sampling) (Bachman 1994; Stark and Flitcraft 1988a; Coleman 1994; Island and Letellier 1991; McGibbon *et al.*

Table 2.2 Sexual abuse

Country	Rate (%)	By gender of perpetrator (%)			By gender of victim (%)	
		Male	Female	Both	Male	Female
Australia	–	–	–	–	9	28
Austria	–	–	–	–	19	36
Belgium	–	–	–	–	–	19
Canada	–	–	–	–	8	18
Costa Rica	–	–	–	–	13	32
Denmark	–	–	–	–	7	14
Domin. Rep.	33	–	–	–	–	–
England	16.2–46	82	10	1	20*	80*
					27	59
Finland	–	–	–	–	4	7
France	–	–	–	–	5	8
Germany	–	–	–	–	4	10
Greece	–	–	–	–	6	16
Ireland	–	–	–	–	5	7
Netherlands	–	–	–	–	–	33
Norway	–	–	–	–	9	19
New Zealand	–	–	–	–	–	32
S. Africa	–	–	–	–	29	34
Spain	18.9	–	–	–	15.3	22.5
Sweden	–	–	–	–	3	9
Switzerland	–	–	–	–	3	11
USA	–	96–98	4–5	**		38
					20*	80*

Notes:
*   These present an estimate of the distribution of gender within samples of victims of child sexual abuse.
**   Of a small study of female sexual abusers, 70 per cent had been precipitated by male partners, and the levels of violence and the types of act perpetrated were similar as those for men, for instance, sadomasochism and bestiality (Wolfers 1992).

1989; Mooney 1993; Yoshima and Sorenson 1994). The estimated rates for Thailand and Hong Kong are lower than those for the other countries mentioned (18 per cent to 19.5 per cent, and 14 per cent respectively (So Kim 1994; Hoffman *et al.* 1994).

To be more specific about the numbers of women suffering domestic violence, almost half a million British and Welsh women are assaulted in 'domestic disputes' each year; there are an additional 100,000 home-based assaults (BCS 1992).

In the United States, approximately ten women are murdered each day by their intimates or ex-lovers (National Crime Survey 1993); battery is the leading cause of injury, mutilation and death for women and ranks higher than car accidents and cancer combined (Stark and Flitcraft 1988a). Its prevalence is endemic, with one out of every three women suffering a violent relationship during the course of their lives; one in two will be abused (New York State: abuse is defined here as incidents of physical violence rather than a full-blown battery relationship). This is three times higher than the rate for breast cancer in the US, which afflicts one woman in nine.

Many claim that the violence in heterosexual relationships is mutual, so a mutual battery syndrome, including a battered man syndrome that does not refer to gay partnerships, should be the focus of research and intervention efforts. The founder of this school of thought is Murray Straus, who pioneered empirical research on domestic violence in the US. He has consistently found fairly equal rates of violence by his measures between husbands and wives, at face value suggesting a dramatically revised picture of mutual battery rather than one of victimisation of women.

While not claiming that men are never battered or sexually abused by their female partners, a close examination of Straus' work dissolves the mutual and male battery syndrome claims. The Conflict Tactic Scale (CTS) that Straus and his colleagues use is riddled with major problems: the two most relevant ones are that he does not make distinctions between self-defence and attack, nor does he attempt to calculate severity (for example, according to the CTS all punches are counted equally; when a 13-stone husband bashes his 9-stone wife once with his fist, knocking out a tooth, this is not as bad as when she pummels his chest (leaving no mark at all) because of the number of landed punches and the irrelevance of severity of injury). Moreover, Straus' mode of information collection (by telephone) obviates the possibility of creating a safe environment for responses, most especially for battered women whose telephone use is often tightly monitored by the abuser. For a detailed and thorough excoriation of large-scale mutual and male battery assertions, see the article by Dobash and Dobash (1980) listed in the bibliography.

The struggle for power in 'romantic' relationships can be lethal. Men and women do murder each other (there are no available statistics for homicide within gay and lesbian relationships), although, once again, men kill women far more often than the other way around. Moreover, if the woman seeks to end the relationship, the likely denouement of her murder increases.

In a study comparing partner homicides in New South Wales, Chicago, and Canada, the female to male murder ratio for married couples went up by two to five times when the women left their husbands. For co-habitating couples, the rise of the female to male homicide ratio is not so dramatic – it 'merely' doubles and triples at the end of the relationship (Wilson and Daly

1993b). These statistics, which defy adjectives such as tragic and terrible, are the culmination of a long-term and growing abuser dependency and obsession with power and control; the pattern of this obsession and dependency is the Western romantic script.

India, while not at all the exclusive repository of the murders of married women, has a particular confluence of economic, rule of law and cultural factors which manifest in a unique form of bride murder: dowry death, often by burning. The extent of the problem, defined as a suspicious death in the first seven years of the victim's marriage, is vastly underrated at 300 to 1,319 cases per year. All government interventions are seen to have utterly failed.

Women's rates of murdering spouses is higher for the US than other industrialised countries. One theory posits that 'women's lethality will approach men's when women's valued resources (e.g. their children...) are threatened or when they are socially empowered to do so (e.g. matrilocal residential patterns)' (Kruttschnitt 1993, p. 259). There is evidence to suggest that the legal structure of family law (most notably, the availability of divorce), impacts homicide rates. The rate of women murdering men is higher in countries where divorce is unobtainable, such as India, and lower where it is easily obtained, such as in the Netherlands. However, there is very little support in the Interpol data Kruttschnitt uses that women are more lethally violent as a result of emancipation: homicide rates did not vary much with a nation's level of development or degree of modernisation, which she relies upon as an (admittedly problematic) index of female emancipation. Also, women's variation in being murderers is more parallel to the variations in men's rates than fluctuating according to any other factor – in other words, men's and women's rates are, overall, driven by the same cultural and other sociological mechanisms (Kruttschnitt op. cit.), namely, in no small part, male-dominated institutions such as law, government and the economy.

The American rates of women murdering their (ex-)partners may be due to retaliation against the higher risk of murder they live with. 'Women in the United States today face a statistical risk of being slain by their husbands that is about 5–10 times greater than that faced by their European counterparts, and in the most violent American cities, risk is 5 times higher again' (Wilson and Daly 1993a, p. 90).

The hypothesis of self-defensive murder of abusive spouses (and otherwise keeping a low profile) is borne out by the data. When examining murder rates overall, women tend to stay at home. In the United States, women account for a small share (10 per cent) of homicide arrests. 'They are more likely to kill their intimates (spouses or partners) than are men – who are more likely to kill acquaintances or strangers – and the victims of women's homicides are more likely to have initiated the violence than are the victims of men's homicides' (Daly 1994, p. 125). England and Wales Home Office statistics show that men are more likely to murder the women in their lives (37 per cent of female homicide victims had been killed in 1994 by a partner or ex-partner) than are females to murder the men (8 per cent of male homicide victims, again in 1994, were murdered by a spouse or lover or former partner), and that men are more likely to kill in general. For those indicted on homicide charges of all kinds, the percentage of male to female suspects has been remarkably constant over the past ten years; in 1985 88.7 per cent of those indicted for homicide were male, and 11.2 per cent female, and in 1994 the rates were 89.5 per cent and 11.2 per cent respectively. Men also run a higher risk of homicide than women (60 per cent of all murder victims are male) and are two and a half times more likely to be killed by a stranger.

According to England and Wales Home Office statistics men are violently victimised at twice the rate of women (from 1988 to 1992, for example, men regularly outnumbered women as murder victims at a ratio of about 2:1). The perpetrators are, as noted above, mostly male.

Globally speaking, women's involvement in public oriented violent crime is a fraction of that of males. 'Female violent criminality in the public domain of various countries ranges from the lowest rate of 5 per cent in Latin America to as high as 23 per cent in Thailand' and hovers around 10 per cent (Ben-David 1993, p. 347).

To help explain these phenomena, women's smaller percentage of victims and perpetrators in the public realm is in no small part due to the separation of public and private spheres for men and women. Although the two spheres are interconnected structurally and functionally, women do spend more time in their home space and men spend more time on the street, and the streets are even more bloody than the homes. Home is more of a haven for men, and men keep the public space so bloody: the police force, the government, the military, religious institutions, the economy, technological research facilities, in short, every institution in society that is associated with power is dominated numerically and philosophically by men.

Then there is rape and sexual assault to consider. Although men's rape of men is endemic in prison, overall, rape and sexual assault victims are female and the perpetrators are male. Rape is also endemic, as has been demonstrated of battery and sexual and physical abuse of children. It is widely believed that rape is one of the most under-reported crimes due to impediments to obtaining a satisfactory (for the victim) response from the criminal justice system and to internalised cultural factors, such as blocks to defining an act as rape if the perpetrator was known to the victim or accepting guilt for a crime committed against oneself. By the time women in the United States get out of college, one in four will have been raped or the victim of an attempted rape, 57 per cent of the incidents having taken place during dates, and with 84 per cent of the women knowing their attackers. Sexual abuse inside marriage is often the last abuse to be named by women seeking refuge in domestic violence shelters, even if the sexual attacks are sadistic. The issue is often muddied by the fact of fearful acquiescence to sex after being beaten into submission in the past; consent loses its meaning altogether when a woman is living with the everyday possibility of brutality. During the course of their lifetimes, 14 to 25 per cent of married women in the United States can anticipate at least one incident of rape by their husband (Russell 1982).

According to official Home Office statistics for England and Wales, between 1990 and 1992, 16,000 females reported indecent assaults per year (10–15 year olds were at highest risk) and 4,000 rapes per year (10–15 year olds also at highest risk, with those in the 16–24 year old category following closely behind). Males reported 3,000 assaults per year in this same time period, with 10–15 year olds suffering the highest victimisation rate adjusted for age population (male rape is conflated with female anal rape under the term buggery, and this offence was reported by 1,200 victims per year. The highest risk age group was also 10–15 year olds, who comprised 37 per cent of the victims).

The perpetrators are overwhelmingly male. For all those tried for rape in the Crown Court in 1993, 891 were male, and only one was female. In 1994, the Magistrates' Court proceeded against 1,782 people on rape charges: two were female, the remaining 1,780 were male (Supplementary Table Criminal Statistics 1994).

In sum, men, as private citizens, are far more violent than women. But men are not only violent one by one, but also in collectives of governments and the military. Well over two-thirds of the world's governments are fully and officially documented as practising torture and other human rights abuses (Amnesty International), and many other countries, such as China and Indonesia, escape official finger-pointing due to the economic and/or political (military) interdependence of first world countries.

The body count is lengthy and the means of inflicting pain horrifically inventive. The torturers are men, specifically trained for their jobs. The only documentation of women employed as torturers of children or adults comes from Nazi Germany. However, we do need to bear in mind that some women do kill their infants, abuse their lesbian lovers, beat their children, etc. (see Welldon 1993).

Not only are children severely abused at home by parents or other guardians, but also by state actors in state owned and operated detention centres. Children are currently tortured and put to death, often in summary executions in the following countries: Bangladesh, Brazil (paramilitary forces are paid by shopkeepers to kill homeless young), Bulgaria, Chad, Colombia, Ecuador, Guatemala, Indonesia, Israel (where torture sometimes results in death of Palestinian youth), Turkey and Yugoslavia. This list represents those countries for which fully documented cases of torture and murder of named children by government actors are available (Ndiaye and Rodley 1994); there are many others without the formal documentation.

Wars bring death to soldiers, but to civilians as well, and to more civilians than ever before (85 per cent of casualties in the wars of the 1980s were civilians).

Many deaths, some intended and others not, are attributable to men's collective political activities and suffered by civilian populations. For example, after the United States' carpet bombing of Vietnam during the war against Vietnam in the 1970s, the reduced arability and utility of the land still causes deaths today by, amongst other things, starvation, and the defoliates used to clear the jungle still poison and deform. Land mines laid down by the Khmer Rouge in this same conflict, and by warring factions in many other countries, continue to be tripped by civilians, many of them children tending animals, resulting in loss of feet, legs, hands, arms, and life.

Wartime allows for the confluence of the patriarchal conflation of sex and death to manifest. Where there are soldiers, there are prostitutes and sexual slaves. Avatars of the victim end of these dynamics, the Chung Shun Dae (the Korean 'comfort women') were enslaved by the Japanese in the Second World War in Japan's occupation of Korea. Women typically were forced to service 30 to 40 men a day (sometimes well over 60), were refused medical care, were not fed properly, and disembowelled or otherwise murdered when they tried to escape or made eye contact with their captors. Unsurprisingly, most of the women died in their slavery; those that did survive have endured the life of the outcast back in their home country. In our modern day in Europe, there have been multiple accounts of forced prostitution (in other words, officially sanctioned, repeated rape) in Bosnia and rapes in detention camps for the alleged purpose of discipline.

Whether in private or in public, individually or in collectives, men are, to understate the case, exceptionally violent. This is the context for this study and as Straus has shown, the cultural context, as outlined in his Cultural Spillover Theory, is more than implicated in private, one to one, violence. Answering the question of why men are so violent is beyond the scope of this book. My concern is to address domestic abuse and violence or battering. Of course it is impossible to address the question of why men are so domestically abusive without looking at the context. This question will be the subject of the next chapter.

3 Aggression and violence

How theoretical models help us understand why men abuse women

It is surprisingly easy for researchers, including myself, into what is known as family violence to lose sight of the most obvious, and that is not only that many families are extremely violent places to live in, but that the world is a very violent place, full of cruelty and ruthlessness. It is worth asking if it is valid to isolate family violence from this context or whether, first, one ought to ask why it is that people are so violent to each other. Perhaps the question should be why is it that men are so violent. In general this question may be the most fruitful to pursue, and I shall give my reasons for so doing. Not that the question of violent women is irrelevant. In fact it is being made increasingly relevant today by those who assert that the problem of battered husbands is as serious, or should be taken as seriously, as that of battered wives. My opinion is that whilst I do not dismiss the claims of those who assert the reality of female violence, this is part of a backlash against the successes of feminism during the past 30 years. That it might represent such a backlash should come as no surprise, a backlash having followed every advance in women's emancipation. That said, it remains the case that the problem of violent and abusing men is as high on the agenda as it has ever been. The articulated level of social concern is unprecedented, although this has not so far been matched by an equivalent level of public funding either to support the victims or to intervene with the offender.

It may come as a surprise to the reader new to the problem to discover that male abusiveness to women is not a recent phenomenon. Nor, contrary to what one might think, is this the first time in history that it has been a major cause of social concern. The first recorded campaign is that led by Mary Wollstonecraft in the late eighteenth century, although the phenomenon itself had been recorded, and indeed recommended for application to recalcitrant disobedient wives, in the Old Testament. There were campaigns by early feminists in the nineteenth century around the time of the famous rule of thumb judgement which ruled that it was permissible to beat one's wife providing it was carried out with a stick no thicker than the thumb. Emmeline Pankhurst and the suffragettes instigated a similar movement prior to the First World War. The feminists of the 1930s began another prior to the Second World War. Currently we have a major campaign which has lasted for almost 30 years, which began in the UK with Erin Pizzey at Chiswick Women's Aid and was taken up in almost all industrialised nations. The surprising thing is not that the present campaign should have such a history, but that so little seems to have changed in these centuries as a result of earlier campaigns. Why is this? It is not that the role and status of women have not undergone a radical transformation. This has certainly occurred. It is that such changes as have occurred seem to be due to factors other than public concern about the plight of women, such as the needs of production brought about by the shortage of men. Although these changes, which I will address, have left a seemingly ineradicable mark on women's behaviour, they seem to have had little bearing on men's behaviour, and in particular, their violence to women.

There are a number of ways in which clinicians have understood violent behaviour in relationships. In recent years the issue of abuse, particularly of women and girls, has become the focus of a heated debate with the rise of feminist inspired scholarship determined not to allow what is seen as male hegemony to dictate models of treatment which further undermine the cause of women and which replicate the original abuse. In effect, feminism has to a large extent succeeded in taking the issue out of the encapsulated world of the consulting room and metapsychology and into the political arena. The ideological implications of different models have been subject to searching analysis (see for example Roy 1977; Schecter 1982; Horley 1991; Wilson 1983; Saraga and Macleod 1990; and many others) as feminists have attempted to make explicit the ways in which supposedly neutral clinical disciplines describe and therefore construct models of femininity which are sexist and reinforce women's oppression. This is not to say that there is any consensus within feminism about why men abuse women. However, there is little doubt that feminists of all persuasions have had to address the issue and that there is a consensus that men's abusive behaviour is a central issue for feminist efforts to achieve equality with men. The most elaborated feminist analysis, of non-clinical origins (although it should be required reading for all clinicians), comes from the sociologists Emerson and Russell Dobash (1980). Their argument is deceptively simple. It is that men abuse women, the world over, in order to ensure the provision of services from them, to guarantee continued caretaking. Abuse is instrumental. Its aim is to gain control of the woman so that she will do as the man wants when he wants. I will refer to this work more. I should say, however, that the paradigm has become a central part of my own thinking as I have attempted to integrate it with ideas arising from orthodox clinical practice.

What I will attempt to do in this chapter is to examine the way in which clinicians have understood why it is that it is usually men or males who abuse women and children (including boys). The emphasis here will be on how male aggression has been understood, not why it is directed at females. A related issue, which I will briefly address is how each model of understanding violence – aggression which causes physical damage with intent – implies a model of the human mind or is based on an explicit model of mental functioning. This is quite important insofar as these models of functioning determine to a large extent the degree of optimism with which one views the prospects for change in behaviour and the strategies for achieving it. My additional interest is to explore the nature of rage. I am in no doubt that the core task of effective clinical work requires us to be successful in helping patients to metabolise and or mitigate their rage. This applies to the general population of patients and especially so to abusers. As we see from everyday reports of murder, road rage, casual killings, street violence, rioting, crowd violence and other phenomena it is clearly also a social problem of major dimensions. It is important for this discussion that we begin by drawing a surprisingly deceptive distinction between feelings and behaviour. Anger and rage are not violent or aggressive although the subjective experience of one of them may be a necessary condition for the kind of violence and aggression with which I am concerned. Any attempt to understand violent behaviour must also at least imply a psychodynamic theory, that is, a theory of mental functioning and the origins of these feelings of anger and rage. As we will see later, this distinction between feelings and behaviour is crucially important in clinical or re-educational work with abusers, but it also has profound significance for our view of what we might, for want of a better term, call human nature.

Male aggression has many forms, some much more dangerous to men than to women, as we saw earlier. It is usually men who wage war on each other, although women are used in war by men in the most appalling ways. Theorists from ecologists (the first and by far the most notable being Lorenz (1966)) to psychoanalysts (beginning with Freud (1930); see also Storr below) as well as medical practitioners backed by physiological research have opined about the origins and sources of male aggression. It has been an inexhaustible source of inspiration since recorded speech began. Aggression is such a neutral word. It gives the lie to what is man's unique capacity for cruelty. No other species rejoices in the suffering of its victims. As Storr (1968, p. 90) put it

> it is inconceivable that a cat could so identify with a mouse as to enjoy the latter's fear. Yet men, with hatred in their hearts, take pleasure in prolonging the agonies of helpless victims and show extreme ingenuity in devising tortures which cause the maximum pain and the minimum risk of a quick ending...the enjoyment of another's pain is...peculiar to human beings.

I think Storr is right in this. It provides a starting point for my enquiries in that it raises the question what it is that is unique to humans that we have this capacity to inflict suffering and derive enjoyment from it. There is a complex question here about whether aggression is innate (what one might call the genetic theory of causation based on instincts), primary (Freud's death instinct) and indiscriminate, or whether it is induced (the so-called frustration theory) or learned (the social construction theory) and also whether it has a special place in relation to women. This is also important in terms of how we position ourselves in relation to treatment efforts. If male aggression is the problem, and it is indiscriminate, then this should be the focus of our enquiries with an awareness that women hold 'pride of place' as a category of victim of this aggression. If the problem is something unique to men's relation to women then we can address what it is that is unique and deal with the aggression as a gender issue. Of course there is another position, which is that men are uniquely cruel, full stop, and that our cruelty or violence towards each other has different sources and meanings from our violent maltreatment of women.

I have to say that the literature on violence or aggression is vast (20,000 publications according to De Zulueta (1993)) and it would be a lifelong task to read it let alone reach any independent conclusion about its cause. What I have read, which is a not insubstantial portion of the total, has on the whole, not been very useful in my clinical work with violent and abusive men. The reasons for this are complex, and may be as much to do with me as the discourse itself. I have to say that psychological research into violence or aggression achieves a level of reification and sententiousness which is simply not clinically useful and this has to be the acid test of its value (the most comprehensive coverage of psychological theories is provided by Archer and Browne (1989) and by Archer (1994)). Gelles (1982) discovered fundamental incompatibilities between research and practice in family violence cases. The level of generalisation required by research methodology is simply too high for it to be useful in individual cases and research generally seeks closure whereas the clinician has to be open to new information. Perhaps the most important point is that psychology research in particular did not help me to understand the origins of my own rage and violent desires in a way which adequately accounted for my experience. At one level I was comfortable with accounts which took away from me any feelings of personal guilt or responsibility, those which derive it from instinct, whilst I was also profoundly uncomfortable with them because I knew that I was responsible for my behaviour and that I made choices when in a rage which limited the potentially damaging consequences of my behaviour – giving the lie to the idea that I was out of control however much I might find retrospective comfort from this notion. On the other hand I was uncomfortable with those accounts which explained that my rage was a result of early childhood experiences for which I had no responsibility. It was because my parents were inadequate (undoubtedly true) and I needed to recover those trauma and work them through in order to be free of the worst of my raging moods. At one level I could accept that this was true but I also felt that both my reading and my personal experience of many years' analysis did not deal with what felt like a central issue, which is that I actually derived satisfaction from raging, regardless of the consequences.

Bonnie Buchelle (1995, pp. 275–85) has described the four analytic or dynamic models of anger and aggression which clinicians use to inform therapeutic interventions. These are (1) drive theory; (2) ego psychology; (3) object (another word for person) relations theory; and (4) self psychology. In general, drive theory and ego psychology tend to be related in practice. Essentially, drive theory, which is predicated on the notion that activity is motivated by the satisfaction of the instinctual drives (with people as means to that end), sees aggression as innate and wishes to 'destroy, retaliate or hurt others…are expressions of the aggressive instinct'(ibid., p. 276). The amount of aggression is a constitutional given in each individual. This is often twinned with ego psychology in which successful management of anger or aggressive feelings is dependent on the presence of healthy 'ego' defences against instinctual expression. Drive theory and ego psychology derive directly from Freud's work, particularly his early studies. Object relations theory, which sees activity as motivated by the need to form relationships (and only secondarily as satisfying needs, hence Guntrip (1973) was able to say that whereas in 'drive theory…the object points the way to satisfaction', in object relations theory 'satisfaction points the way to the object'), views the aggressive drive as part constitutional and part socially constructed and deriving from a bad or conflicted past relationship, usually infantile. This relationship is internalised, becomes a kind of template, including a representation of the self and the other person (object) and a feeling which binds them together. In later life these internalised (object) relationships get transferred to other people in an illusory way and can become troublesome. Self theory assumes that anger and aggression are a result of experiences of empathic failure during childhood and infancy. These failures stem from the inability or unwillingness of the primary carers to be emotionally responsive to the infant, and the infant experiences this as a form of abandonment which causes rage. Clearly this has close links with object relations theory although it is more based on privation than the latter, which is conflict based. Although Buchelle does not mention it, there is another model, attachment theory, which is closely allied to both object relations and self theory. In fact it takes object relations theory to its limits in its assertion that people are motivated (driven) entirely by the need to seek relationships with others (objects) and that all psychopathology is based on the early failure to do this satisfactorily. This model is totally privation based in that it posits that rage and destructiveness always result from early failure, on the part of the primary carer, to respond appropriately to the infant. I will examine this in some detail later.

It is appropriate to begin with the efforts of Freud (1920), the founder of modern psychology and the father of psychoanalysis, to understand human aggression. Perhaps the most famous of his attempts to deal with this issue is contained in his book *Beyond the Pleasure Principle*. Begun in 1919 and finished the following year, this book has a central place in analytic thinking. There is no doubt that the despair it reflects is a product of Freud's awareness of his developing oral cancer and his depression about the Great War, the 'war to end all wars'. Whatever its personal motivation, in it Freud grapples with the question of destructiveness. The reader might know that he had reached a position in his work some years earlier in which he had concluded that people are motivated by the search for pleasure and the avoidance of pain. However, he had been constantly confronted by commonplace clinical facts, such as patients who repeat the same painful experience over and over again without conscious volition, and others who seemed addicted to masochistic experience, or deriving pleasure from pain. Even this admittedly simplistic statement of his position reflects his difficulty. How can pleasure be the main driving force when it is clear that people are seemingly driven to self-destruction? He concluded, in what was a major revision of his work, that eros, or sexual energy, the life instinct, was opposed by another force, thanatos, or the death instinct. The organism (you and me) is driven by an instinct to die, to return to an inanimate state. This instinct is innately self-directed, that is towards self-destruction, or masochistic, but under various pressures connected with psychological development is turned outwards and becomes sadistic. Hence, masochism is primary and sadism is secondary. This idea of an instinct for death has generated furious debate ever since, and has contributed to serious splits within the analytic movement. It is no idle matter. Its implications are profound. We might call this theory the biological one, in that it posits aggression as being innate or genetic i.e. a drive. This notion of the death instinct has been most successfully taken up and elaborated by Melanie Klein (who could be said to be the founder of object relations theory) whose theory of mental functioning and individual development places innate destructiveness at the very heart of the human psyche. She believes that the death instinct is expressed and experienced as envy, primarily envy for the breast which contains all that is needed for the infant to grow and thrive. The envious child contains the wish to destroy that which it covets, because it cannot stand the pain of lack and the desired object possessing all the goodness and keeping it for itself.

Klein's influence has been extensive and profound on the way clinicians view aggression and destructiveness. There is little doubt that she is the most famous, and influential, of post-Freudian analysts to take seriously to heart the notion of an instinct for death. She embraced and elaborated the idea with fervour. For her, this instinct was evident in the universal experience of primary destructive envy. It is important to point out that this is an expression of the instinct, not the instinct itself, just as for Freud sadomasochism and the repetition compulsion were manifestations of the instinct, not the instinct. The instinct cannot be seen. It is to Klein that we owe our understanding of the nature of the splitting of the object (person) into good and bad and this is worth elaborating a little. In essence she posits that, in order to survive, the infant has to develop two mothers or primary carers. One of them is good and nourishing and loved. The other is frustrating and toxic and hated. The split in the mother which becomes internal to the child's developing idea of the self enables the child to go on feeding and to survive at a time when it does not have either the emotional or cognitive capacity to integrate the good and bad mothers. For Klein this bad mother is an inevitable consequence of birth and life. The bad mother comes to contain all the impulses and components of the child's death instinct.

The idea of the death instinct causes me great problems. I have no diffi- culty with the idea that we are in some sense programmed to die like all organic matter, and ultimately to return to an inorganic state. Death is the ultimate goal of all life. Without it there could be no evolution, no survival of the fittest. Death ensures the survival of the species. From a simple biological point of view, therefore, there is undoubtedly an 'instinct' for death in the sense that we are programmed for it. The central question for a psychotherapist or analyst, or a counsellor of violent men, is whether there are psychological parallels for the biological programme, and what form these might take.

Another way to think about aggressive and violent behaviour is the frustration or instrumental hypothesis (Berkowitz 1969; 1989) which is actually a paradigm derived from a theory of deprivation but which also implies a particular model of psychological functioning and human motivation (in fact, the problem of human motivation, which is at the heart of any model of the mind – what is it that makes us do anything – is always implicitly addressed by the way one construes aggressive or violent behaviour). Within this paradigm, humans are not seen as innately sinful or bad or as being born in a state of original sin. Anger and aggression are a product of the frustration of needs or wants – drives – which heightens the drive level and sparks aggressive behaviour. This model, clearly Freudian, in its pure form sees humans as need driven, with activity being oriented to the satisfaction of those needs and frustration as a necessary condition of aggression. The orthodox analytic model, on the other hand posits aggression as innate (although secondary – masochism and the death instinct being seen as primary then turned outward as sadism) and aggressive responses as being capable of stimulation by a variety of circumstances, not only need or drive frustration. For example, traumatic experiences which occur during the formative period of childhood are seen as persisting in the psyche – in ways which I will elaborate – and being acted out in adulthood in a variety of destructive ways. Let me once again emphasise that the way we understand destructiveness, whether we call it aggression (which I hasten to differentiate from constructive action – aggression – directed towards the pursuit of goals and which is not intended to cause harm to others) or violence has profound implications. Clinically, the implications are manifold both for the aims of treatment and strategies for achieving change. The most obvious one being that if we regard destructiveness as an expression of the death instinct and innate, then the best we can hope for is to strengthen the ego's capacity to contain and hold the secondary sadistic desire and attempt to develop sublimations or displacement activities into which this can be channelled. Additionally we can attempt to develop the individual's capacity for holding passivity (the primary source of anxiety) and all the pain that this implies. I shall say more about the move from passivity later. From within this model there is little hope of sadism being mitigated in any substantial way at species level. Alternatively if we hold to the frustration/aggression hypothesis there is a great deal we can do providing we hold to the notion that desire is socially constructed, not instinctual. I shall return to 'frustration' shortly.

All these remarks have a bearing on what is for me a more important point, which is to do with the way that differing explanations for destructiveness actually are ways of constructing it. We can never know the 'truth' about destructiveness. That would imply that there is something called human nature which is somehow fixed – a familiarity with the history of psychological thought shows that this is a view which is patently false. Human nature, like the self, is constantly undergoing a process of invention and reconstruction. If aggression and destructiveness are the products of failed environmental provision then we can operate to change the environment or to change the individual's needs or expectations. Let me say at once that I am not setting up a dialectic. These are not mutually exclusive clinical goals. Indeed one will be doing all of this with all patients, including abusers. Also, in the clinical setting one could hope that the person could learn some impulse control, i.e. develop adequate ego defences. Of course this explanation fails the acid test of accounting for sadism and self-destructiveness.

In his widely acclaimed book *Individual Psychotherapy and the Science of Psychodynamics* David Malan (1979), following Bowlby and therefore deriving his ideas from attachment theory, links many manifestations of destructive behaviour with the phenomena of loss, separation and maternal deprivation. In so doing he is following in Freud's footsteps, particularly the important paper 'Mourning and Melancholia' (1917) in which Freud traced the origins of depression in the failure to mourn the lost object because of powerful conflicting feelings of love and hatred towards it. It is well known that loss, whether through bereavement, unemployment, bodily functions or parts, property or marriage breakdown can evoke powerful feelings of aggression in its victim (see Parkes 1986). Malan pays rather more attention to the guilt associated with the aggression or hatred than does Freud and in fact suggests that this may be the main motive behind the process whereby the person turns the aggression against him or herself. At the time of 'Mourning and Melancholia' (during the First World War) Freud was already struggling with the problem of the origins of hostile impulses. He says 'the ambivalence is either constitutional i.e. is an element of every love-relation formed by this particular ego, or else it proceeds precisely from those experiences that involved the threat of losing the object' (Freud 1917, p. 256). So whilst there is agreement that the loss of the object or its love or the threat of its loss can precipitate feelings of hatred there is no speculation about the origins of this capacity. We know that Freud eventually concluded that destructiveness was a product of the death instinct.

Konrad Lorenz (1966) says that aggression between members of the same species – human – is millions of years older than friendship and love. Malan develops this theme by speculating (and he makes the point that this is the best we can do, that no one is in a position to answer the basic question of the origins of aggression) that the first relation between a mother and a baby will be an aggressive rather than a loving one and that the 'initial interchanges between them...are in some way analogous to the courtship rituals in other species, namely an elaborate procedure by means of which the more fundamental relation can be first neutralised and then converted into a bond of love' (Malan 1979, p. 191). As he himself says, 'this is in many ways an appalling thought'. 'Is it' he asks, 'simply primitive and fierce, or destructive, sadistic and revengeful? No-one knows...there is an alternative however...that these qualities enter *when the initial exchanges go wrong*' (ibid., p. 192). This is a comforting thought. It takes us to the point, which Malan reached, of optimism about the potential for therapeutic change in the most destructive of man's capacities as it hypothesises that hatred is a distortion of or is in some other way connected with love. Where I do not feel so about the link between love and hate, I am uncomfortable about the connection with the implications of the 'initial exchanges', for two reasons. First, it inevitably involves blaming the primary carer for destructive adult behaviour (not that I am saying they have no responsibility) and second, in clinical practice its implications may be inherently dangerous for patients with violent desires and, perhaps more importantly, their victims. From this amoral point of view one can, and indeed Alice Miller does, end up feeling sympathy for and forgiving even Hitler (Miller 1991). This is partly endemic within the psychoanalytic paradigm whose main aim is to understand the meaning of behaviour, not to judge it. However, it does place an enormous responsibility on women, who are universally constructed to be the primary carers. Are women to be made collectively culpable for mankind's headlong rush to prove ourselves nature's greatest mistake? Not that there is any doubt about the fundamental hypothesis of maternal deprivation or object loss being a precipitator for destructive and disturbing feelings of rage or anger – there is simply too much accumulated evidence for this to be dismissed. However, my own belief is that maternal deprivation and profound object loss are universal and we do not all – especially women – go around destroying things or people.

I made this point rather forcefully in *Why Men Hate Women*, that any explanation of human aggression must take into account its gendered nature. If women are subject to the same influences described by the hypothesis, then one has to account for why it is that most human aggression (as we saw in the last chapter) is instigated by males, or why it is, in terms of that hypothesis, that women are not equally violent. Actually this may not be so difficult as it first appears. A simple hypothesis could be that female children are subject to the same influences but that differential child rearing methods, gender role learning and culturation determine that female aggression and destructiveness follow different developmental pathways from those in males. In this case we should expect to see some common outcomes of displaced aggression in women which parallel the violent behaviour of men, some other forms of destructiveness. I realise that this question is rather different from the one of where the destructiveness comes from but this will not be avoided. (Perhaps the seminal work on this issue is that by Estella Welldon in her book *Mother, Madonna, Whore* (1993). At its simplest, her thesis is that rather than attacking women, females attack their own bodies or psyches as the mother/woman with whom their psyche/soma is identified.)

'When the initial exchanges go wrong.' The statement has its origins in attachment theory and it is apposite to state the central tenet of that model before proceeding further. Whilst attachment theory shifts that analytic paradigm, the basic idea is actually very simple. It is that people need each other and that each individual is born with an attachment system which makes it necessary for him or her to develop relationships with more powerful and competent others with whom he or she can feel safe and protected. This is the primary system which motivates infant behaviour, to stay close to that powerful, protecting other. The bond is the attachment and the behaviour is oriented to staying within range of the attachment figure. There is overwhelming evidence (see Marrone 1998) that the quality of the first attachment, the primary bond, is of profound importance for later mental and social health. Attachments (particularly early ones) become internalised as 'working models'. These models or representations are:

> cognitive maps, schemes or scripts that an individual has about himself (as a unique bodily and psychic entity) and his environment. Such maps can be of all degrees of sophistication, from elementary constructs to complex ones....one function of these models is filterability of information about oneself or the external world...several models of the same thing may co-exist, split off from each other. Models enable an individual to generate interpretations of the present and evaluate alternative courses of future action. In attachment theory an internal model is a representation of oneself in relation to significant others. A model is based on at least two judgements: 1) whether or not the attachment figure is assumed to be a person who in general will respond to a request for support and protection; and 2) whether or not the child judges himself as a person to whom anyone, particularly an attachment figure is likely to respond in a supportive way. Models are formed in the course of attachment related events (i.e. interactions with significant others) and they begin to be formed in the earliest months of life and can be re-shaped in later life.
>
> (Marrone 1998, pp. 71–4)

This is a radical departure from traditional theory in that it clearly asserts that any pathology, or indeed health, is a consequence of social processes, not internal phantasy or fantasy, or developmental failure. These are not denied but are seen as a consequence of early failure in the environment not the infant. The infant is located in a social environment from the very beginning, indeed is constituted by that environment. I am a fairly recent convert to attachment theory but there is little doubt about its clinical usefulness. What concerns me here is how far we can use it as an explanation for aggression. Felicity De Zulueta (1993) addresses just this point although it should be said that it is an attempt to understand all human violence and aggression. She concludes that differences between men in terms of anti-social and violent behaviour can be correlated with differences in child rearing and early attachment experiences, at least insofar as those adult men who have a history of such behaviour seem to share certain basic experiences during childhood.

Insofar as we are talking about violent experience in childhood this is not supported by my own research. In a population of almost 300 men with a disclosed history of violence seen regularly in a clinical setting fewer than 35 per cent had either received corporal punishment or witnessed violence between their parents or with other family members. I can be fairly sure about these given that each was seen regularly for some time. The sample is even higher (over 1,000) if it includes those seen only for assessment or consultation. It should also be noted that in agencies working with violent men who might be said, by virtue of their preferred model for understanding (Everyman, London, pers. comm.), to have a vested interest in showing a higher figure, no more than approximately 50 per cent of their clientele can be found with such a history. There are also important questions about whether there are discernible differences in the early attachment as between boys and girls and that such female violence as there is can be explained by early attachment experiences.

Before I discuss attachment theory in more detail I must stress my misgivings about its clinical implications particularly in working with violent perpetrators. To put it at its simplest it transforms perpetrators into victims, at least offers them dual status, and thereby entails the risk of minimising the offending behaviour and the damage to the present victim. I will say more of this later. Whilst I do not dismiss the theory, indeed wholeheartedly endorse much of what it has to say, I cannot accept that the hypothesis of distorted love which it proposes can adequately explain the roots of human, especially male, violence (see Chapter 7). Here I must say more about De Zulueta's work and I will do so at some length as hers is an important book about the understanding of violence derived from attachment theory. In it she is attempting to prove that violence and rage derive from experiences of loss and psychic trauma. She presents a great deal of evidence for her hypothesis. However, there is a major departure from normal definitions of what constitutes trauma. Her argument is quite complex, depending as it does on present theories of self psychology, findings from research in post-traumatic stress disorder and infant observation studies. Attachment theory research has developed to the point where it can categorise the nature of a person's attachments and even make predictions about an infant's future attachments from knowing the mother's history of her relationship with her own parents. Attachments can be defined as secure (type B) or insecure. Insecure attachments are of two types: type A, the insecure avoidant or detached, and type C, the insecure ambivalent. Each of these types has been further divided into sub-groups but detailed description is beyond the scope of this book. A third type of insecure, disorganised-disoriented, has recently been identified (Main and Solomon 1990). De Zulueta makes the point that studies generally find that approximately 20 per cent of all infants can be defined as belonging to type A, a type which is consistently found to be prone to violent and aggressive behaviour. She also quotes a study in which 20 per cent of American men acknowledge that they have used violence in their intimate relationships with women. This has to make anyone sit up and take notice although it has to be said that there is no way of knowing if those same men had suffered trauma as children even though they are by definition type A, insecure/avoidant. Where De Zulueta's definition of trauma diverges from that commonly held is her inclusion of the theory of attunement, a theory which is rapidly gaining ground in self psychology and psychoanalysis as being the process at the heart of the development of the self. Attunement is what is observed to occur between mothers and infants who develop secure attachment. It is a condition in which the mother is attuned to the infant's internal states and responds appropriately enough – in a way which enables the infant to develop a stable sense of self. Where this attunement goes wrong, when the mother is not in tune with the infant's states, the infant will not develop a stable sense of self but will be traumatised in a way which leads to one of the types of insecure attachment and leaves a residue of deep narcissistic rage and sadness. On the face of it De Zulueta makes a strong case and many abusive men describe their pre-abusive states in language which is resonant of failed attunement with their victim, their primary attachment: 'she doesn't understand me'; 'she wasn't listening'; 'I couldn't get my point across'; 'I just feel as though she doesn't see me'; 'I just wanted to be heard'; etc. I should also say that many men are completely unable to articulate such awareness and will often say that they have no idea what they were feeling prior to their attacks. However, the question is whether an insecure/avoidant attachment strategy is a necessary or sufficient condition to cause men to abuse women and children or become violent. A necessary condition is one without which the behaviour could not occur. A sufficient condition is one which will on its own cause the offending behaviour. The fact is that there is not one primate or human infant study in which it is seen that an insecure attachment model can be seen to be a sufficient condition and De Zulueta's work makes this clear. Is it necessary? In fact her well researched work seems to eventually lead her away from her initial enthusiasm for attachment theory as an explanation of violence. After eventually getting around to the importance of gender differentiation as the major organiser of social meaning, and after acknowledging that most violence is perpetrated by males (because females internalise their aggression), she says:

> But perhaps even more important to this study is the realisation that it is essentially the dehumanisation of the 'other' that is at the root of all human violence: this process appears to be almost intrinsic to the development of male–female role differentiation that exists in patriarchal culture. The result is that men become 'men' at the expense of the female 'other'. The psychological template for sexual abuse and racism is the inevitable result of such a cultural system.
>
> (De Zulueta 1993, p. 277)

In fact she explicitly acknowledges that masculinity is the problem, 'men are more likely to be abusers and females to be victims' (p. 237). She makes the point repeatedly that 'culture has a need to deny the importance of human relationships, an attitude that contributes considerably to the present difficulty in understanding violence' (p. 277). However, she has already made the point (and made it very well) that it is only men who have this need, that women in general are culturised, shaped to value intimacy and relationships. Approvingly, she quotes Kaplan who 'describes the woman's model of development as the "self in relation" model'.

> It posits that, for women, the core self-structure is a relational self that evolves and matures through participating in and facilitating connection with others and through attending to the components of the relational matrix, especially affective communication.
>
> (De Zulueta 1993, p. 237)

'As Kaplan explains, this is achieved...by...the girl discovering that her sense of self is enhanced by moving into relations with others' (ibid.).

Of particular interest is the finding that in most primate species the males are more aggressive than the females and that when maternal deprivation has also occurred the males tend to become extremely hostile (ibid., Ch. 4).

Although it is clear that failed attachment or traumatic attunement is not a sufficient condition for adult violence – or of direct interest here, male abuse of women – we are left with the question of whether it is a necessary condition. In other words, does a man have to have suffered from traumatic attachment in order to become violent to women? To date there is no research evidence for this. The difficulty is that it is impossible to find hard data about the infantile histories of the vast majority of men who present for treatment for abusive behaviour. Of course it is easy to classify them as being in the insecure category – their present behaviour towards their primary attachment is sufficient evidence of this. However, available research shows that children who fit this category have parents who are more than simply neglectful – they are actively abusive. Their mothers are described by Main *et al.* (1979) as 'interfering, neglectful, rejecting of close bodily contact, angry and threatening. They often mock their children or speak about them sarcastically. Ratings showed a strong association between avoidance and maternal anger.' Another study shows that infants who are physically abused tend to belong to the insecure attachment group (Egeland and Sroufe 1981).

So is failed attachment a necessary condition for later abusiveness? Does a person have to have suffered a failed attachment of type A (detached), type C (ambivalent) or type D (disorganised) in order to later act abusively or even act aggressively as an infant? I have already pointed out that only approximately 35 per cent of the disclosed abusers with whom I have worked have also been physically abused or have witnessed abusive behaviour in their family of origin – sufficient evidence that it is not a necessary condition *providing that we do not include early failed attunement as an abuse.* The reason for this is simple: it is almost impossible to get information about whether there was a failure of attunement during infancy. We urgently need research into this issue. At best it can be inferred and it would clearly be invalid to infer from an adult's abusive behaviour that such a failure had occurred. This would be faulty logic of the sort which says that if all dogs are quadrupeds and a horse is a quadruped then a horse must be a dog. However attractive such a conclusion may be the question is simply too important. It seems clear to me that those men who act abusively and particularly violently do so in a far more intense way when there is 'clear' evidence of failed attunement. In my experience it is one of the main criteria for predicting a high risk of future violence and such evidence may be often available in accounts of relationships with parents. This accords with research by Eron (1987), Morton (1987), Patterson (1982); Patterson and Dishion (1985), Patterson *et al.* (1989; 1991) and others which shows that early bad experience with parental harshness, cruelty or simply unsupportive behaviour coupled with behaviour which teaches and reinforces aggression is correlated with later criminality and violent offending. It is equally clear to me that we risk perpetrating an injustice to women if we isolate men's violence from other forms of abusive behaviour or if we begin to make scales of seriousness – a practice all too common in abusive men who have a vested interest in minimising the seriousness of their behaviour. The point I am making is that many of the men with whom I have worked could not be described as batterers or physically abusive, although they may have been profoundly abusive in other ways. Although it requires the use of the Adult Attachment Interview to determine, and I have not used this in assessment of abusers (it is too time consuming and expensive), my impression is that these men could not be fitted into the category of having been the victims of failed attunement. However, I am in no doubt that they are acting out a developmental failure concerning self development/ separation/individuation. The only person who can assess the seriousness of the abuse is the victim. What remains from De Zulueta's sensitive and extensive study is that failed attunement or early deprivation or abuse is a major contributor to violent and aggressive behaviour. She fails to demonstrate, however, her central hypothesis that failed attachment or traumatic abuse is the cause of violence. Whilst not denying its biological underpinnings, attachment theory places itself clearly with those who hold to environmental explanations for violence and aggression as opposed to an instinctual or drive theory. It places the responsibility firmly on nurture rather than nature and sidesteps the idea of the death instinct or primary sadism.

One interesting aspect of the attachment theory of violence is its understanding of the role of reversal (or identification with the aggressor) in causation. Briefly this posits that when someone is traumatised they can deal with it by inflicting the same trauma on someone else – treating others as we have been treated. In other words they become the perpetrator as a way of triumphing over the internalised abuser and forcibly projecting the distress of being the victim on someone else. This is the familiar theory of the 'cycle of violence' even if it derives from a more solid theoretical base than hitherto.

At this point I should like to mention a fact much quoted by non-clinical feminists and certainly often repeated by those who work with violent abusers. It is that a large majority of the latter are physically violent and otherwise abusive only to their immediate intimates, usually only their wife and children, even though, as my own experience informs, they often feel violent to others. I mention this here because it undoubtedly offers qualified support for attachment theory but, it needs to be said, it simultaneously undermines it.

Let us try to work a way through this. If early trauma is the cause of violence through reversal then one ought to be able to predict the pattern of that later violence. What does the theory lead us to expect? In a general way one would expect survivors of abuse to inflict abuse on children insofar as it is as children that we are hypothesised to have suffered the trauma of lack of attunement or have been physically punished or abused. Reversal would then be perfect if the victim were a child. However, although there is evidence for the intergenerational transmission of internal working models, it is not the case that all children who were physically or sexually abused go on to become adult abusers of children. In fact, as we saw in Chapter 2, the perpetrators of child abuse (where the victims are approximately pre-latency) are of both sexes, at least where substantiated, convicted or disclosed, abuse is concerned. In addition the gender of the victim seems to be insignificant and there is no doubt that women inflict serious physical abuse on children (Welldon 1993). However, as the victims get older the gender of the child becomes very significant indeed, as does the gender of the perpetrator, with the balance being heavily weighted towards female victims and male perpetrators and the abuse becoming increasingly sexual. Finally, in intimate adult heterosexual relationships it is female victim and male perpetrator. It is simply impossible for me to account for this pattern from within an attachment paradigm. I believe we need to look elsewhere for explanations. The fact of intimate abuse clearly supports attachment theory insofar as one would predict that survivors would attack those with whom they become intimate, form attachments, as adults. The contradictions are many. First, the majority of abusers of older children are male and most of their victims are female – so the abuse becomes gendered and sexualised. This would not be predicted from the theory. Second, the majority of men who inflict physical abuse on their intimate partners have not actually been physically abused or, insofar as we can tell, witnessed physical abuse in their family of origin. It may be the case that ordinary (?) corporal punishment should be included in the catalogue of physical abuse in which case a great many more men would fit the category of survivor or victim of child abuse. However, so would many more women. Furthermore, although slightly more boys than girls are physically abused, more girls than boys are sexually abused. Attachment theory accurately predicts neither genders of perpetrators nor the variability of kinds of attacks on children, nor the difference in the gender of the child victims. It does in fact predict that men and women would be equally violent and that the gender of the victim is irrelevant which suggests that boys and girls would be abused equally.

In summary, attachment theory suggests that our positive emotional capacities for empathy, connection and love and hence to develop and sustain nurturing and healthy relationships as adults may only develop adequately if a mother (or primary carer) makes a consistent and loving connection to the infant from birth onwards. This is undoubtedly true. However, apart from being essentialist and identifying mothers as easy targets for blame for all social ills, it fails to account for male violence to women and will continue to do so until it extends its theorising to include sexual and gender development.

Finally we need to take a look at socialisation or cultural theories of violence which account for violence or aggression as a learned strategy for resolving conflict, achieving satisfaction, resolving identity confusion or building self-esteem. These form an important part of any clinical approach to dealing with violence which recognises the import of the interaction of cognitive, social and cultural factors in producing violent responses. I have already mentioned the frustration/aggression concept of Berkowitz (1969; 1989). The underlying notion is the traditional psychoanalytic one of aggression as a natural drive which can lead to violent responses in the absence of adequate internal controls. These internal controls – the ego – have been seen as the natural focus of research (Redl and Wineman 1951; 1952; Redl and Toch 1979) particularly in isolating the factors which lead to faulty ego development. In general it is seen as being a consequence of inadequate socialisation during childhood. Research which shows that violent criminal offenders tend to come from conflict ridden homes and have a history of traumatic, cruel and harsh parenting (Farrington 1991; Arbuthnot 1987) supports this view as does the work of De Zulueta (1993). Such findings clearly suggest the need for a developmental perspective. Berkowitz's original formulation was that frustrating experiences act as instigators of aggressive behaviour by heightening the drive level and sparking aggressiveness. The drive is frustration instigated rather than innate and indiscriminate as in psychoanalytic theory. The inadequacies of this model are obvious in clinical practice. I have not seen a single violent abuser who has not shown the capacity to contain frustration and aggression in situations where, at home, he would become violent. It is also obvious that aggression is not the only response to frustration, whether for abusers or 'normal' men (see Bandura 1973). This clearly points to the need to include cognitive and emotional factors in the model, which Berkowitz himself has done (1989). That aside, the clinical implications are clear – working to strengthen the ego and develop the capacity to think whilst containing strong feelings to enable effective goal satisfying behaviour – what might be called ego training. This necessitates understanding how the man perceives frustrating situations and how he actively interprets them. In attachment theory terms, understanding how abusive men perceive frustrating events needs to be elaborated in terms of their internal working models of the self in relation to significant others. The frustration/aggression model has led many workers with abusers to focus on so called 'triggers' which induce frustration. I have to say that I have found this approach largely sterile simply because the list of triggers is endless; as soon as one is dealt with, another one appears. The triggers can change according to the frame of mind of the man – one day he may abuse because his partner has not cleaned the house; another day he may do so because she is cleaning when he does not want her to. My experience of the shortcomings and inadequacies of unpacking and analysing triggers in my early clinical career with abusive men, led me to develop the theory elaborated in *Why Men Hate Women*. This is not to say that it cannot sometimes be useful, particularly in helping the man to see how decisive is his behaviour, rather than 'out of control', but it is not sufficient as a model for understanding the motives for abusiveness and promoting change.

   At this point I need to state my own understanding of the role of frustration in abusiveness. Actually, I could as easily address its role in all forms of criminal violence perpetrated by men. To put it at its most simple, frustration is an essential construct in understanding abusiveness. Analysing triggers is usually a waste of time for the reasons I have already stated. Every abusive man I have ever encountered has been frustrated, some more, some less. The most serious abusers are the most intensely frustrated. Careful history-taking will usually elicit a lifelong tale of coping with a deep sense of unresolved frustration that the man himself cannot name or even differentiate. Often he will describe states of unbearable tension, of feeling wound up, explosive, etc. This is a visceral as well as psychological state. Provocations or triggers evoke extreme responses which reflect this frustration, not the trigger. Abusers blame their immediate environment for this frustration. They do not take any responsibility for it. It is something which is being done to them and the noxious precipitator has to be removed or destroyed. What are the origins of this frustration? Although, as I have already said, we need further research, I have no doubt that for serious batterers, it has its origins in the early relation with the primary carer. Of course, this frustration may be physical in origin; he may have been deprived of the breast or sufficient food presented at the right time. All, however, will have received enough or they would not be alive to abuse. What they have been deprived of – frustrated by – is an essential quality of care and attention, which may have included actual emotional or physical abuse. They are left with what Kernberg (1986) describes as

> a deficiency in genuine feelings of sadness and mournful longing; their incapacity for experiencing depressive reactions is a basic feature of their personalities. When abandoned or disappointed by other people they may show what on the surface looks like depression, but which on further examination emerges as anger and resentment, loaded with revengeful wishes, rather than real sadness for the loss of a person whom they appreciated...their controlling behaviour is a defense against paranoid traits related to the projection of oral rage. They envy others and...tend to depreciate and treat with contempt those from whom they do not expect anything.

They have usually been subjected to 'chronically cold parental figures with covert but intense aggression' who have caused 'intense oral frustration, the first condition for his need to defend against extreme envy and hatred'. They are hungry, empty, frustrated, envious, raging, contemptuous and terrified of their own neediness and dependency. They have a basic dread of attack and destruction. My understanding of this basic emptiness is that it is the absence of a primary good working model as described by attachment theory. In its stead is a deeply disturbing model, characterised by neglect or deprivation and persecution and pain. This causes deep frustration, envy and rage which leads to attacks on any object (person) who is seen to possess what was first lacking. As a consequence, as adults all good things are attacked and the feeling of emptiness and frustration becomes chronic and crippling leading to a permanent feeling of impoverishment and hunger. This leads to all relationships being experienced as frustrating. These men – and I stress they are the most serious abusers – are unable to take anything from anyone because to do so will lead to the stimulation of envy and the subsequent destruction of what they 'take in'. Nothing will satisfy them. As we shall see later, I believe there are other origins to this frustration which are developmentally older (Chapter 6). Before leaving this subject I want to point out something which most people are already aware of – men's capacity and predilection for sexualising this basic frustration. I believe it accounts for the existence of pornography, rape, masturbation and most sexual perversion. The stimulation of an erect penis is a short-term solution to most problems. It should be clear that helping abusers to develop a capacity to recognise, name and then tolerate frustration is a major theme of treatment. To put it bluntly, control and power, and the abuse used to gain and maintain them, are simply frustration pre-emption strategies.

The most prominent of the socialisation theories is that developed by Bandura (1973; 1977) which has been called 'social learning'. In contrast to a theory based on drives, Bandura describes behaviour as originating in the learning environment of the individual. Learning occurs through observation of models and the reinforcement of behaviour through the provision of rewards or punishments. One may learn violent or aggressive behaviour from three sources: the family, subculture (e.g. peer group) and culture (reading, TV, films etc.). To some extent research supports the general principles of social learning theory. Boys who witness violence in the home are more likely to be severely violent when they marry (Kalmuss 1984). I have also observed that the most seriously violent abusers are those men who observed their fathers being violent to the mother and were also the victims of parental violence. However, this does not apply to women who also observed paternal violence nor is it related to a woman's being subsequently victimised by such abuse (Pagelow 1984). It is also clear that many boys were abused or witnessed such abuse and do not become abusers, just as I have worked with many abusive men who were not abused (although they were victims of corporal punishment – endemic in the UK and many European cultures) nor did they witness abuse. It has to be said, however, that these were not men whose violent abuse was of the most intense kind. Also, social learning theory or 'modelling' simply cannot explain why it is that although females are more likely to be sexually abused than males they rarely commit sexual abuse as adults – a critique which also applies to attachment theory.

Perhaps the most wide reaching research of recent years is that by Straus. His development of the Cultural Spillover Theory is a significant contribution to our understanding of the impact of the cultural context on violent and criminal behaviour. His research (1991) shows that rates of all forms of violence are correlated with the level of institutionalised and therefore syntonic violence in the immediate culture. In this case he was able to control for differences in major variables because his sample was each individual state in the USA with its own laws determining what sort of violence, for example capital and corporal punishment, was permissible. This finding (see also Baron *et al.* 1988; Goode 1971; Dobash and Dobash 1980; Hanmer 1978; and Hanmer and Maynard 1987) is crucial for those of us who hold to a model of abuse which sees environmental factors, particularly social learning, as determining variables in the intensity and frequency of abusiveness, particularly violent abuse. It is clear that boys internalise values and norms which give permission for the use of violence to manage difficult situations. Foulkes' (1964) description of what patients bring to groups emphasises the pivotal role of the 'foundation matrix'. The dynamic matrix is the web of communication and relationship within a group. This matrix emerges out of the specificity of the interactions and history of the group but it derives its meaning from the underlying matrix of meanings which emerge from the shared cultural and biological history – the foundation matrix – of the individuals within it. This is the system of shared symbols and meanings which members bring to the group. They are acquired during the development of the child to adulthood. As Foulkes puts it:

> They are transmitted verbally or non-verbally, instinctively, and emotionally twenty four hours a day and night. Even the objects, movements, gestures and accents are determined in this way by these representatives of the cultural group. On top of this, but all permeating, is the particular individual personal stamp of the individual father and mother.

To this one would only add that since the time he wrote this, the pervasive influence of the mass media has reached a new level of intensity.

From her extensive study of the evidence De Zulueta concludes:

> Primate and anthropological studies show that the most effective way of transmitting socio-cultural values is through the infant-caregiver attachment system. In a culture where corporal punishment is the norm, such as in the USA, the potential for violence in the population is very high; this becomes manifest in high rates of child abuse, murder, rape and legitimate violence.
>
> (De Zulueta 1993, p. 277)

A full account of individual violence and abuse needs to include a theory of motivation derived from attachment based psychoanalytic thinking (including gender role learning and development), social learning theory, and a theory of the influence of the wider system of culture, its norms attitudes and values. High levels of institutionalised violence combined with underlying psychodynamic structures for containing frustration, hatred and helplessness, historically (i.e. retrospectively – see Chapter 7) constructed from within discourses about gender provide the breeding ground for man's need to control women and abuse them in the service of that control. Infantile or childhood experience of abuse may be neither a sufficient nor a necessary variable to produce violent abuse of women, but combined with a universally constructed view of women as suitable targets and an accompanying ideology, it is explosively predictable.

4 Special problems in the treatment of abusers

Abusers' subjective accounts

When I began to consider dedicated work with abusive men, I had fairly strong ideas about its causes. I had initially been trained as a gestalt therapist and later, as a result of a personal analysis, had taken a lengthy training in psychodynamic therapy prior to becoming a group analyst. For that reason I approached the problem as a clinician. In effect this meant that we were dealing with a psychopathology, a form of sickness, and the favoured intervention would be treatment. I had been forewarned in the available literature that abusive men are prone to denial. I could not have foreseen how intensively this is maintained, nor the creativity which men use to bolster their position. The vast majority of abusers share a number of features in their presentation. By far the most important is that they accept no responsibility for their behaviour although, paradoxically, they share a deep need to find meaning in it. The majority are also deeply confused about whether their behaviour is actually wrong, and veer between explanations which blame the victim and minimise the wrongness, those that blame drugs or alcohol and maximise the wrongness and explanations which rely on insanity. The rationalisations they employ to explain their actions leave a deep-seated feeling of dissatisfaction and discomfort.

The justifications and excuses which abusers use are myriad. Lest the reader is unable to differentiate between the two I shall outline the understanding of them as they were first used by the sociologists Scott and Lyman (1968) in their analysis of the process of what they call 'accounts'. An account is an explanation which is given by the perpetrator of socially unacceptable behaviour when he is challenged or questioned about it. Excuses are accounts which accept the wrongness of an act but deny full responsibility for it. For example, 'I lost control of myself' is an excuse. Scott and Lyman define a justification as an account which denies or minimises the wrongness of the act but assumes full responsibility for it. Ptachek (1985) goes along with the distinction between excuses and justifications although I personally find both his and Scott and Lyman's explanations confusing. My confusion derives from the notion that any justification assumes, not denies, the wrongness of an act, even though it may be minimised, but its main effect is to place the blame on the victim. Scott and

Lyman define two types of excuse: loss of control and victim blaming. In practice the most common justification, *not excuse*, is to blame the victim, which has the effect of minimising the wrongness. But why blame the victim if there is nothing to account for? As far as I can tell, neither excuses nor justifications deny the wrongness of an act but they are both attempts to negotiate an identity which does not damage self-esteem or the esteem in which others hold you.

The notion of 'accounts' is extremely valuable in clinical work as one struggles with abusers' attempts to negotiate a non-deviant identity, the main motive for excuses and justifications, by using a vocabulary of motives which is culturally legitimated and syntonic. However, the idea of excuses and justifications merely serves to confuse and obfuscate the issues because in my experience they are not qualitatively and clinically distinct categories but are distinguished by reference to their location in respect of two crucial differentiating factors, already given by Scott and Lyman. The first is the location of responsibility. In effect so long as the abuser can locate responsibility for his actions other than with himself he need not vary his self-image, and therefore can avoid the need for change. By far the most important aim of his account is to enable him either to totally deny or minimise his responsibility. This can be seen as a continuum from at one extreme 'I am totally responsible' to the other which is 'I am not responsible at all'. The second is the judgement of the legitimacy of the act, whether it is wrong both criminally and morally. The continuum of legitimacy or wrongness goes from 'totally wrong' to 'not wrong at all' although it is rare for this last to be used unless the man defines his behaviour and therefore the consequences as accidental. In my experience an abuser's assessment of 'wrongness' is dependent in a somewhat complex fashion on his apportionment of responsibility to the victim. For example, if the victim is seen as being totally responsible by way of her 'provocative behaviour' then the act will be seen as minimally wrong. The man's motives for denying responsibility or minimising wrongness, and this is his goal, are to avoid the guilt and anxiety associated with integrating his abusiveness into his self-image. In any case he will devote more energy in his account to denying responsibility. He will be far less concerned about admitting the wrongness of his behaviour when he can displace responsibility. The vast majority of abusers feel afraid, impotent and helpless much of the time in the face of what they experience as their partner's abuse. This derives from the belief that significant others bear you ill will, are unsupportive or persecutory etc. which is an element of an internal working model which predicts others' ill will towards you. This is similar to the 'attributional bias' mentioned earlier, the over-attribution of hostile intentions to others (Dodge 1980; 1991; Dodge *et al.* 1990; Weiss *et al.* 1992; Toch 1969). On the whole abusers believe themselves to be passive and submissive, and for many this is indeed true. As they struggle to protect their partner from their violent feelings their experience is that they are passive in the relationship. That aside, their self-image does not include being violent.

Apart from these two continua, the man is also involved in attempts to find explanations for the events, and he usually has available a range of possible causative factors which will dovetail neatly with his accounts. These causal factors have the effect of locating responsibility. They range from 'not self i.e. drugs, alcohol' to 'other i.e. victim'. If the man gets drunk or batters when he is using drugs he will deny any personal responsibility, accept that the act is wrong and attribute the blame to drugs. In explaining or seeking meaning for their behaviour or events, the vast majority of men will give different accounts consisting of excuses and justifications. In most cases these alternate accounts will be internally inconsistent or contradictory, as it is not possible for justifications and excuses, as Scott and Lyman define them, to be internally consistent and congruent. This is particularly clear when a man uses what Scott and Lyman call the excuse of 'victim blaming' through, for example, provocation. This excuse is also clearly a justification for behaviour, in that it accepts that battering or physical abuse is wrong but redefines this particular episode as non-abusive by virtue of having been provoked. In other words the abuser also retains the right to define the legitimacy of an act by its context. It is in this way that private rationalisations reflect and construct political ideologies, particularly where the justification consists of judgements of the victim's performance of what might be called appropriate wifely duties or feminine behaviour.

Fortunately, in spite of the great number of accounts given by abusers, they can easily be collapsed into positions with respect to each of these variables. It is in the process of doing so that the man will begin to see the inconsistencies in his accounts and that the process of destroying his rationalisations begins. Frequently, a man will say that he has no idea of why he behaves in the way he does. However, it is often the case that this is a euphemism for loss of control. The majority present themselves as confused and bewildered by their behaviour. More often than not this can be seen from the outside as a simple defence and an attempt at self-deception. However, most men are quite genuinely bewildered and confused and their experience is of being out of control. One factor which needs to be understood by the reader is that contrary to the stereotype, abusers are generally mild mannered. Naturally, we know of one such exception, and that is in relation to their partners. Apart from this known exception they do not differ from the male population in any particular respect. In fact, according to self-reports, the majority have great difficulty in being angry or assertive in any situation other than in their homes. Nonetheless, most are aware of a high level of arousal in other situations. According to some research (also validated by our findings at the Men's Centre), and often repeated by workers in the refuge movement, men who abuse women are less abusive than the male population as a whole. There are in existence treatment programmes for men who abuse women which regard abuse as simply one more expression of male anger, or hyper-masculinity – a perspective from which maleness, whether socially constructed or innate, may be seen as red in tooth and claw, containing primitive sexuality, needs for dominance and aggression which require constant restraint. In such programmes the violent abuse of women, including rape, is treated as if it were the same as random attack on another man. This approach has high face validity and is also an attractive alternative to the approach espoused here. Its primary attraction is that it obviates the necessity for a close examination of gender – in fact for any examination at all. Women are present only as an absence. I believe this approach is worse than merely neutral: it may actually be dangerous to women in the same way that claims of massive rates of hidden husband abuse by their wives threatens funding programmes for refuges. The most damning flaw of all 'anger management' is the assumption that anger is a cause of abuse, when any abused woman will tell you that anger is a form of abuse. It is not that there are no common factors in men's maltreatment of women and their violence towards men, but that these are less important than the differences. As I made clear in Chapter 1 the social context and the psychology are actually so different as to make it hard to understand why a clinician would treat them as similar unless it is that he is uncomfortable with the implications of the diversity. I will say more of men's violence to men later.

As to men's accounts, the majority of men will use more than one of the above explanations for their behaviour and their accounts will be full of internal inconsistencies. For example, it is not uncommon for a man to say that he was drunk (maximally wrong but minimally responsible), but that in any case she was being provocative by failing to act like a wife should (minimally responsible, minimally wrong) and he just didn't know what he was doing (minimally responsible, maximally wrong). On top of this, in any case, he had not really hurt her and she and the children still love him (denial of injury by minimisation therefore minimally wrong but maximally responsible). Clearly, he does not need the provocation account when he has already used 'drunkenness' or any other account which emphasises loss of control such as 'temper', drugs, depression, unhappy childhood etc. The fact that most batterers or abusers frequently mix excuses with justifications in a contradictory way is probably responsible for much of the confusion and bewilderment they experience. I believe (see Ptachek 1985) that this also reflects their desire to believe something which relieves them of guilt and responsibility whilst simultaneously trying to deny what they suspect, that they are lying to themselves. However, it is also undeniably true that in presenting accounts the abuser is attempting to find an explanation *for behaviour which he himself does not understand* but is desperate to explain. I will postpone, for now, a description of the ways in which we deal with these explanations in favour of a detailed examination of the significance of each. In *Why Men Hate Women* (Jukes 1993) I advanced the argument that whatever the particular motivations of each man for inflicting abuse on his partner, or on stranger women, there is a commonality in the unconscious of men, and in the construction of masculinity which helps us reframe male abusiveness in a form that enables effective intervention to prevent it. That said, it remains true that men offer many explanations as to why they abuse women, and I have received criticism for not sufficiently accounting for individual men's subjective accounts of their behaviour. I will correct that in this work.

Loss of control

This understanding, however it is framed (I blew up, I went berserk, I lost it, I didn't know what I was doing, I was drunk, drugged etc.) is advanced so often that it deserves special consideration here. Serious consideration of it will throw up some major moral dilemmas for clinicians, because there is no doubt that at the time of their attacks many of those abusers who make the claim (rather than simply lying or negotiating a non-deviant identity) are actually 'having the experience' of being out of control. That they are mistaken about the reality, not their experience, and that it is simple to show them the fault in their thinking and their motivation for it, does not obviate the necessity for us to understand the experience or explain it in terms which enable us to mitigate the rage and prevent further abuse. This issue is central to the current debates about criminality concerning personal and social responsibility and its implications for punishment as against treatment strategies. Economic decline in the Western world and the widespread fears and symptoms of social disorder this engenders makes this a heated and angst-ridden discourse. Apart from that, loss of control also raises questions which go to the heart of our understanding of emotional life. In fact, it asks precisely what emotions are and whether they are innate or socially constructed. The notion of loss of control is an explicitly animalistic conception of emotional life with the emoter as a passive observer and experiencer, not an agent or self.

The 'loss of control' as an excuse is very complicated. James Ptachek (1985) identified five different dimensions to the controversy about whether abusers are 'out of control': the clinical, the social scientific, the legal, the political and the moral/philosophical. My particular concern in this chapter is the clinical dimension. What this involves is questions about psychological and emotional abnormality or pathology and the extent to which the violence (or, in different kinds of abuse, sexual impulse) is innate or instinctive and beyond the abuser's ability to control (see Monahan and Steadman 1983 for their finding that there is no evidence of a link between mental illness and violence). This discourse has crucial social and clinical implications because to the extent that abusers are really out of control, *they cannot be held responsible for their behaviour*. This view is exemplified by the following quotation:

> When the self is threatened in any way – loss of identity through inner confusion or through domination by the object, a blow to self-esteem, an insult or humiliation, a loss of emotional supplies – aggression will be a prominent component of an overall response and, other things

being equal, violent action will occur aimed at negating the source of assault on the self.

(Glasser 1982)

Here, there is a clear implication that there is an ineradicable connection between the stimulus – the threat to the self – and the response – the aggression – aimed at the source of the assault. In common with all such statements, the assumptions that threat or frustration leads to anger which in turn leads to aggression or violence is unquestioned. But, as Bandura (1973) has argued, aggression is only one of a number of responses to frustration, or threat I might add, and all the men with whom I have worked use different responses to threat and frustration at other times both inside and outside the home. In fact it is not possible that all men who abuse have not used other responses to such stress. Aggression must therefore be a selective response. In the frustration/aggression hypothesis there is a clear assumption that emotions are innate and invariable, whereas, as we have seen from sociological and anthropological research, they are socially constructed and malleable. We feel what our culturation allows us to feel, and act in ways which our culture defines as appropriate for that feeling. Why is that women the world over are not attacking men when those threats seem so much more frequently to be directed at them? The fact is that these connections, between threat or frustration and aggression, are self-evidently false unless we can demonstrate the presence of psychopathology. Even then the burden of proof rests with the espousers of this position. Let me re-iterate, however, that frustration is a central component of the personality structure of the abuser. What remains is to describe its role and, crucially, its context.

The question of 'what is a feeling?' is a central one to my position. I am bound to say that I can find psychoanalysis quite obfuscating in this regard. On the whole, it does not take a critical position, seeming content with feelings as physiological states of arousal. My own thinking on this has been much influenced by cross-cultural anthropological research and by the work of Roy Schafer (1976), a radical psychoanalyst and psychiatrist. Put briefly, Schafer believes that feelings are complex ways of thinking and that they are essentially a form of activity or willed action; they do not happen to us. They are not things or substances of the self but actions and active fantasies pursued by the individual. An emotion does not exist apart from the behaviour by which we bring it into the world, such as naming it, choosing words, gestures etc. States of arousal are just that and they are ambiguous; emotions are not. They belong firmly in the world of the symbolic, whatever roots they may have in the imaginary as states of arousal.

Let me illustrate this with an example. It concerns a man, Peter, who, in a group, was giving an account of his anger with his partner because she had told him she was afraid of him. In common with all the men I work with, he had reacted to this statement with anger and shouting, thus precipitating more fear in her. She had then told him that he was a psychopath (an antisocial personality, which is actually partly true of everyone and more than a little true of him). He had reacted to this projection with more anger, verbally abused her and left the house. Actually this was quite an achievement for him, previously he would have inflicted serious physical damage on her. It is not difficult to see how this behaviour of his fits Glasser's model of a 'threat to the self'. In fact hers can also be made to fit quite well. As an aside I should mention that abusive men have great difficulty in dealing with projections of his nature, or simply with accusations which are not projective. It seems to me that the threat they feel, apart from the dread that their worst fears of themselves are being confirmed, is derived mainly from their predilection to identify totally with the projection, that the part is seen as being the whole. I have no doubt that this reflects a failure on the part of the primary carer to adequately process his destructiveness when he was an infant – she or he probably responded with anger to his anger and he did not develop the equivalent of psychic muscle or the capacity to process strong emotions. This identification of the part with the whole is parallel to what abusers do with parts of their partners prior to and during abusive attacks – she does something he experiences/interprets as bad so she is *all* bad. Teaching the skill of negative assertion (for example, in this case, Peter could have said something like 'yes I can see that sometimes I behave in a scary way') can be very useful in helping men to actually listen to their partners on such occasions.

However, to return to Peter. After almost all the other men in the group had noisily identified with his predicament, he was asked what the anger was about. He replied that he felt manipulated and controlled (an experience of many abusive men which I will take up elsewhere), although it was clear that he was struggling to articulate his experience and this description seemed inadequate. When it was pointed out that this was not an answer to the question of what was his anger for, he tried again. It was an expression of his frustration that he was not allowed to express himself without being accused of being frightening when he himself did not believe he was being so. So, someone suggested, he also felt misunderstood. He replied that this was so. Again it was pointed out that this was not an answer to the question: what was his anger for? By this time he was becoming quite confused and clearly frustrated. At that point it was suggested that maybe his anger was his way of telling her that she had good reason to be afraid of him and that she had better not tell him things about himself which were unfavourable and which he did not want to hear. His understanding was that his shouting and leaving her were expressions of his anger. He was being given another construction which was that his behaviour was his anger and that it had a purpose, not that his anger was a cause of abuse but was actually his abuse. He was splitting his feelings and his behaviour in a way which is actually very confusing for him and his partner. His anger is not a primary experience to which he then attaches meaning. His anger is a form of meaning; it is itself a construction of thoughts and physical actions which produce a state of arousal called anger and which taken together are instrumental and purposive. They derive from his attitudes and beliefs about himself and women concerning his rights and her role in relation to them. Central to these are his beliefs that his partner has no right to disagree with him about who he is, no right to define his behaviour differently from his own, no right to define her experience of him and no right to tell him things which are painful. In general his main expectation is of deference and submission in all things. The crucial point is that without these cognitive symbolic structures her words would be meaningless, and these are learned structures, not innate. I believe the structure precedes the state of arousal which then is selected, defined and labelled to become a feeling, although the sequencing is unimportant when it is clear that in any case the state of arousal is completely ambiguous.

I came across an interesting piece of research (Gottman 1994, p. 144) into arousal patterns between married couples under stress, which was carried out in a laboratory. Gottman claims to demonstrate, amongst other things, that men are more physiologically aroused than women by conflict and that these arousal patterns cause different and more aggressive behaviours. What is extremely interesting to me is that these arousal patterns, which Gottman argues are innate, seem only to occur in men when they are in conflict with women. The range of behaviours which he describes men using when in conflict with women are simply not used when men are in conflict with each other. My own observations repeatedly confirm that men can have control of these patterns of physiological arousal (which they mostly describe as undifferentiated 'tension') and that they are not simply a function of the autonomic nervous system, but also of their attribution of negative intent (negative interpretations) to their partner's behaviour and their perception of the consequences of acting in threatening ways. Even though there is an innate state of physiological arousal in conflict situations (frustration) and it is greater for men than women, it is quite clear to me that this is not a prime determinant of behaviour and that the arousal is completely ambiguous as to meaning until it is selected and defined through thoughts and memories (internal working models) which lead to intentions, selection of alternative responses, judgement of consequences and then actions, even though this may eventually happen in a millisecond. It is important to recognise that most abusive men start small, after consciously considering their intentions and the consequences of abusing. However anguished they may have been prior to the first few times, after a while the last form of abuse becomes a baseline for as much further abuse as they believe is necessary to achieve their goal.

Whatever the particular form or content of the account, I believe the experience of loss of control is a dynamic one and is the product of complex psychological interactions rather than a rigid reified structure of the Jekyll and Hyde type implied by perpetrators' accounts. This is not to say that abusers cannot split off or become dissociated from a part of themselves which is then perceived as a Hyde character, whether this is subjectivised as a 'bad temper' or uncontrollable impulses or rage, or as brought on by drink or drugs or stress etc., and dealing with this dissociation or denial is crucial in treatment or re-education. I will try to show that the perception of 'loss of control' is motivated. It is not an event in which the man is a passive victim of uncontrollable impulses or feelings, but in which he is an agent of the behaviour in which I include feelings and his understanding of it.

The concept of internal working models has central importance here. In my understanding, views such as those expounded by Glaser are actually a contribution to the construction of a vocabulary of motives which provides a theoretically syntonic link between individual rationalisations of unacceptable behaviour and the politics of criminality, or in terms of my interest here, gender ideology. To some extent it is the legacy of Freud's inability to detach himself from a physical model of psychological functioning that issues of personal responsibility for criminal behaviour are so confusing. The idea that behaviour has 'causes' rather than 'meaning' provides a means by which individuals can divest themselves of responsibility for their actions. The notion of an 'id' forever at war with society or culture locates agency away from the self. To some extent, therefore, accounts are an attempt to locate explanation in this impersonal agency, in the face of which the self is helpless. Madness is not a substance, an essence. We should recognise it for what it is. It is a state in which people act (by which I also mean feel) in ways which are socially disruptive. We should, and indeed do with abusers, speak the language of desire and meaning. This does not remove madness from the lexicon but makes of it what it is, a social rather than a psychological phenomenon. The central issue is responsibility, and in spite of the apparent complexity of Scott and Lyman's elaboration of the process of 'accounting' this remains a primary concern of an abusive man in treatment: to deny responsibility. He is only concerned with legitimacy when it becomes clear to him that he may need a back-up to his primary account, the sole aim of which is to deny responsibility. However, I am in no doubt whatever that when men use an account which centralises 'loss of control', some of them explicitly, they are completely sincere. The fact that it is embarrassingly easy to deconstruct it and show the vast majority of men that they were completely in control at all times, is neither here nor there. The promotion and management of a non-deviant identity, which 'loss of control' accounts are intended to achieve, is not solely a social phenomenon. It is also an intra-psychic process. 'Accounts' are intended to produce a persona which is consonant with the self-image.

Jan Horsfall (1994) writes extensively about what she believes from her literature search to be a common denominator of abusers; they all suffer from low self-esteem. I believe she is profoundly mistaken in therefore concluding that low self-esteem is implicated in the causation of battering. Apart from the mechanistic nature of this as an explanation (the batterer as victim) there are many people who suffer from low self-esteem who do not batter, most notably women. More importantly, however, by locating the origins of this low self-esteem exclusively in childhood (where it undoubtedly begins) she unwittingly colludes with batterers' accounts which displace or even deny responsibility. Self-esteem is a function of the relationships between the ego-ideal and the self-image. Most batterers or abusers do not consciously wish to be identified as abusers or think of themselves in this way. However, they know that they do it and that they dislike it. What, then, to do? What they do is to attempt to erect an indestructible scaffolding of accounts which project responsibility and protect their self-image. Short of total denial, which is a rare phenomenon similar to a dissociated state, they are only too aware of the discrepancies and contradictions in the scaffold. This 'causes' deep confusion, which is a functional escalation and which most abusers feel. It is not that abusers do not suffer from very low self-esteem but I am convinced that this is as much, perhaps more, a function as a cause of their abusive behaviour. They feel bad about themselves because they know they are doing bad things. However, not all suffer consciously from low self-esteem although they may experience other states of mental discomfort – their partner is a convenient container for the low self-esteem which the abuser forcibly introduces into her.

I have also come across a minority who, whilst not in denial about their behaviour, feel no guilt, no confusion, no doubt whatsoever about either their behaviour or their integrity. In every case these men have been abused as children in a way which would now be classed as serious abuse and lead to statutory intervention. Their accounts are buttressed by almost impenetrable and articulated ideologies about gender and the appropriate role of men and women. They genuinely suffer from the hyper-masculinity which other authors mention in their descriptions of abusers (see Adams 1988). It would not be difficult to diagnose them as pre-psychotic authoritarian personalities. They share a legacy of brutal early experience with their parents and later with peers. It can be quite frightening and frustrating to be in the presence of such men, and on the whole they are not treatable within the paradigm outlined here. I have attempted with six extreme types and failed with them all. Without exception they dropped out of treatment. This invariably happened when they were confronted with the scale of their denial and too much anxiety was aroused. Any crack in the bubble of their narcissistic perceptions was simply too much for them to cope with.

As to the majority, low self-esteem is not a source of the problem, but a route to its solution. The easiest way to cure guilt is to desist from the behaviour which causes it. Self-esteem can be bolstered either by modifying the demands of the ego-ideal or by behavioural change in the direction of one's expectations of oneself. Naturally, change is not quite so simple as this. In addition, many abusive men have a powerful set of identifications with male authority figures, which they may either act out or be in conflict with (see Moberley 1989). The ego-ideal may include expectations of masculine behaviour which conflict with or are in agreement with the paternal superego. Where they conflict the person will be struggling to dis-identify with the father, but inevitably lapses will occur.

Abusive men who use out of control explanations for their behaviour will frequently report 'I am afraid of myself'. This statement is rather odd, and requires urgent work with its user. Actually, it is rather clear that any man who uses loss of control accounts will experience anxiety of this nature. The superficial interpretation of it indicates that the man experiences himself in danger of being overwhelmed by some innate, not-self impulse or instinct. When asked what it is that they are afraid of the answer usually is that they are afraid they will do something terrible to their partner or themselves. This is, in fact, a high risk with abusers of the 'out control' type. Clearly, the greater the threat to the self-image, or the greater the dissonance between the ego-ideal and the image, the greater the shame and guilt the man will experience and the more intense will be the denial used. Under the circumstances, homicide or suicide are a real risk and special care should be taken by counsellors. In these cases it is advisable that the man's doctor be informed of the man's attendance in a programme and that a close watch be kept for any signs of incipient depression with suicidal content. Practitioners need to be aware of the risk of double homicide/suicide. Facilitators must be ready to advise of the need for medication with all men in abusers pro- grammes, but perhaps especially with 'loss of control' cases where there is a total denial of memory of violent incidents.

Frequently, men will use 'loss of control' and substance abuse in their accounts. Taken together they form a defiant challenge to attempts to undermine his denial. Alcohol, drugs, food allergies etc. are all employed in accounts from abusive men. They do not often form the basis of an account unless there is clearly an addiction problem. There is little doubt that substance abuse is widely accepted by policy makers and institutions as being a major causative factor in all forms of criminal behaviour, not simply men's abuse of women and children. As we shall see in the next chapter, however, like all forms of denial used by abusers it is very simple to deconstruct substance abuse. For example, I have never seen even a confirmed alcoholic who is abusive every time he is drunk. It may be true, and often is, that he is drunk every time he is abusive, but this gives the lie to the notion that alcohol 'causes' violence. I am sure that many women are often drunk and do not abuse their partners or commit crimes and that many drunken men will walk home safely whilst drunk and not assault anyone until they are at home. If alcohol causes violence without any intervening variables it would do so every time with everybody. In their review of studies of the relationship between alcohol and criminality, Taylor and Leonard (1983) found little to support the hypothesis that alcohol is a powerful indiscriminate disinhibitor of violent impulses. Gelles (1974) is clear that drunken behaviour is learned and he uses anthropological data to show how drunkenness varies widely in different cultures. Why is it that alcohol and other substances are so often implicated as causal in cultural constructions of abuse? As Finkelhor (1986) says, in order for a man to be abusive in any form he must have both the motivation to abuse and overcome his internal inhibitions against abusing. My own view accords with that of Gelles (1987) that men use alcohol in order to provide a post facto explanation and justification for their abusiveness. This is only possible when alcohol is socially constructed as a disinhibitor of violent feelings and desires – culture prescribes which actions and feelings can be disinhibited when drunk.

Where will it end if I say yes?

In anti-abuse programmes we frequently begin a session with a quick round to find out if any of the men have been abusive since the last session. Although it is rare for any of our clients to physically abuse when they are in a programme, there is always someone who has broken a basic element of the pre-treatment contract all men have made with the Centre – that he will not argue with his partner or become verbally or emotionally abusive. Although it is not invariable, most abuse begins with arguments. Not that these are necessary, but I have observed that the man often needs to start an argument in order to progressively access those parts of the bubble which he yearns to articulate and discharge – most notably his frustration and frustrated rage. In the early stages we teach him how to recognise the beginning of an argument and he agrees not to do it and instead to analyse why he wants to argue. A very high proportion of these arguments arise because of a conflict of wants, needs or interests. They are often, apparently, simple things, such as whether the radio will be on in the car, which TV programme to watch etc. Often in the past these arguments will have led to physical abuse and men are bemused that they can behave in this way over what they themselves describe as 'little things' when they never abuse over the 'big things'. As one man once said to another who had expressed his confusion over this, 'perhaps if you dealt with the big things you wouldn't abuse over the little ones'.

In discussions about the almost reflexive way in which they refuse their partners what they want (projecting the frustration) and insist on having their own way, the men will frequently ask, almost shocked, 'but if I did that where would it end?'. One man described an incident in which he and his partner were going to see a house they were considering buying. He was driving (which most men do when they are in a car with their partner – the need to be in control explicit here) and asked her to map read. She apparently had always disliked the radio on in the car and said that she would if they could have the radio off. (Note that she is asking for permission. She has already learned that her comfort is less important than his.) He always insisted on having it on, and usually had his way as in this case. He did not reply so she reached out and turned it down, he turned it up, she turned it down, he turned it up and so it went on until, in a rage, he stopped the car and said he was going to drive back home if she did not stop. (One hopes this is redundant, but I will point out that this is appallingly abusive. To all intents and purposes she is his prisoner in the car and he is not only threatening her with more severe consequences but punishing her for her refusal to accede to his wishes.) A colleague cut to the chase and asked him why he did this, why it was so difficult to simply allow her to gratify her wishes. His reply was, 'but if I do that where will it end?'. In the discussions which followed he insisted that we agree that where it would end would be with him 'under the thumb', being dominated by a woman.

The intensity of these discussions reveals the level of anxiety which this outcome evokes in abusive men. For them it is tantamount to emasculation ('giving her my balls on a plate'; see Chapter 5). In fact one such group ended with a detailed and rather hysterical discussion about the Bobbit case, in which a women cut off her abusing husband's penis. Readers can draw their own conclusions.

One of the more important issues which crops up repeatedly with men is that they are unable to construe relationships in any other than sadomaso-chistic terms, that is in terms of dominance and submission. The concept of partnership is completely alien. They are initially able to think only in terms of master and slave. It does not take early childhood experience of a dominating father, or even the presence of a father, to engender such perceptions. It can just as easily develop when the child thinks the mother is too much in control of the father and the most surprising events can trigger the conclusion that 'I will never let a woman do that to me'. One client recalled that he reached this conclusion when his mother decided that she did not like the house they were living in, and in which he and his father were content. He was shocked when they moved house and never forgave his father. His weakness on this occasion, as he described it, encapsulated my client's contempt for him from that day forward. As those who have read *Why Men Hate Women* will know, I believe that in any case this decision, to 'never let that happen to me', is inevitable for little boys. In fact, the decision is not so much to dominate as to resist domination, to avoid the experience of being a victim of female power. However, it is not, as Freud thought, castration which is the underlying anxiety. Indeed, anxiety is too small a word for what these men feel. Terror or dread would be more appropriate descriptions. It is the terror of being annihilated by a witch who is presumed to want him dead or immobilised – the primitive root of sadomasochism and the male/female divide – what I believe to be the most basic internal working model of abusive men. As we shall see, in common with many female authors (see Maguire 1994) I believe this is a defence against even more primitive fears deriving from the yearning to merge with the 'mother' with consequent fears of being lost in her. Paradoxically, this sadomasochistic model seems to have the effect of institutionalising men's feeling of powerlessness and many, certainly abusive ones, will spend the rest of their lives acting like persecutors and experiencing themselves as victims.

So, 'where will it end?' is not the question that a man in a programme should get answered. More relevant is the question 'where are you beginning?'. His question, however, has a subjective validity that needs to be addressed. He needs to be helped to understand it for what it really is at this early stage in his re-education. Because (as he already knows) the answer would actually confront every one of his beliefs and attitudes about men and women, the pillars of his identity. It would evoke so much anxiety that he will give up his attempt to change and justify it with the accusation that he is being asked to give up his masculinity. This is true, but at this stage all he can see is sadomasochism and a masculinity which is predicated on being on top of a subordinated and oppressed femininity. The hope is that he will eventually see these constructions for the chimera they are and that the question will lose significance. The question is an attempt to provide himself with a justification for not changing, for not giving up the power he knows he has and the pleasure of punishing his partner when she fails to accord to him the princely status (Balint's harmonious interpenetrating mix-up, or Winnicott's good enough mothering) he believes is his birthright (and actually is the birthright of us all for a while). All this seems incredibly easy when it is written down, but in practice it requires constant challenge and hard work to effect lasting change in men's fears of their fantasies of subordination to women. Freud, genius that he was, saw that the ultimate challenge for the psychoanalytic process was men's fear of the loss of their masculinity. As far as where it will end is concerned I would like to try to communicate some of what we try to do with the issues this raises, the real conflicts about needs and wants.

The first thing that abusive men have to learn is that they are not ready to deal with real conflicts because they are so much in the habit of expecting and getting their own way (not that they believe this!) that they have no way of knowing what is important to them. As Kaplan 1988, quoted in De Zulueta 1993 put it:

> In patriarchal society, men are given permission to expect gratification of individual needs and to use their dominant status to seek such gratification.

Actually I believe Kaplan understates the case. If 'seeking' does not provide, then men are more than willing to use abusive and controlling behaviour to achieve gratification. From inside the bubble of wanting and expecting control everything is equally important to an abusive man, whether it is watching the TV programme they want or deciding which school the children go to or, equally importantly, not wanting anything at all except to be left alone. They have no means of making meaningful discrimination between their desires and more importantly, their expectations of their partner. Men who abuse care for only one thing – their own comfort. They relate to every situation from this attitude. More importantly, they believe this should be the primary concern of everybody else. Of interest here is the fact that even outside the home they have this same attitude. It is often thought that abusive men are different in public from their private abusiveness. This is true, but it is still the case that publicly they exercise self-control because they know this is in their own long-term best interests and that public abusiveness will have serious consequences for their strategic comfort. Within the home, the difference is that they believe their behaviour has no long-term negative consequences and that they can act entirely selfishly. Nothing is negotiable or discussable for them, they either have their own way or as they often say, they give in to their partner's or children's demands . This 'giving in' syndrome has to be confronted. Abusive men will often defend their desire to get what they want, and acting abusively to achieve it, by referring to the number of things their partners do which they do not interfere with. This is patently misleading, and in any case is symptomatic of their desire to live the life of a single man with all the benefits of a full-time servicer. It is not that they do not care, but that they cannot be bothered at that moment because it would interfere with their present comfort.

So it is quite easy to answer the question: 'where will it end?'. Hopefully, it will end with the man realising that there are other people in his environment and that their needs and comforts are just as important as his own. Inevitably, if he can learn to value his relationship, this means he will have to make decisions which are in his partner's, not his own, interests and the long-term interests of the relationship. Partnership means just this, that one acts in its best interests. This is a very demanding objective for him and he will fight tooth and nail to defend his right to put his comforts above that of his partner and their children. The realisation that he is not the centre of the universe can be a profoundly painful and depressing one. It is knowledge he has always simultaneously possessed and repressed – known and unthought. Freud used to say that the trouble with self-analysis is the counter-transference. What he meant by this is that it is hard for us to tell ourselves the truth because we love ourselves too much and want to maintain a positive self-image. This is a healthy form of narcissism up to a point. With abusive men the counter-transference can seem at times to be quite delusional.

As we shall see later, male secondary narcissism as a defence against what I call 'the bubble' (or what Balint 1963 named the 'basic fault'), is a pivotal issue for clinicians working with abusers. Disavowal or denial of reality, or distortion, especially concerning one's own 'bad' parts or behaviour is the key to maintaining a good self-image. In work with abusers denial and distortion are the staple sources of our interventions. We use a simple four-part model of denial, which we also present to clients in the initial stages of their treatment. The four parts are:

1   Denial of abusiveness
    This is where you completely deny that you are abusive in any way or in
    a particular way, whether physically, emotionally, psychologically or
    financially. You will also deny that you wish to be dominant in the rela-
    tionship. In the extreme it involves your not remembering your attacks
    on your partner or otherwise forgetting abusive incidents or behaviour.
    Although it may be impossible to remember all abusive attacks, we
    believe that the more you remember and take full responsibility for, the
    lower the risk you will represent in future.

2   Denial of responsibility
    This is where you are able to acknowledge that you are abusive in all the
    ways you have been in the past, but you continue to insist that your
    behaviour is caused by factors over which you have no control. The most
    common of these are:

    a   drugs and alcohol
    b   provocation
    c   loss of control

3   Denial of frequency, intensity and severity – minimisation
    This is when you lie to yourself and probably to your partner about how
    abusive you know you are. You tell her you didn't hit her so hard or so
    often and you tell yourself the same thing. You tell her you didn't mean
    to do it and try to convince her that her experience of your behaviour is
    false and even crazy.

4   Denial of consequences
    This is when you refuse to see the effects of your behaviour on your
    partner and your children. You refuse to see that your partner's increas-
    ing confusion, fear and incompetence are caused by your abusiveness
    and that she fears you. You may hate her for her increasing dependency
    and use this as a justification for further abuse.

I will present some vignettes illustrating each form of denial to show how
these are handled in a group setting. Generally speaking these forms of
denial are in decreasing order of seriousness and treatment tends to be
sequential as it progresses.

Total denial

This concerns a man who had presented after he had been arrested for
grievous bodily harm (GBH) following an attempt on his partner's life. He
had strangled her to the point of unconsciousness and had been interrupted
by the police, summoned by a concerned neighbour. This man, a social
worker in his early thirties, was of mixed race and had suffered a great deal
of racial abuse in his lifetime. He was a very angry man, and at almost six

and a half feet tall and weighing 17 stones, mostly muscle, was a very intimidating presence. He had been arrested and held overnight in the cells prior to being charged and released on bail. The charge itself is interesting. His partner is convinced that if the police had not arrived she would have been killed. More surprisingly, when he arrived home (his partner had not been informed by the police that he was released, not uncommon in my experience) and was reluctantly admitted by his partner he was astonished when he saw the state she was in. Her face was covered in cuts and bruises and there were bruises on her neck. Of course he knew that he had attacked her, he was not crazy, but he had no memory of his attempt to strangle her. She had informed him, and he had denied any memory of it. In any event, he was at this point reasonable, and very afraid of what he remembered having done, in itself bad enough. She told him she was taking out an injunction and asked him to get his things and leave the house. It was some weeks later that he presented to the Centre for help. By this time he and his partner were in contact again and had resumed sexual relations. The charge against him had been reduced to actual bodily harm (ABH). She had allowed him into the home and it was clear from my conversations with her (when she was enquiring about our services on his behalf) that she had felt intimidated into having sex with him but felt that having broken the terms of the injunction by allowing him into the home, she could no longer go back to the courts to have it enforced. When I first saw him he was still in total denial of his attempt to murder her. In fact, by this time he was convinced that it was all made up by his partner to get him into more serious trouble.

This man raised interesting and important questions for me concerning the nature of denial. He was not denying that he had been and still was very abusive to women. He denied responsibility for his abuse, being convinced that she was very provocative like all the previous partners whom he had abused. He minimised it and until now had denied it had any serious consequences for him, the relationship or the children. The most important question concerns the relationship between real denial and mendacity. I believe that I can now tell whether a man is lying when he presents his account. When he is in genuine denial my belief is that I feel as bewildered as he does. This was the case with this man. His motives for the denial seem fairly clear. He is a professional carer. Somehow he has learned to live with the notion of himself as abusive provided he accounts for it with explanations centring on her provocation. This fragile economy simply would not sustain the notion of his having attempted to murder her.

Denial then is a function of the gap between the ego-ideal and the self-image. The greater the gap the more likely that denial is employed to bolster or maintain the self-image and reduce the guilt and shame of failure and the devastating blow to self-esteem. I'm afraid that I have no miracle solutions to denial. It requires constant confrontation and challenge. What is clear to me is that the risk of lethal abuse is highest in those who maintain denial at this level. In my years of working with abusers I have come across only five who were able to do so and they all failed in the treatment programme. In one case the man committed a serious life-threatening attack and was sent to prison for five years after terminating his treatment. Assessing lethality is an essential and high-risk activity for facilitators of anti-abuse programmes.

Denial of responsibility

Loss of control

A client recounted an incident in which he had designed an extension for his house. He had drawn up the plans and presented them to his partner with a declamation that this was what he was going to do. His plan involved a full extension across the rear of the house. She had responded by saying that she didn't want that. She wanted it to go across only a portion so that the present kitchen area would remain unchanged. He had immediately responded by shouting that she was fucking stupid, throwing down the plans and verbally assaulting her further. The context of this is that he had been repeatedly and seriously violent to her on many occasions. I believe it was only because he had entered the treatment programme that she felt safe enough to demur at his declamatory style. This false safety is an issue which all abuse programmes have to address. However, when he recounted this incident and was asked why he did it he replied, 'I just get overwhelmed. It just happens, I don't have time to stop and think about it.' He sounded very convincing and was undoubtedly sincere in the sense that he was not dissembling. He has a history of psychopathic violence of an intense and vicious kind, having been involved in fights with weapons in pubs, on streets and, on one occasion, kicking a police officer to unconsciousness. He is and was a seriously disturbed young man of 33. Although he sometimes suffered mild depression (actually a good sign) in general he felt fine. He did not present himself because of his violence but because he was about to get married, for the second time, and he was beginning to feel bored with his partner of 18 months. He reported that this was a familiar pattern. As soon as he had won a woman he would lose interest in her and start to look for sexual adventures with others, which he would invariably find and act out. He could not understand why he kept doing this and it had begun to worry him because he wanted a family. He also had realised that he would feel the same about anyone. Could I help him to stop, he wanted to know. It emerged that he was also seriously violent to his partner and he was worried about her leaving him, in spite of the fact that he was bored and spent most of the time wishing she were someone else.

It was at this point in his assessment that his violent history began to emerge. It was an endless catalogue. If another driver cut him up, as he saw it, he would chase them, stop them and assault them. If someone nudged him he would attack them. A look would often be enough. His face was badly scarred from knife and bottle fights. He was, when I first saw him, the living embodiment of one's worst urban nightmare. When he made his remark about getting overwhelmed and not having time, my initial reaction, internally, was complete agreement followed by despair. I thought about his history and began to have serious doubts about my assessment of his capacity for change and my decision to accept him for 'treatment'. I thought to myself, 'yes he's a psychopath and he probably can't stop himself'. The group was reduced to silence. They were familiar with his history. In addition he was quite a threatening character. His demeanour was that of a man who is secreting a weapon. Completely self-assured, quiet but attentive (one might say watchful), confident, careless to the point of ruthlessness. I sensed that the group was unwilling to confront him, even if they had been able to think their way through the impotence he was evoking in us all. Of course I could have made an interpretation about the transference. His relationship with his father provided enough grounds for doing so. However, I believed that dealing with his denial and passivity was far more important. The question was how? The standard technique for dealing with this particular form of denial, which has many variations, is to enquire about whether he ever feels the same sensations without becoming violent or otherwise abusive. In response to this he replied that it never happened, that he always was like this. He was clearly making a strong bid for an 'out of control, crazy' position. This is completely unacceptable. It is essential for the facilitator to show such a man, and his group, that he can exercise control and simply chooses not to, or at least to appear not to. Of course the situation is more complex than this. He is not simply attempting to negotiate a non-deviant identity, although one might think being crazy is a poor choice of alternative. He is also attempting to shore up an increasingly fragile self-image which does not include the truth of his abusive desires. Some detailed questions elicited the information that coincident with his 'uncontrollable' reaction he was aware of a funny feeling in his stomach. There is no doubt, by the way, that his reaction was constant so it is hardly surprising that he should insist that he felt he had no alternative. He abused his partner every time she resisted or contradicted his demands with needs of her own. It turned out that this funny feeling was familiar to him in his everyday working life when he had conversations with clients who wanted something which he thought was inappropriate or unnecessary. He frequently thought they were stupid too. However it was clear, and he was able to acknowledge it, that he did not react in the same way to them as he did to his partner. When he was asked why he said he would obviously lose his job if he did. In a sense it was downhill from then on. He acknowledged that we had established that he had the capacity for control. Why then did he not exercise it with his partner?, he was asked. At this point the impasse emerged. 'I don't know', he replied. He seemed very downcast.

I will leave this vignette for the moment. It has served its purpose of illustrating how to deal with this particular form of denial. However, I could not do so without first acknowledging that his ignorance is certainly genuine.

Men, abusive or not, cannot think clearly in the bubble. I believe it would be correct to say that a Kleinian might interpret this confusion as a defence against awareness of overwhelmingly painful envy of a primitive kind. The fixation point is certainly too young, developmentally speaking, for adequate reality testing or cognition to take place at an adult level and when a man abuses he regresses to the point of the fixation and the encapsulated psychosis. Before I move on, let me simply draw attention to the depth of this man's frustration.

Alcohol

This is by far the most commonly used form of denial of responsibility. Men will say that they were drunk, or had been drinking at the time. This is really quite easy to deal with. All it requires is the simple question 'do you always attack, hit, threaten her when you have been drinking?'. Often the man, (who is calculating all the time, looking for advantage or seeking to avoid damaging revelations) will realise that he is in danger of being trapped. If he says 'yes' he will probably be defined as having a drink problem requiring separate treatment (and be removed from the programme) and if he says 'no' he is losing his main negotiating strategy in his attempt to appear 'normal'. It really doesn't matter which he chooses. If he says 'yes' the follow up question is 'when you drink and your partner is not there do you always attack someone else?'. If this were true he would not be in the programme, he would almost certainly be in hospital or jail. The likelihood of his replying in the affirmative to this question is very low. Often there is a joke made about alcohol which causes violence towards one's partner. We frequently talk about that bottle having her name on it – in the manner of the bullet with a name on. Such humour can be very effective in undoing this particular form of denial. Once it is established that he can drink without being violent we are back in the land of cognition – of decisiveness, motive and goals where he can begin to map his internal world and create conscious dissonance and conflict about his abusive behaviour. The process is the same with drug abuse.

Minimising

Severity, intensity and frequency

This is the commonest of the forms of minimising. A slap becomes a gentle push; a punch becomes a slap; a beating is a punch or a fight. With other forms of abuse, verbal threats and screaming become an 'argument'. Descriptions of abusive behaviour need to be constantly challenged because abusers will always be economical with the truth. Dealing with it requires a no tricks confrontation method and the courage of the conviction that one is being misled. Additionally, and more importantly, isolation as a defence (that is, seeing the violence as the only form of abuse and without a context) is employed in order to minimise the overall severity of abusive behaviour. As we have seen, it is crucial (at least if you intend to employ a pro-feminist approach to abuse) to contextualise violence both within a framework of abusive behaviour and a social and political environment with a highly elaborated, if not articulated, ideology which determines the construction of femininity. Of course you may choose not to do so but stopping men from being violent without also stopping threatening behaviour and other forms of abuse is of little use to the women involved. It may be comforting never to be physically harmed, but living in the constant expectation or fear of it is just as damaging psychologically and emotionally.

It seems to me from having listened to many men who work with abusers that they fail to realise the clinical implications of not contextualising the abuse. Seeing the violence as the problem inevitably traps one in a paradigm which carries with it profound implications for treatment. At the very least it involves a strong focus on impulse control and anger management. Of course this does not necessitate that one would ignore the construction of masculinity in respect particularly of learned aggressive behaviour. However, what would be missing is, from my point of view, the crucial element of the construction of femininity and the central role of men's control in this process. The point about the man's being allowed to isolate his violence is that he will continue to see only this as being abusive behaviour. As many women have testified, and many men with whom I have worked, violent abuse is only a small part of his oppression.

Do not think I am minimising violent abuse – far from it. It is the most important behaviour to prevent, and as quickly as possible. However, isolating it from its context will make it much more difficult to prevent. It is actually only the most extreme of the abuses a man will use on a woman after all his other abuses have failed to achieve the desired objective – whatever that is, either tactically or strategically. The man must be helped to see that this is the case and that his oppression of his partner is an ongoing applied pressure on her to behave in ways he wants. If he is not willing to give up the underlying forms of abuse it is unlikely that he will ever give up the willingness to physically attack her.

The context also included the political, social and economic conditions outside the relationship insofar as they are gender biased. It is my belief, for which I have no research evidence, that a man who can be helped to see how his individual abuse of his partner is a part of a worldwide system of oppression of women will the more effectively give up abusive practices. One is often confronted by a man saying that 'all men do that though' when they are talking about a form of abuse which is more socially syntonic than physical violence. Take, for example, the common situation where the man is in charge of the family finances. He is the only one who knows the true financial position of the family. In this way he gets to control what is spent and when. He decides what is the disposable income and to whom it goes. I can think of many examples where the woman has requested that she be told of the family finances so that she could undermine his control of her and he has begun to do so reluctantly. The frequency with which he will do something to enable him to stop this and blame her is surprising. Often he will provoke an argument about her stupidity or lack of understanding of the way banks or credit card companies work. Or he will explain in a way which makes it so difficult to actually understand, by making it appear excessively complicated, that his partner will feel foolish and give up her attempts to get from under his yoke. Of course it is difficult to get accurate information about how many men are in total control of the family finances, but it is certainly true that the vast majority of men are who attend groups with the Centre. In the circumstances it is easy to see that each man's claim to be doing nothing unusual is difficult to deal with.

For those of us who are already used to thinking in terms of partnership and gender politics and women's oppression by men it is clear that there is a connection between the individual ideology which allows a man to control the family finances and the worldwide economic discrimination against women. Men will fight very hard to maintain this power because ultimately all power is economic. Equal control of the finances would actually make her as powerful as him. Of course if she had it genuinely, by that time he would no longer mind. It is very important to enable the man to see that his motives for maintaining control in this way are as direct an expression of his need to be in control of his partner as is his physical violence and that they are mutually dependent. The issue is not the violence but the control and the power and his inability to live with the castration symbolised by her equality. Equality in relationships is not fragmented – it is either total or it does not exist. There can be no areas where the man retains the right to be in control. If he has this right then he retains the right to re-assert control in any other area. This is the importance of dealing with context and of breaking down the defence of isolation used by all abusers. I will take the risk of repeating myself by saying that the abuser cannot be permitted to retain his belief that his violence is the problem. This can only be achieved by challenging all his abusive behaviour.

Denial of consequences

Cliff, a designer, talked in the group of his partner's recovery since he had left the home, of how she had gone to college and seemed to be really getting her life together. Martin, one of the very few sociopaths ever to complete a programme, intervened and pointed out that David was simply reinforcing his denial by saying that since Christine was doing so well so shortly after his abuse of her, then his abuse must not have been so bad. He also correctly named the form of denial, of consequences, and confronted David's smugness in his report. David was very downcast but took the confrontation well and acknowledged its validity.

This is a very subtle form of denial – the minimising of the consequences of abusive behaviour – but it is very insidious and it is important to constantly remind group members of the long-term effects of their actions. One simple way of doing this is to insist that they read literature from the women's movement documenting first-hand experiences. We present a reading list to participants and regularly remind them. We also ask them to tell us about their reading and if they are not doing it we want to know why. Resistances such as this occur all the time. Minimising the consequences relates also to the children and the relationship. It needs to be addressed in relation to other family members and the abuser himself – particularly the effects on his self-esteem and self-image. I have remarked elsewhere that the low self-esteem of abusers, which is by no means as common, at least consciously, as some would believe, is as often caused by his abusiveness. I do not believe it is ever implicated as a cause of abusive behaviour.

Another area where consequences are denied, and often the most tragic, is that of children. The evidence is now overwhelming that children who are raised in homes where there is a lot of conflict and where fathers are violent will grow up with potentially profound personality and behaviour problems ranging from psychopathy to addictions and criminality. Additionally, their capacity for establishing trusting intimate relationships will be seriously impaired, often beyond repair (see Zulueta 1993). I recall one couple in which the man, who was a real charmer (see Horley 1991) insisted that he and his partner, who owned and managed a business together, were a great team. He believed, and unfortunately continues to do so, that any failings in the business (which was performing disastrously) were entirely due to his wife's hysteria and her pre-occupation with her children's (his stepchildren's) problems. He was just a saint who was doing his best to keep everything together in the face of her constant provocation and her concern for her 'bloody children'. This in spite of the fact that he had, to my certain knowledge, physically attacked her on at least 19 occasions over a six year period and frequently screamed at her in a threatening, drunken rage no matter what the social context or whether the children were present. The children were very disturbed and largely as a result of his treatment of their mother. From my point of view it seemed clear that as far as he was concerned there should be room for only one child in her affections: himself. He may well have been the most disturbed of them all.

Sulking

Before I examine sulking I would like to digress slightly and talk about men's love for women. It is apposite here because in my opinion abusive men are incapable of loving a whole object and yet there is a type of abuser, much written about in the literature on abuse, who claims that he abuses because he 'loves her too much'. Loving too much is a particularly insidious form of control. I prefer to call it idealisation. Either the woman or the relationship can be idealised. The desire is to have a perfect relationship with the woman never behaving in a way which threatens the idealisation by evoking the primary frustration. When she does the man will begin to abuse. In my experience the most common form of abuse the idealiser will use is sulking. This type all too often is completely unaware of his ambivalence or his destructive feelings towards his partner or women. He just wants everything to be perfect and is at a loss to understand why it is that she cannot see that everything would be fine if she did not complain or get depressed or anxious – which he experiences as reproaches. However, it is impossible for her not to get depressed or anxious. She is living in a psychological prison in which there is no room for her to express who she really is. She is only acceptable to him when she attempts to live up to the idealisation and create a non-conflictual relationship similar to that described by Balint (the harmonious interpenetrating mix-up): an impossible task.

To avoid confusion, let me say that most abusers sulk to some extent. All idealising abusers sulk and it is the first and most important form of abuse for them. It is a little known fact that sulking, with which most of us are familiar, either from experience, or as parents, or both, can take on a degree of severity such that it becomes a clinical phenomenon (see Malan 1979). Briefly, a sulk occurs when someone feels rejected and instead of getting openly angry, or sharing the hurt, retaliates by rejecting. The 'perceived' cause of the hurt, the rejecting other, is indirectly invited to approach in order to restore the situation by making some form of reparation but the person in the sulk consistently rejects any attempts to make them feel better. In extremis there is a chronic form of this where the person in the sulk is simply unable to express love in any form. It is remarkable to me that sulking has never been mentioned in the clinical literature on abusers. In my experience, a very high proportion if not a majority of abusers are prone to severe attacks of sulking and, in fact have been in a sulk for most of their lives, deriving as it does from the basic fault (or the encapsulated psychosis, the primary frustration) and the desire to punish the inadequate primary carer (mother). Much of the rigidity which I will write about, and have already described elsewhere (Jukes 1993b), is symptomatic of sulking. I would not be surprised if this causes some disbelief. Sulking is generally thought of as something which children do but not as part of the adult behavioural repertoire. In reality many, if not all, adults do it at some time in their lives with more or less seriousness in their relationships with important others. My belief is that it is a major blight on the capacity for happiness of many adults, both men and women, and it is closely connected with envy and the desire to destroy or spoil the contentment of the frustrating object. In abusers it is a serious clinical phenomenon, with serious tissue consequences for the women who live with sulking men. The first thing to do is to describe what a sulk is, how it feels to the sulk, and how it appears to and is experienced by the others in the sulk's life. Second, I will account for its developmental origins, before finally elaborating its role in men's abuse of women.

The experience of sulking

As most of us know from first-hand experience there is little doubt that being in a sulk is profoundly unpleasant. I cannot count the number of times I have interpreted an abuser's sulk and to have him agree, often with great surprise and laughter, that he is indeed sulking and had not recognised it. However, when I suggest that he give up the sulk he replies that he is unable to do so and that even if he could he would not want to (this is a primary quality of sulking) as it would mean 'letting her get away with it'. What this boils down to is that he feels like a victim, that the object of his sulk has done something which he feels is so unfair and unjust that the idea of her going unpunished is unthinkable. In fact, his experience is that he cannot get out of his sulk, not that he will not. As often as not he wishes he could, as the isolation and alienation he feels is unbearable. The sulk, however, is not the origin of the alienation – that is more a by-product of the failure of primary care and the consequent weakness in the self-system and the dissociation from all tender and loving feelings and the need to be attached. However, his sense of the justice of his behaviour, and his certainty of the conscious intent of his victim's sadism (the over-attribution of negative intent, again), is such that he cannot bear to yield to concern and ruth even if he is aware of any.

The punishment he wants to administer is a form of emotional torture, it is a tallion revenge. Often he would like to inflict serious physical injury, sometimes including killing, but cannot do so, not only for fear of losing the object (a fear which is one of the causes of sulking), but also because her death would deprive him of the pleasure of making her suffer and the possibility of eventual gratification of his unmet needs. The gratification is in inflicting suffering, and all her entreaties, her fear, her pleading with him, her tears, are, apart from causing intense guilt and anxiety, actually pleasurable for him. They are the gratification, the reward which he seeks. During a sulk, pain and rejection are the only currencies in which he can trade. He can neither take nor give anything good, in fact has no wish to. His desire is to spoil. During a sulk the man will show enormous rigidity in his behaviour and demeanour. He becomes what the partner of one man referred to as 'a wardrobe!'. This pungent image conveys the rigidity of a sulk as well as any other I have heard. I have come to the conclusion that, apart from the origins of the sulk, the feeling of being a victim is usually illusory or is based on a childlike frame of reference which offers distorted interpretations of others' motives and/or limited options for resolving difficulties in relationships.

The internal object relations of men who sulk is interesting. Even after the hurt, imagined or otherwise, has occurred, the man will experience that his partner is still inflicting pain on him because she is not suffering, or not enough, for the damage she has done. This is delusional in most cases, although his experience is real enough. The initially 'perceived' hurt evokes the repressed sadomasochistic relationship with a primary carer (who is probably not gendered) and this evokes the internal sadomasochistic dialogue, felt as being with the present object although deriving from and linking with the unconscious internalised primary carer, in which his retaliations stimulate attack and more retaliation and so on in a process of projection.

I believe that with this understanding it is possible to explain one of the more enduringly opaque elements of battering and abuse, why it is that the man does not stop and cannot explain why it is that he feels he cannot. The experience is that she (the real object) continues to punish him. How do men articulate this? More often than not it is a version of a powerful drive to achieve what he believes to be justice. The difficulty is that justice is tallion during such regressed episodes. If the original hurt (by the primary carer, whether from disharmony, weaning, separation, individuation, frustration or whatever) was experienced as a life-threatening event then, apart from any complications arising from guilt or concern, the urge is to push the real object into life-threatening anxiety (projective identifications). This explains to me why it is that most abusive attacks stop when the object becomes completely passive, a state which unfortunately does not preclude death. Her simply breathing or standing can be a precipitate for more abuse. Apart from the psychodynamics of this, it is appropriate to elaborate on the power and control issues involved. The passivity of the victim gives him what feels to be absolute control of her, and only when he feels he has re-established this (re-established because it is the illusion of his primary infantile omnipotence) will he cease that particular attack. More often than not the man is a victim of his partner failing to live up to his expectations, and feels deeply hurt and angry. However, it is my experience that he needs to feel like a victim in order to be abusive and express and ventilate his sadism, a sadism which is continually reinforced by his unreconstructed and failed expectations of women.

David Malan is not sure about whether the aggression in sulking is sadistic, although I am fairly sure of it. Many programmes of intervention with abusers, especially those which emphasise the socio-cultural basis of abuse, recognise the pivotal role of male expectations. Writers of a socialist feminist persuasion (see Wilson 1983; Segal 1987; 1990) make it clear that they see men's violence and abuse as a response to the strategic failure of men's power over women, both individually and collectively. It is easy to understand how they reach this conclusion. My own work leads to a different understanding, which could simply be stated as follows: that abuse is both the source of power, and the final and definitive tactic by which men maintain it. Abuse is, therefore, an expression not so much of its failure but of the power itself. My work at the Men's Centre, which recognises the importance of deconstructing men's expectations of women has, however, demonstrated that the most important of men's expectations of women are not in awareness or accessible to consciousness. This has crucial implications for the limitations of cognitive/behavioural intervention. Let me illustrate with a case history.

A case of chronic sulking: Brian and Zelda

I recall one man, Brian, who initially came into an anti-abuse programme because he periodically attacked Zelda, his partner, when she became angry with him. It was clear from his account that she was emotionally disturbed and moreover, from my conversations with her, that she knew this to be true. However, the history of the relationship turned out to be very interesting. When they had met, 30 years previously, she had been a junior executive in the company in which he was a manual labourer. Now she is in a state of fairly chronic depression and finds it hard to maintain a job as a domestic cleaner. He, meanwhile, after much encouragement and support from her, has qualified as an accountant and holds a senior post in the same company.

Her behaviour as he described it seemed bizarre. Whenever there was a problem in the relationship she would get very angry with him because he was profoundly passive. The bizarre element was that whatever the problem or content of the upset she would end up 'accusing him' (his words) of loving his mother more than her. He was completely nonplussed by her demands that he talk about this as the source of his passivity and her pain. On the face of it, it seems pretty weird for a man of 49 to have to deal with this constant accusation, particularly when, after many years of his partner's 'nagging' about it, he had, rather sadly, broken off all contact with his family, and particularly his mother and father.

Initially I had disagreed with him, but after talking with his partner about her accusation it seemed that she was pretty disturbed and described herself in this way. As a result we began to focus on his violent responses to her in an effort to deal with his abuse in isolation. After some time it became clear that he had now begun to abuse her by telling her that I agreed with him that she was 'crazy'. In general it had not been very difficult to help him to the point where he could see from the schematic outline of their relationship that her anger with him was almost certainly the consequence of his years of emotional and physical abuse and vampirism. He completed a programme of treatment and had made a decision that he would never physically or emotionally abuse her again. The group was fairly confident that the physical violence decision was firm, although there were some reservations about his capacity for emotional abuse, particularly in the light of his unresolved passive abuse. The outstanding major difficulty for him was his response to Zelda's accusations about his loving his mother more than her, which still occurred with great frequency. In spite of these reservations, the plan he had made detailing all the methods he would use to take responsibility for his feelings and behaviour was sufficiently convincing.

After about two years he contacted me again. He had not attacked Zelda during the intervening years but her accusations about his love for his mother had continued, though less intensely. He was still having great difficulty with this and had reached the point where, feeling very hurt and angry, he reflexively withdrew from her, sometimes for days. He told me that Zelda had agreed she needed some counselling but had done nothing to pursue this. I read in my case notes of my earlier discomfort about agreeing that Zelda was disturbed and determined that this time I would accept that there was something in her hypothesis, even if she was unable to articulate it in a way which allowed him to work with it. I was more comfortable with this as it was in accord with our principal working hypothesis, which we share with clients, that all the problems in the relationship are the consequence of his prior abusive behaviour, and that causation is linear not circular or systemic. I took him into once-weekly individual therapy and we began to talk about his early childhood. As I have already said, we do not do this as a matter of course in anti-abuse programmes. Our focus is group based and more empirical and pragmatic. He talked particularly about his relationship with his brothers, one two years older and the other two years younger. He described how he had always felt alienated and isolated and talked about the loneliness of his childhood (he presented the typical attachment history of someone who had suffered not good enough mothering). He told me of two incidents in which he had gone to school. The first was when he was five years old and somebody was sitting in his desk at school and he had simply left without a word and gone home. The second incident was precisely the same except that he was 13. In response to my interpretation about the effect of his mother's pregnancy and his brother's birth his eyes filled with tears. He said that he had felt unwanted and could never win his mother's love or appreciation. He had been aware of a chronic feeling of rejection. He described how he had never taken part in family life, preferring instead to stay in his room reading or playing on his own. He could see how he had continued the same pattern with Zelda. One additional piece of information he volunteered was that both he and Zelda had agreed, before the marriage, that they did not want children. When I asked him if his withdrawing from Zelda, and from his family, were symptomatic of sulking, he smiled broadly. I believe this was the first time that he had ever had a word for his experience and began a marked shift in his relationship with Zelda and his general mood.

The point of this vignette is that it illustrates that Zelda had been right all along. Brian really had cared more for his mother throughout his marriage. His feelings had been frozen, fixated on his deep hurt and rage about her pregnancy and the rejection this meant. He had gone into a sulk and had never come out of it. All the symptoms which David Malan mentions, and a few more, had been acted out in his marriage. I would mention in particular his inability to express love, his withdrawal and the constant invitations to Zelda to approach and repair the damage followed by his rejection of her. He actually was unable to tolerate things being good for any length of time and felt compelled to spoil. He interpreted any act of hers which interfered with his comfort, or frustrated his expectations, as a sadistic rejecting attack. This was the point at which he externalised his chronic sulk. It became clear that he always struggled with impulses to reject her, and that he constantly expected rejection. The fact is that Zelda was proven to be substantially correct in her accusation about Brian's feelings for his mother. Zelda had suffered for his feeling of rejection by his mother at the birth of his younger brother. It was not so much that he loved her more, rather that he blamed Zelda for his frozen anger and hurt and had punished her for it since they had married. She had inherited a chronic sulk. Marrying a woman who did not want children, and reducing her to a state of depression and low self-esteem so that she was a virtual prisoner had ensured that not only would she not be able to reproduce the original trauma but also that he could punish her for it.

I frequently find myself asking men like Brian if they love their partner. In spite of the constant carping and complaining, the bitterness of many years of experienced victimisation, the hurt, rage and vengefulness, it is surprising how often the answer is an unequivocal 'yes'. In these circumstances, however we might understand the neurotic or dependent nature of this love, it can provide the basis for real change, the motivation to work to make his partner happy. In practice, as far as sulking is concerned the most important issue for abusive men is their inability to forgive. For example, Brian was able to articulate that when he withdrew into his hurt and rage at her rejection of him, he felt unable to move towards her unless she made some act of reparation. Actually, this was quite misleading, as he came to see, because it was not that she could do something to repair the damage he felt she had caused, but that he could repair it by inflicting as much suffering on her as he felt she had caused. This, of course, is the point of the invitation to approach followed by the rejection of her approaches. Only when she had suffered enough would he cease his abuse of her. The problem is that it was impossible for him, as for most men in this situation, to say when enough was enough. The gratification of inflicting sadistic torture, without any guilt because it is 'justified', can be compelling and difficult to renounce. Add to this the power of being in control of the rejection, rather than the victim of her rejection, a substantial masochistic satisfaction in maintaining the experience (illusory though it is) of being an innocent victim and it is not difficult to understand why it may be hard to stop.

Justice can be a very important issue in these circumstances (and, incidentally can provide the basis for a creative adult sublimation, as witness the man for whom it became the source of a successful career as a probation officer although it did not prevent his becoming abusive to his partner). Again, though, the problem is, 'whose justice?'. From within the sulk, there is only one kind; old testament, tallion justice. Eye for an eye, tooth for a tooth vengeance.

If forgiveness is the key to ending this particular source and form of abuse the primary question is what we, as clinicians can do to stimulate such forgiveness. Balint (1967) makes some interesting comments about love and hate, which are worth paraphrasing here. He believes that all hatred is distorted love. He also believes that it is easy for love to be converted into hatred when the loved object frustrates or causes one pain. However, he believes that converting hatred back into love is very hard because the essential requirement is that the object of the hatred has to change. In other words the hated object has to make an act of reparation towards the one who hates. Clearly this is very hard to do, although parents do it all the time. It is more than I believe we have a right to ask of a battered woman who in any case is in no way responsible for her partner's hatred or his maltreatment of her. I also believe that Balint was wrong in his conclusions. I think that hatred can be mitigated in the therapeutic process without the analyst or therapist having to provide a corrective emotional experience or a reparative object relationship – although this is inevitably on offer with any therapist who is minimally competent. My experience teaches me that men can also learn to mitigate their hatred by other means and that analytic cognitive/behavioural techniques can be very productive of this process. More than any other method, I believe group analysis offers the opportunity for this hatred to be articulated and metabolised.

I believe we also have to ask obvious questions about why abusive men do not seem to possess what might be called a 'normally expectable capacity' for forgiveness. This issue has been much written about in psychoanalytic literature, particularly that of Melanie Klein. In general, forgiveness is thought to develop from the capacity for concern about damaging the object of one's hatred. The issue of forgiveness is closely connected with another concern in work with abusers, the development of the capacity for empathy with the victim of their persecution. I will address this first.

Developing empathy

If I might go back to the case of Brian and Zelda. Why is it that men seem never to think about what women feel? Clearly this is related to the issue outlined earlier: it is a very basic failure to develop any idea that other people have internal worlds and minds of their own. It is as if we men do not have problems in relationships with women – it is always the women who have problems with us. For example, Zelda's thinking about Brian's mother and his inability to see it as anything other than her problem. One of the reasons this was never resolved was because she took his passivity as a sign of assent to her belief. He was just glad when she was not raising the issue. He simply never thought of it as his problem. Clearly this is only true if there is no relationship between them. In a real partnership any partner's problems are the problems of the partnership and Brian should have at least taken the initiative in raising the issue of how much of a problem it was for him that Zelda was having such a problem with her belief.

Men's not thinking about what their partners might think or feel is overdetermined. However, it is closely connected with the capacity for empathising with women or even being remotely interested in the fact that women also have an internal world (assuming the man is aware that this is possible). In general this is made difficult by the ways in which masculinity is formed and developed, and the fact that the identification with the mother is eschewed in order to attain a masculine identification. It is as if the capacity for identifying with women is thrown out with the particular identification with the mother, at least in heterosexual men who fall within one standard deviation of the mean. In fact, the situation is more complex than this. It is not true to say that the abusive man does not possess anything related to the capacity for empathy. Rather, it is his capacity to identify with the suffering he inflicts which underpins his abusive behaviour insofar as it is sadistic rather than instrumental, and as I have made clear I believe that sadism is always present. The problem is that he derives pleasure from the identification with the object of his abuse, as do all sadists. There is an enormous gap between empathy and identification. It seems more appropriate in these circumstances to ask how we can help him move from pleasure (this word always provokes protest from abusers. I often end up conceding to satisfaction, a word with which they have fewer problems) in inflicting pain, to guilt and concern about it. I do believe this is important, and that the capacity to tolerate guilt and to use this creatively to inhibit aggressiveness or sadism is essential in helping abusive men (actually anybody who suffers from an excess of ambivalence).

Dynamically, all these issues are connected: remorse, guilt, empathy and forgiveness. In object relations psychology (Klein 1975; Winnicott 1969; Fairbairn 1952) they are all a function of the child's success in negotiating the depressive position and successfully developing concern for the object. Developmentally, the depressive position is the route out of the paranoid position which precedes it. For the benefit of those who are not familiar with Kleinian thinking I reproduce below the main points of Laplanche and Pontalis' definition of these positions (1980).

> The paranoid position describes a mode of object relating during the first four months of life in which the aggressive instincts exist side by side with the libidinal ones and are especially strong. The object, a partial one – mainly the mother's breast, is divided into two parts, good and bad...and anxiety which is intense is of a persecutory type.

The resolution of this anxiety is predominantly a function of the relative strength of the aggressive and libidinal instincts. The depressive position is established around the fourth month of life and is characterised by the child's ability to 'apprehend the mother as a whole object (rather than as a part e.g. the breast)'. The splitting of the object ceases during this phase, in healthy cases, and denial is attenuated. The child 'knows' that the good and bad part objects are actually one and the same i.e. a whole object, mother, and anxiety is associated with

> the phantasied danger of the subject's destroying and losing the mother as a result of his sadism and it is overcome when the loved object is introjected in a stable way that guarantees security. Ambivalence is thus

established in the full sense of the word...depressive anxiety is only successfully overcome and transcended thanks to the two processes of inhibition and reparation of the object.

Reparation here is of fundamental importance. Laplanche and Pontalis have this to say about it:

the subject seeks to repair the effects his destructive phantasies have had on his love object. The phantasied reparation of the exernal and internal maternal object is said to permit the overcoming of the depressive position by guaranteeing the ego a stable identification with the beneficial object.

What they say about Klein's idea's concerning defective mechanisms of reparation is of particular importance in our efforts to understand abusive men. They go on:

to the extent that their operation is defective, mechanisms of reparation may come to resemble sometimes maniac defences [feelings of omnipotence] and sometimes obsessional ones [compulsive repetition of reparatory acts]'.

Does this not forcefully remind one of the habitual repetition of abuse followed by the hearts and flowers stage so ritually acted out by abusive men?. It would seem self-evident that men who are abusive, and not only violently, are both insufficiently inhibited in their aggression and that their reparative mechanisms are defective. Lest I stray too far from my point about the development of concern, let me turn to what Winnicott (1969) has to say about it:

The origins of the need to make reparation are in the child's anxiety lest he should lose the object he needs to keep him alive and his guilt at the damage he has inflicted on the object – mother.

Interestingly enough abusive men do not seem to suffer from either the anxiety that they will lose the object – they are very omnipotent and fail to believe her capable of leaving – or from the guilt at the damage they are causing their partner. Of course this cannot be wholly true or they would not present in treatment. However, they generally maintain verbal denial of concern about either issue for some time into treatment. This is more to do with their inability to tolerate both the anxiety of loss or abandonment and the realisation that they have no control over their partner if she should decide to leave. In addition it enables them to feel powerful if they can maintain the 'I don't care' position in the face of what are actually overwhelming feelings of powerlessness.

Programmes for abusers, whatever their orientation, whether the 'soft' co-counselling tendency or the 'hard' perpetrator tendency, all agree that establishing empathy with the victim is important if the men are to permanently give up abusing. Many techniques are used to foster at least the foundations of an empathic understanding. These range from showing films about abuse, of which many powerful ones are extant, to therapeutic work enabling the men to be aware of times in their lives when they have been bullied or have felt powerless and afraid. What we are attempting is really rather ambitious. There is no doubt that from a Kleinian perspective we are dealing with some of the most primitive psychological processes leading to the development of pathology and overlaid with a lifetime of learning and introjecting linguistic and symbolic constructions of male and female behaviour. Even an optimistic psychoanalyst would balk at aiming for resolution of these issues in any less than five years of five times a week sessions. Yet I and many other therapists like me attempt to achieve this impossible task in less than a year of once-weekly group sessions. Actually it is not quite true to say that this is our aim. More reasonably we are aiming to stop the behaviour which is the visible manifestation of these processes of development in the hope that if we can break the vicious circle the reparative process will continue afterwards and be self-perpetuating. That the man can learn that his low self-esteem, anxiety and chronic guilt (or his chronic guilt avoiding strategies) will be seen and felt to undergo significant change when he changes his behaviour towards women.

I am now at the point where it is possible to see sulking in a developmental framework. I described earlier how Melanie Klein saw the major dynamic crises of the child as outlined in her elaboration of the paranoid and depressive positions and how the resolution of them leads to the development of whole object relations. The literature describes how the child resolves the paranoid position when she or he becomes afraid that her or his attacks on the object may lead to its destruction (whether in fantasy or reality) and this leads to the development of guilt and concern and the depressive position. I believe that sulking is what bridges the two. It is a phase in which anger and destructiveness still hold most sway; concern for the object is also present but not in sufficient quantity to mitigate the destructiveness or the need for revenge. The need for revenge originates from the child's experience of being traumatised. Every sulking abuser I have ever met has suffered a serious rejection, loss or abandonment early in life that threatened the destruction or fragmentation of his internal world. The sulk differs from the depressive position in that destructiveness is more evident, rather than the guilt and self-reproach of depression. The child or sulking adult wants to harm the object but is aware of the need for it and has the desire to preserve it. Fantasy attacks on the object have the effect of also laying waste to the infant's or sulk's internal world, leaving him with no internal good object to mitigate the dread of utter loneliness and life-threatening separation. The reconstitution of the good object is the only route out of this anguished dilemma. It is unfortunately followed by another attack as envy and vengeful feelings re-emerge with the reconstitution of the good object. The repetitive destruction and reconstitution of the object who does not retaliate is probably the only way of eventually mitigating the destructiveness. Here we are into Balint territory and the concept of corrective emotional experience. However, this cannot be provided by the abuser's victim and he has no right to expect that it should be. Unfortunately, this is his expectation.

I wish to point out an interesting difference between the position of Balint and that of Klein in their understanding of what it is that mitigates the hatred. Balint points to the need for the hated object to change and make reparation. Klein points to the need for the subject to repair the damage. This is profoundly important. Perhaps in the analytic setting it is possible to offer a relationship which is designed explicitly to correct the damage which caused the basic fault. In work with abusers it is my experience that in general this is a generally fruitless task – they are usually too defended for a corrective emotional experience to have any effect. The key to change lies in exposure to a group setting in which their abusive behaviour is defined as the key problem and the underlying damage is addressed largely unconsciously through the medium of the group dynamic matrix. In individual analysis or therapy, the therapist usually has to sit and wait out the sulk, which is inevitably acted in the consulting room. It is also acted in the abuse group and later I will address how this issue is approached in a group setting.

5 Isolating the violence
Variations in clinical approaches

The simple purpose of all forms of treatment for abusive men is to prevent them from abusing. One is attracted to any theory which seems to offer a simple cause for abuse on which one could focus all one's clinical energies. Life, however, is rarely like that. Abusive men are very complex, behaviourally, cognitively and emotionally. If I might use a military metaphor, one needs to work on all three fronts at once. However, in my own way I believe I understand the final cause of men's abuse of women, particularly when we are focusing on the psychology of abusers rather than the socio-political, cultural or family context. As I understand it, all abuse reduces to men's capacity for and our need to devalue women, which of course connects it directly to the socio-political context. I am convinced that if we can stop a man from devaluing his partner he will stop abusing her in every way. It sounds simple, but unfortunately is not. The motives for devaluation are complex and deep seated. They go to the heart of the construction of masculinity in Western culture, and its bedrock – castration anxiety as a metaphor for the loss of desire (socially constructed as the loss of masculinity). Fundamentally, the method of work I use is the talking method. Although role playing and other behavioural forms may have a place in the facilitator's repertoire, I am convinced the self is constructed through language and that the spoken word is the key to change.

I should begin by outlining what is meant by devaluation. No doubt we are all familiar with the term in its economic usage. There it means that a currency is made to be worth less than it previously was worth. Ultimately, of course, as in Nazi Germany prior to the Second World War, the currency can become utterly worthless. The paradox of this process is that whilst the object is almost terminally devalued people become, at one and the same time, completely obsessed with it. So it is with abusers. The processes by which devaluation occurs in human psychology have the same end result. A person, in this case a woman or women, is deemed to be less valuable, to possess less intrinsic value than previously. In the extreme, as with currencies, this can mean that the woman or women is perceived as being without value at all, as not possessing or holding any qualities which one might desire.

Of course devaluation can be selective, for example sexual, intellectual or maternal. When a man devalues his partner he begins to see her in negative ways, as being stupid as in the case of Steve below, or ugly, or smelly, or disgusting, or simply as not being attractive in any way at all. Equally, he can see her as vicious, dangerous and threatening, or, in a word, bad. The process is self-perpetuating and escalating. One bad thought can lead to another in an almost obsessive way. Many men have told me how it got so bad that they could not bear to be in the same room with their partners and how going to bed became a torture which they had to face every night. Steve, for example, had requested help to stop becoming bored with his partner. He had gradually developed the habit of going to bed a little later each night, on the pretext that he was watching something on TV, until he was sure that his partner would be asleep and he would not have to face the emotional torture of her desire for sex or his guilt about not desiring her. He was beginning to find her physically repugnant even though he insisted he loved her, wanted the marriage and children with her. It takes little imagination to empathise with the anxiety this was causing him, let alone the pain it caused her. Another client, Alan, would never ask his partner for any advice or help with problems, whether they concerned her or not. He was convinced that she had no contribution worth making or listening to. I could give literally thousands of examples of this. Every man I have ever worked with suffers from the same problem and inflicts the same pain on his partner. The assumption that women are brain-deficient, senile or otherwise similarly intellectually handicapped is endemic.

The most fundamental motivation for contemptuous devaluation of this sort is fairly obvious. If the woman is/has nothing of any value then what could the man possible want from her? Why should the man want to be in this position of living with a woman of whom he desires nothing? Can it be, as I believe, that it is because he can then hold to the illusion that he has no need for her, hence no dependency, no vulnerability? She cannot then be a source of frustration and envy as she does not possess and withhold what he yearns for and is incapable of taking even if he could acknowledge she had it to give. Above all, it renders her powerless and chronically insecure although it would be a rare abuser who could acknowledge that this is an intended consequence of his treatment of her. She knows, whether or not it is true, that if he feels this way her position is fragile at best, disastrous at worst. She may redouble her efforts to please him, because of course everything she does is devalued as she, herself, is. The control and power this bestows on the man can be limitless as the woman goes to increasingly desperate lengths to demonstrate her value and receive what we all need, validation, legitimation and a recognition of our fundamental worth, the absence of which can cause self-hatred, depression, anxiety and despair. In a relationship in which he is not actually violent the woman may find it easy to leave him. However, where violence is also being inflicted, and it usually is, this becomes increasingly difficult as she slips into the 'battered woman syndrome' of helpless victimisation.

One might ask whether it is really true that the man feels this way about her. The answer is probably no, but it rests on what we define as true in the murky world of the unconscious and human desire. He certainly believes it is true when he is ruminating in a spiral of negative blemishing. However, on those increasingly common occasions when a woman has or finds the resources to leave such a man, his collapse into depression, panic and fragmentation can occur with a speed which is frightening to see. We are of course in that confused world of transitional or projective space where qualities of one's own are denied, repressed and then forcibly (in an emotional sense) thrust or projected into another. We are then free to exist as if we have actually got rid of them. Unfortunately, at least for the man if not the woman, her departure will necessitate his repossession of that which has been disowned – the dependency, confusion, low self-esteem, anxiety, helplessness, vulnerability etc. The gain for him is that the projections help him to maintain his psychological equilibrium. From his point of view this is of immeasurable value. I could fill a book with stories of vampire-like men who build successful careers on the emotional bedrock of their partners and then abandon them when they no longer fit the bill required of a successful man. The novelist Fay Weldon has made rather a successful career from fictionally documenting the exploits of such men and their hapless victims. Psychotherapy should and must deal with these primary gains. Treatment of abusers, first and foremost should deal with the secondary gains, which are no less important in maintaining the man. These gains are overwhelmingly concerned with power and control over the woman and the maintenance of service provision by her – washing, ironing, sex etc.

Steve, who I mentioned earlier, had asked for help with his boredom with his partner. A discussion had taken place in his group about boredom and every man identified with Steve's dilemma and his history. They had all used pornography, they had all flirted with other women, some had had affairs, but they all became bored and had great difficulty in sustaining desire for their one partner. Steve wanted to know how to stop being bored so that he could stop repeating his history of constantly changing partners. It was suggested that if he ceased his endless devaluation of his partner he might begin to see her as desirable again. It was pointed out to him that it was hardly surprising that he found so many women attractive when he was living with someone who he found so unattractive (for the present I will set aside any consideration of splitting). Steve's reply was, 'but I'm bored with her because she has no attractive qualities'. Another man retorted that it was probable she had no qualities because he was bored with her. There is a crucial difference here. The sub-text was the suggestion to him that what he could not tolerate was desiring her, that for whatever reason he was afraid of his love for her. It was at this point that a discussion took place of the issues outlined above, about devaluation and dependency, power, need and vulnerability – the fear of loving. Because he was terrified of loving her, or any woman, he needed to devalue her in order to define her as unlovable and justify continuing his search for the perfect woman so long, of course, as his partner remained at home whilst he conducted this search. The boredom was a result of his withdrawal of his desire. Of course it expresses his fundamental ambivalence also, an ambivalence which he could not contain or tolerate and which always emerged whenever he became close to a woman.

This discussion illustrated to me once again the power of groups for abusers. The group had asked him what he was afraid of that he needed to withdraw from his partner. Remember he was working for everyone at this point. It manifested his fear of intimacy and his need for control and his fear of the loss of it. He volunteered, and remember this man is substantially sociopathic, 'if she left me I'd be completely devastated. I don't know how I'd survive.' When I replied that it seemed inevitable if he continued with his present behaviour, the violence, the boredom, the devaluation etc., another man in the group turned to me and erupted: 'what you're saying is that we've got to hand over our balls on a plate'. Fortunately I was not the only one to laugh at this.

This castration anxiety is a very serious problem we encounter in our work with men who abuse women and children. I have reached the conclusion that this is true whatever the nature of the abuse. Unfortunately, I cannot claim authorship here. Freud reached the same conclusion in his work with men over one hundred years ago (for a slight twist on the theme see Chapter 6 below). The root of this fear, as it is expressed in abusers groups, is that they will be emasculated if they do not dominate a woman. The central role of the domination of women in male psychology is complex. I will leave aside for the moment any consideration of its developmental causes in favour of an attempt to describe both its experience and its treatment (notwithstanding Freud, who was rather despairing when it came to his own efforts to deconstruct it with his patients). It has some connections with the issue of 'where will it end if I say yes?'.

Abusive men are abusive whenever they are confronted with any requirement from a woman that they cease to locate themselves as the centre of the universe. Many men demur when confronted with this. They will frequently say things such as 'but I let her do lots of things she wants to do'. This is indeed true. However, it is not the case when her desires contradict or are incompatible with his. So his 'letting' her actually costs him nothing. It interferes with nothing. His basic position, which he will rarely articulate, is that he is not willing to sacrifice anything for the relationship. Why should he when he gives her his presence, the greatest sacrifice of all? Such men rarely feel held in a relationship, they feel trapped. When her desires are a challenge to his secondary narcissism he will feel uncomfortable (frustrated) in a way which initially is very difficult to differentiate. He will not have bothered to attempt to differentiate it unless he is actively encouraged to do so. His experience is of rapidly differentiating this discomfort into a feeling of anger or rage and then becoming emotionally, verbally and maybe physically abusive. What precisely is this discomfort? Anger, yes. Rage, yes. This is why he presents for treatment or re-education in the first place. Let me make clear that this is the focus of our efforts to change him notwithstanding any remarks I might make about underlying processes. What emerges later, as his rage and anger are deconstructed back to their original discomfort, is powerful anxiety and depression connected with the primary frustration. This may take some time. A great deal of prior work is needed to undo the violent behaviour and the beliefs and attitudes which underpin it. Most of our work centres on men's denial of their abusiveness. In part this is a problem generated by the treatment process itself, at least in the form in which it is practised at the Men's Centre. It arises because the emphasis is on stopping the violence before understanding it and if we are successful the man will begin to experience a lot of discomfort. It is hardly surprising that this evokes resistance.

I mentioned earlier that the definition of abuse we use is formed from a mindset which integrates many different frameworks. I suppose it is best encapsulated in what we present to our clients as the working hypothesis. This will come as something of a shock to any reader who is immersed in systemic thinking or marital therapy. It is that 'you are 100 per cent responsible for any difficulties in your relationship, this includes your violence and any of her behaviour which you use to justify your abuse'. I hope to show, if I have not already done so, that this idea is not as ridiculous as it undoubtedly sounds. I will return to this later. In the circumstances our definition of abusive behaviour can be experienced as rather extreme. I can only say that in my long experience of its use, it comes as a revelation to men who abuse. In general they are relieved that someone has finally recognised that they have a serious problem. Its one drawback is that it does a lot of the work that they themselves should be doing. Taking full responsibility also includes recognising their abusive behaviour.

The crucial point is that when men present for treatment or re-education they do so in the firm belief that their violence is the problem which needs attention. Although not all men who present do so for actual violence, it soon emerges that they have all been violent but simply have not defined their behaviour as such. The first aim is to undo the isolation – their belief that violence is the problem. This is neglected in some treatment programmes where anger management is the focus, but I believe that anger management colludes with the abuser's definition of the problem and fails to achieve one of the main aims of intervention: to make the woman safe. A close examination of isolation is a good way to begin to articulate the model we use in our work with abusive men. It is a special problem with abusers and it is a ground from which I can begin to introduce the theoretical framework underlying our intervention strategy and contrast it with the available alternatives.

Isolating the violence

I have elaborated the defence which is most common with abusers of females, whether sexual, violent or other: the defence of denial. This was elaborated as a denial continuum along which we assess each client's progress towards a violence- and abuse-free existence. If there is one difficulty which it is paramount to confront with abusers it is the form of denial which can be called isolation. One major problem in its clinical treatment is that it is a culturally syntonic form of denial and is used just as extensively by politicians, policy makers, law enforcement agencies, the courts, the medical professions and professional clinicians. I have also made the point that abusers insofar as they acknowledge they have a problem (usually not very far) routinely define this as being in some way about their violent behaviour towards women. One of our first tasks is to disabuse them of this notion: the notion that their violence is the problem. Although, for obvious reasons connected with the safety of the abuser's victim, his violence is the first behaviour issue we address and attempt to change, we begin by clearly stating that as far as we are concerned his violence is symptomatic of a more fundamental problem. This problem is his need to be in control of his partner, and his violence is instrumental in achieving and maintaining this control. My belief is that his isolation of his violence is part of the problem and his difficulty in resolving it. We do not believe that violence can be effectively confronted or prevented if it remains in isolation. Sooner or later it will re-appear, for however long the man remains violence free.

I am implicitly critical of orthodox, analytically derived models as a ground from which to work with abusers. In effect my critique is that analytical, dynamic psychotherapy or marriage guidance or family therapy (I realise that these cannot be conflated theoretically) collude with men's violence to women by using the same defence as the abuser. They isolate the violence, and even if they define it as the problem, which most do not (it is usually seen as expressing more fundamental insecurities in the man, such as depression, impulsivity, low self-esteem, attachment anxiety or dependency anxiety etc.), by so isolating it, and defining it as a behavioural problem, they underpin the real motives for its continued use. They implicitly collude with its ideology whilst explicitly condemning the means. I think that this is fundamentally dangerous, not only for the women directly involved but also for women in general who end up sharing responsibility for their attacker's behaviour. In effect, this is an attempt to articulate why it is not only mistaken but dangerous to isolate the violence. I also want to understand the motives for this therapeutic isolation and examine the similarities with abusers' motives. I would like to begin with a clinical vignette which encapsulates the issues before going on to elaborate what I mean by isolation for abusers.

Robert is a 35 year old man, married for ten years to Tabatha. They have two children aged five and three. Some months before, Tabatha had sought counselling for her communication problems with Robert. Her counsellor had invited him in for a couple of sessions after Tabatha disclosed that Robert had been hitting her. Although the counsellor recommended that Tabatha continue to receive counselling to deal with the trauma of Robert's violence she referred Robert for treatment for his behaviour. I should say that this in itself is quite unusual for an analytically trained therapist, as Tabatha's is. However, she had been in regular contact with us and was familiar with our work and our philosophy. Although she did not support it wholeheartedly, she agreed that Tabatha (as a woman) could not share any responsibility for Robert's violence.

In common with most of our clients, Robert began by freely expressing his belief that he did not belong in treatment. I should add that Robert had no choice but to attend. His enlightened employer had made it clear to him that to some extent his career depended on it. When I began the structured interview for his initial assessment, he admitted that he had been violent to Tabatha but far less so than I was already aware of from my contact with her counsellor. He disclosed two incidents during the marriage, but I knew of at least five. As far as he was concerned, this was not the problem. If there was one it was that there was a difficulty with communication in the relationship. He acknowledged that he shouted at her and got angry a lot, occasionally calling her hurtful names. 'I sometimes have a problem with my temper', he acknowledged. He believed that Tabatha provoked him by nagging and interfered with his desire for a quiet life; he is passive and uncommunicative and these were her motives for seeking counselling. As we have seen, minimising is routine for abusers and after making a mental note of it I proceeded with the interview. In one section we cover the couple's arrangements for dealing with family finances. In response to my questions Robert indicated with some intensity that as far as he was concerned both he and Tabatha had equal access to money and that family finances were a joint responsibility. At the same time he insisted that his giving her an allowance for personal spending did not contradict this understanding. He insisted that if she was unhappy with the amount she had only to ask for more. He saw no contradiction between this and the idea of financial equality. He added for reasons which will become clear that she spent all this on herself whereas he never spent money on himself. 'If she didn't buy me clothes I'd be here naked', was his comment.

In summary, Robert is an abusive man, more than some and less than many others. In fact, his physical abusiveness is, in my experience, less severe than the norm in its frequency. Tabatha had never been forced to visit a doctor or hospital as a result of Robert's violence, and his worst attack had consisted of slapping her face whilst sitting on her, and frightening her by telling her that if she did not stop screaming he would throw her from the sixth-floor window. He is clear that he would not have done, but that he had to convince her of his intention to do so. He succeeded. Tabatha stopped screaming. Of course it is not for me to judge the level of violence, only

Tabatha can do that and this was a paralysing, frightening experience for her. I want to make clear that so far as our programme is concerned there is no distinction between levels of violence. All violence is unacceptable. Furthermore, as has been said, it is no indication of the severity of the underlying problem, which is the strength of the desire to control the woman.

I would like to consider briefly how Robert and Tabatha's problem might be dealt with by other clinical specialists. I realise that this necessitates some simplification and that there would be many variations on the themes I present. However, I will attempt to avoid caricature.

Psychiatry

Psychiatrically, the situation is complex. The number of individual pathologies implicated in 'marital violence' is bewildering. Poor impulse control is a common diagnosis. Importantly, few abusive men are diagnosed as suffering from any recognisable pathology although 'personality disorder' is beginning to be quite fashionable and there is some evidence that most abusers suffer from some form of personality problems. There is little doubt that if one takes Clecky's 16 factors as a guide to diagnosis (Clecky 1964) many abusive men will be found to be suffering from an antisocial personality disorder and this is confirmed by my own experience, although many more would fit a diagnosis of a different personality disorder, such as schizoid, passive/aggressive or aggressive/sadistic. One is, however, entitled to question how much this is a diagnosis rather than a social or moral judgement. Perhaps the most popular diagnosis in recent years has been that of borderline personality (Bolton and Bolton 1987, p. 67) and there is recent research which indicates that many abusers do labour with a borderline personality organisation (Dutton and Starzomski 1994, pp. 203–22). A new diagnosis came to my attention recently when a female victim phoned for advice about what to do about her non live-in boyfriend who had been physically abusing her for eight years (giving the lie to marriage being a precondition for abuse). He had gone to a psychiatrist who had afterwards requested to see the woman, apparently to check how disturbed she might be and presumably in an attempt to explain the man's behaviour. The woman asked the psychiatrist if her boyfriend was sick or schizophrenic. She was told 'no' to both questions and that her boyfriend, who is 56 years old, suffered from aggression. Unsurprisingly, the woman was not impressed with the diagnosis.

In spite of this the psychiatrist gave the man some medication to deal with his problem and told the couple not to expect quick results as the medication took at least six months to work. I assumed she had prescribed lithium salts until I discovered she would monitor him only every three months. The psychiatrist may have been employing a sophisticated placebo and paradoxical intervention strategy.

In another recent case the man, who had already been prescribed antidepressants, was asked to bring his victim to his next session with the psychiatrist. The psychiatrist spent that session attempting to convince both of them that it was the wife's provocative behaviour which was responsible for the man's attacks. The man told me later that it almost ended his marriage, that his wife and he felt crazy after the session because they both knew that it had nothing whatsoever to do with her and there was nowhere to turn for help. He desperately needed to be told that he was mentally or emotionally disturbed. As we have seen, this need is not uncommon and forms part of many men's attempts to negotiate a non-deviant identity through the use of a range of stereotypical and therefore consensually validated vocabulary of motives. In effect when a man presents to us in this way he is offered a choice of being either 'mad' or 'bad' but is informed that he cannot have it both ways. When it is expressed in such stark form most have no hesitation in choosing to deal with the 'bad' part of the self.

What is certain about these psychiatrists (both women incidentally) is that neither of them had available any way of making sense of men's violence which did not involve isolating it from its wider contexts or laying at least partial responsibility for it with the victim. Those which I have in mind here are the gender context and the man's routine abusive, but non-violent behaviour. They were unable to contextualise it in terms other than the culturally syntonic, and in some cases clinical, stereotypes available to them. The isolation of the man's violence is a fundamental element of these paradigms.

Dynamic psychotherapy

Robert came from a poor family. His father was not an abusive man. In fact Robert thought he was weak and that his mother was the dominant partner. At times Robert had wished that his father would be stronger, at least in intervening when he felt he was being unreasonably dominated by his mother. Financial anxieties were a constant factor in his childhood, often to the point that survival seemed an issue. Robert himself had no reason for seeking therapy. As is usual with abusive men it was his partner's suffering which was the identified complaint. The really important point about this is that even if Robert had presented for treatment, it is unlikely that his occasional violent attacks on Tabatha would have been the presenting problem. The most likely identified problem would be his occasional temper outbursts, for which in any case he believed Tabatha responsible. Most likely is that the therapist would quickly discover that Robert, in common with all abusive men, suffers from inexplicable depressive episodes and would draw the conclusion that these were connected with his ambivalence. I am not asserting that if the therapist became aware of Robert's violence he or she would necessarily think it any less than a serious problem. However, I know of many instances where this has been the case.

Let us assume that Robert is already in therapy when it emerges that he has slapped Tabatha on more one occasion. How many dynamic therapists would not be interested in Tabatha's behaviour preceding the attack? I imagine very few. This is not to say that I would do any differently, but I believe my motives would be very different from the orthodox. In circumstances such as these there is a continuum of responses, all of which contain a large element of transference and a greater or lesser element of reality. This reality usually would include an indication that Tabatha had her part to play in the violent attack, that it was in some way interactional. Orthodox analytically based intervention would consider Robert's childhood and how this might have played a part in his behaviour. However, it is his internal world which would receive attention and in particular his unconscious fantasy structure (for example, his desire to destroy elements of himself, his femininity for example, which he had projected into Tabatha). In a therapy of sufficient duration and intensity I have no doubt that Robert's unconscious sadomasochistic internal object world would be the subject of analysis and this would undoubtedly mitigate his violence as more and more of it was drawn into the transference. A Freudian therapist might say that I am finally doing some justice to analytic therapy.

Well, yes. And no. At least not in the way he might think. Let me illustrate this with a real case. I was consulted by a psychoanalyst of many years' experience, an extremely courageous thing for him to do even though he failed to turn up for his assessment interview. He told me that he was hitting his partner, also an analyst. He informed me, one professional to another, that she understood that it was really his mother he was hitting and that it was an unresolved transference issue from his analysis. In the course of a long conversation in which he attempted to justify his violence I asked how he thought his wife's understanding changed the situation. Did it for example make her any less frightened of him? He was nonplussed by my question. He was living in a fantasy world which had been created by psychoanalysis and in which his victim/partner was not a real person. Actually, I think their mutual understanding of his abuse is mildly crazy. By implying that the problem is not his violence but his unresolved transference, it enables him to continue victimising her until he resolves his transference issues. I am not certain that I would be going too far in saying that he was actually making his mother responsible for his problem.

In my opinion this man's analysis had been a failure. I do not believe that analysis or therapy cannot deal with this issue but that the majority of clinicians may be unwilling to take the risk of making the technical and personal changes required to deal with it. As we shall see, I believe it also will require changes in orthodox ways of thinking. Failure is inevitable if the analyst or therapist isolates the violence from its context. I have already mentioned two contexts which I believe to be crucial: gender and the man's non-violent abusive behaviour. Psychodynamic theory already possesses the elements of the paradigm which would enable it to intervene effectively with violent male abusers, but these elements are marginalised rather than central. However, I think that current mainstream practice is not, in this respect, in the later traditions of Freudian psychoanalysis in which gender became the fundamental problematic.

The resolution of ambivalence, which is the central aim of psychoanalysis, would still not prevent men's violence to women unless violent behaviour was seen as only one form of abuse that men inflict on their partners. Although this abuse reflects and indeed acts it out, his ambivalence is not the only issue. I have no doubt that resolving it, or at least enabling him to take responsibility for it, would mitigate and probably stop his violence qua violence. I am far from convinced that it would so profoundly influence his other forms of abuse precisely because it would more than likely be isolated. The essential pre-condition for stopping abusive behaviour is that it be understood as instrumental behaviour in real time, as a secondary rather than primary process. Otherwise it is seen simply as an expression of underlying pathology the resolution of which is a necessary pre-condition to stopping the abuse.

Marital/family therapy

When I first began this work I had few uncertainties how Robert's violence would be dealt with in family or marital therapy of whatever school. Robert's violence and his temper, if they ever became a focus, would have been seen as the product of the relationship, even if his objectives in using violence were understood. The therapists would not question whether their intervention needed justifying. However, feminist activists in the refuge movement, as well as academics, have pointed out that it is virtually impossible for a woman who is afraid of violence to be honest in the presence of her assailant. This threat dominates all her relations with him. Mercifully, this message seems to have filtered into system and marital therapy discourses in recent years. However, if we assume that his violence is substantiated and problematised by the therapists the likelihood is that they will want to see it in the context of her behaviour towards him. The essential context is the encapsulated relationship which is seen as the source of the violence. This is more than likely seen as belonging to the relationship but acted out by the man. Recently, feminist family therapists have attempted to influence mainstream thinking of the perception and treatment of marital or spousal abuse (what is becoming more commonly known as battering) and to shift the paradigm towards an understanding of the centrality of power and gender politics (Perelberg and Miller 1991).

Humanistic therapies

My impression of most humanistic forms of intervention is that they rely heavily on a cathartic or abreactive model derived from the early Freud

(1893) of *Studies on Hysteria.* In this the person is seen as a sort of hydraulic container of repressed or damned up memories and feelings, the discharge of which will relieve the pressure and therefore the illness. I have a number of reservations about this, apart from believing it a seriously flawed understanding of the causes of abuse. One is that these forms of intervention will encourage the discharge of anger and rage towards its object in the safety of the consulting room in the belief that this will reduce the overall level of arousal of anger and mitigate against its being inflicted on a real person. Recent work with multiple personality disorder and other dissociative illness (Colrain and Steele 1991) provides evidence that the contrary happens and that encouraging the discharge of powerful affects, such as anger and rage, without the cognitive pathways for integrating it, may actually create a 'closed physiological loop' and increase the person's potential for experiencing and expressing it (Peterson 1991).

There is one humanistic model which deserves special mention as it is the basis for many programmes in the USA and may well turn out to be influential in the UK. It is a form of intervention which is indistinguishable from re-evaluation counselling. Practitioners using this model do not believe that abusers require special programmes. The intervention strategy remains the same as if they were dealing with any other presenting problem (this is not unusual, it is also the case with most psychodynamic intervention). Insofar as it is adapted it is from the position that abusers are so either because they have been the victims of abuse in their own childhood (a position indistinguishable from that of Alice Miller's), the so-called 'cycle of violence', and/or are victims of male conditioning: that they are in effect prisoners of gender. In common with many women in the refuge movement, I believe this understanding to be insulting (and potentially dangerous) to the real victims, the battered women. It requires a major feat of prestidigitation and denial in which the real victim, the woman, disappears and in her place appears a transformed perpetrator, now victim. Although there are many other reasons why women's groups refuse to support programmes for men it is hardly surprising that they do so on principle when they are presented with a justification for abuse wrapped up as a treatment programme. One practitioner is on record as saying that what abusers need is to 'get rid of the poison inside them'. The echoes of the early Freudian hydraulic model can be heard clearly here. The notion that one can 'get rid' of any part of the self reflects a profound misunderstanding of the construction of the psyche. It may be made up of fragmented or disintegrated parts, but there is no psychic equivalent of surgical removal. I have written elsewhere of the inadequacy of tender loving care in the treatment of abusive men (Jukes 1993a; 1993b). The reinforcement of an abuser's victimisation, or unhappy childhood, prior to dealing with his present abusive behaviour is collusive at best and dangerous at worst. This conclusion is supported by the years of experience of the Men's Centre and by other British workers with abusers (Wyre

1988b; Cockburn 1990) as well as our counterparts in the USA. Robert would be seen as a suffering person, which he also is, but to regard *him* as a victim of his masculinity, rather than his partner, is a travesty of the truth.

An alternative paradigm

Having stated briefly how different treatment models understand and relate to the problem of male abusiveness I would now like to show how the paradigm which is detailed here, for understanding male violence to women, does not isolate the violence. It requires modifications in technique, whether in group or individual therapy and it also makes demands on the personal behaviour and integrity of therapists which ordinary therapeutic approaches do not require.

I will return to Robert. The reader will see that insofar as he saw himself as having a problem, it was with occasional temper outbursts directed at Tabatha. Our first task was to make him aware of the extent of this problem, which he minimised like all other abusive men. Having encouraged him to disclose the full extent of his physical abuse, which is not easy, the next task is to get his account of his motivation for being abusive. The point I want to make here is that none of the men we have worked with connect their physical abuse with the general nature of their relationships with, or their ongoing everyday behaviour towards, women. In general, their experience is of a fairly ordinary, if not loving, landscape punctuated by occasional outbursts of temper and physical abuse. The majority experience themselves as generous and easy-going people who will do anything for a quiet life. It is this combination of compartmentalisation, the idea of occasional physically violent outbursts against a quiet ground or otherwise good relationship, and minimisation of the violence which I call isolation. The motivation for this, as with all denial, is the reduction of anxiety. More importantly, perhaps, the motivation for abusers is the maintenance of their non-deviant self-concept.

In *Inhibitions, Symptoms and Anxiety* (1926) Freud described isolation as a defence particular to obsessional neurosis. His description of isolation is impossible to better. His analysis is that it is an

> archaic mode of defence against the instinct – namely, the prohibition against touching, since 'touching and physical contact are the immediate aim of the aggressive as well as the loving object-cathexes'; it is the removal of the possibility of contact; it is a method of withdrawing a thing from being touched in any way…and…come into contact with any other thoughts.

Freud was clear that isolation is a particular defence in obsessional neurosis. It is clear to me that his description applies to what abusers do with their violence. However, most abusers are not obsessional neurotics.

Let us return to Robert. What precisely does his isolation consist of? What he was doing was presenting his occasional attacks on Tabatha as if they were isolated events in a peaceful landscape. He eventually wanted help with the 'bad temper' (of which he himself is a victim, not an agent) which caused these attacks. What he had steadfastly denied, and continued to deny for some weeks into his treatment, was that he was in any other way abusive, that his 'temper' was manifested in any other way. In fact it became clear that his peaceful landscape was extremely hilly and that flat territory was hard to discern. During the whole of the ten years of his marriage he had consistently treated Tabatha with contempt, disregard and anger. He had been rigid, cold and unyielding, hardly ever initiating communication with her unless it was to chastise, humiliate or instruct. He could not recall asking her how she felt about anything, indeed was clear, if shamefaced, about his utter lack of interest in her internal world. His definition of her, and of reality (including her experience of him), had always prevailed. If she disagreed or protested he had threatened her. He broke objects, he shouted, he imprisoned her in rooms, he gesticulated wildly with verbal threats and humiliation. If she refused to desist from presenting him with her genuine concerns, angrily or otherwise, he used physical violence to restore the status quo which he called domestic peace. Peace for him was when she was so afraid of him that she did not express any opinions, interests, wants or desires and simply cooked, cleaned, and looked after him and the children without protesting and without indicating that she was in any way dissatisfied with him or life. He accused her of being crazy and sick every time she made life difficult for him by not being entirely preoccupied or concerned for his comfort. This reflected how crazy he felt when she did this. He felt driven mad with rage by what he referred to as 'her provocation'.

To get Robert to give up his vision of the peaceful landscape was not easy. It was achieved, however. He eventually began to think, not about why he sometimes attacked her, which he decided to give up immediately, but about why he wanted to frighten her, which he could see was the aim of all his intimidating, threatening and abusive behaviour. Although he struggled against it, he eventually recognised that what he wanted was complete control of her.

Within this paradigm, it is the need to control which is central. More importantly, it is linked with the social and cultural subjection and domination of women – with women's relative powerlessness in relation to men. Violence and abuse are not defined as a sickness, or as deriving from such, but as the personal techniques by which individual men achieve what society as a whole has institutionalised: the domination and pacifying of women. It was Saraga and Macleod (1990) who first expressed the belief that it was difficult for clinicians to challenge the orthodoxy in dealing with child sexual abuse because it would require that we ask difficult questions about the connections between violence, helplessness, vulnerability and male sexuality. Abusive behaviour is not a problem of impulse control, or its lack, or a problem with aggression, or pathology. It is decisive, instrumental and purposeful – it is to ensure the continued provision of services from women. Of course it has all the deep psychological roots in real abuse, failure of attunement, narcissistic wounds, failure of rapprochement, differentiation, individuation, etc., which cause the frustration around which the bubble forms. However, to a greater or lesser extent, these are problems for all men in relation to women. It can only be pathologised if we recognise some universal elements of masculinity as a failure in development. In effect this was what Freud did in his analysis of the Oedipus complex, although he was much more patronising and judgemental about woman's resolution of the female version (see for example his paper 'On Narcissism' 1914). He did not regard as a problem men's 'normal contempt for women' which he saw (rightly I believe) as the invariable outcome for little boys.

The point about normal contempt is that it leads men to behave to women in ways which they know are normal, because all the men they know do it. This is behaviour which achieves and maintains domination and superiority and reinforces the inequality of women. Men they do not know can be seen doing it, and worse, every time they turn on the television set. There is a constant flow of propaganda in favour of male superiority, which encourages and normalises it. The basic assumption on which normal male behaviour towards women is predicated, is that men (their needs, thoughts, interests, feelings, desires and whatever else) are more important than women. Many of these normal ways of behaving are experienced by women – and we have ample evidence for this – as abusive. Even if we disagree as men with this documented evidence, we are in no position to redefine women's experience of what feels bad, frightening, painful or oppressive.

Let us return to Robert and his eventually becoming aware that he could no longer isolate his violent behaviour from the rest of his relationship with Tabatha. The consequences for him were dramatic in the short term. In about two months he underwent what appeared to be a complete transformation. He softened physically, his face relaxed from its previous expressionless mask. The initial energy for this, by no means certain or secure change, was his awareness of the extent of the suffering he had been causing Tabatha for the duration of their marriage. He had been overwhelmed by sadness and remorse of a distinctly genuine character (there is a phoney remorse from abusers which is easily identified). He had tearfully apologised to her and began to initiate discussion about his abusive behaviour, always a good sign of real remorse and the acceptance of personal responsibility. There is little doubt that his ongoing behaviour towards her also changed, I have that from her own testimony. He stopped responding to her from a competitive/survival mindset and began to do so from a cooperation/advancement mindset. Whereas Tabatha had always contained the relationship and thought in terms of solutions to difficulty, Robert had always thought that if *she* got too bad he could always leave. For him this had always been possible from a seemingly sociopathic position of 'I don't care, she doesn't matter' (which is a defence against shame and humiliation). These roles now seemed to be reversed. Tabatha began to feel safe with him and express a lot of suppressed resentment about the years of suffering and she wanted to leave the relationship. He became very anxious about losing her and his behaviour was solution oriented. He was listening to her anger and the genuine concerns it expressed – what he had always thought of as her nagging.

I believe these changes were possible because the therapists at the Centre refused to accept Robert's subjective account of the context of his violence. We identified it as a personal, social and political problem connected with men's need to control women and without denying the underlying psychodynamics. Orthodox approaches do not do this. Although nobody would collude with Robert's violence, few therapists would contextualise it in a way which dealt with the underlying problem of male control and power. Almost certainly, few therapists would have told him to stop abusing her. Most would want to resolve what they saw as the underlying problem first. Although we see an underlying problem, the need to control (and the underlying fears of helplessness and frustration), we act from the assumption that it is not necessary to resolve this problem in order for the man to change his behaviour. In fact we believe the first task is to stop the acting out in the interest of the victim.

Our experience is that in orthodox dynamic treatment the salient gender issues and their reflexive quality would go unexamined except, at best, as psychological processes. The behaviour context would almost certainly not be problematised because men do not report what they regard as normal male behaviour. The chances are that they would not report it because they themselves are unaware of it. They, like Robert, do not problematise it for the therapist. Why tell your therapist that you had breakfast as usual this morning? Robert might, indeed he certainly would, have reported Tabatha's behaviour and a disturbing catalogue this would make from a normative role perspective with stereotyped gender expectations. She consistently refused to act like a woman or a wife should and complained about being made to do so. There are few therapists who would not see Robert's anger as justified in the face of such provocation. Even if they did not think he should be violent, they would surely understand why he hits her. Most would not see his anger as being a form of abuse. More likely it would be seen as a cause of abuse and again perfectly understandable in the light of Tabatha's provocative behaviour.

Why is it that orthodox clinical approaches (including humanistic) have failed to fully integrate feminist analyses of gender relations? Such an integration would require the undoing of the isolation described above and the re-contextualisation of male violence. It requires a sort of return to the Freud for whom gender and power, not catharsis, are the fundamental problematics. This should not prove so difficult. After all, the most radical analysis of gender was provided by Freud. It was he who problematised gender identity and pointed out its social origins, in spite of lingering yearnings for a biological account. Partly, no doubt, this resistance can be accounted for by straightforward disagreement. However, this deserves debate, and where are the texts from orthodox practitioners which deconstruct feminist analyses of sexual politics, whether the essentialist or constructionist variety? They are thin on the ground and written by women (Benjamin 1990 is a notable example). Whatever the disagreements between essentialist and constructionist analyses of its origins, there is an accord that male oppression is *the* pressing problem for women.

Could it be that another source of this resistance is in the demands it makes on practitioners? Psychotherapy, of most kinds, is a reflexive profession. It makes enormous personal demands on practitioners. Being effective requires a level of personal integrity not asked of other professionals. The alternative is to live a divided life; to say one thing and do another. There is a different quality to the demands that a feminist analysis makes on the clinician. It is not that they are personal but that they require so much hard work, not simply on the internal world, but on our external behaviour, more the province of behaviourism than dynamic therapy. The most difficult thing of all, for male practitioners, is recognising that we have power over our female partners and becoming aware of the ways in which we maintain it. Giving up that power is, perhaps, even more difficult than giving up the controlling behaviours which preserve it (for a detailed description of these see Jukes 1993b). Apart from the personal challenge, the underlying agenda, of a re-contextualisation of male violence as simply one form of abuse by which we as men achieve and maintain power over women, is the political one of attempting to change, fundamentally, gender power relations.

If Freud is correct that the resolution of the Oedipus complex for boys involves the development of normal contempt for women, all healthy men will have this contempt and a belief in male superiority. To the extent that the Oedipus complex is unresolved this contempt will be rather more primitive and misogynistic. Rather than make an assertion (that has been done elsewhere e.g. Perelberg and Miller 1991) one can only ask therapists whether they are aware of any differences in their treatment of men and women and if so, how much these differences reflect gender stereotypes and expectations. How much are patients men and women first rather than people?

As bourgeois activities, firmly located in the meritocracy, therapy and analysis reflect and express the values of our culture. It is not simply that therapists isolate male violence, whether expressed by a serial rapist or a wife batterer. Society as a whole suffers from the same scotoma, the same desire to isolate. The alternative is too much of a challenge to institutionalised ways of thinking, feeling and acting. Serious thought about gender and power would require changes in our most basic institutions which would render present social arrangements unworkable. However, our role is not to act as a gender police force. I believe it should represent a radical challenge to orthodoxy, not become the orthodoxy. So much is banal. It has been said before, and better. The need to repeat it reflects the difficulties it expresses. The freeing of human desire, in all its subversive messiness, is our ultimate aim. This is difficult when you have to worry about paying the mortgage.

Another difficulty expressed by therapists is that to integrate a feminist analysis into clinical practice would so transform activity in the consulting room that it would cease to be a clinical setting and become a consciousness-raising class. These difficulties are undoubtedly real, although not so daunting as to be impossible. Many feminist therapists have already discovered this. I would like to share some of my own experience of doing so.

Perhaps the first and most important demand it makes on the therapist is that he needs to be more directive in assessment. He needs to become thoroughly familiar with feminist analyses and critiques of gender relations. Men will not problematise their abusive behaviour; it is too normal. To do this effectively the clinician will need to be familiar with what women have defined as abusive behaviour. To any man not already familiar with the work of the refuge movement, this knowledge will come as something of a shock. Another change required is that the therapist has to begin trying to think like a woman might think (I would like to say here that I am aware that this might sound like essentialist nonsense). This is far from easy. When it comes to thinking about women, most men are lost in a fog of self-deception about our motives and, more importantly from a woman's viewpoint, our behaviour.

If I might go back to Robert again. You will remember that during his assessment he had steadfastly maintained that he and Tabatha had equal access to and control over family finances. He made much of the fact that they had a joint bank account which required only one signature to withdraw. He also mentioned, rather jokingly that he never spent any money on himself. What later emerged during his treatment is that there was only one cheque book which he carried at all times. It also became clear that his reason for spending nothing on himself was that it placed him in a morally superior position to Tabatha. He could use his self-abnegation as a weapon with which to control Tabatha's spending. What also became clear is that when this issue was eventually raised by Robert, at our urging, Tabatha expressed a great deal of resentment about his years of being in total control of the finances. He had genuinely believed this was not the case. At the time of the discussion he became very angry with her (although he did not abuse her) for not previously telling him that she felt resentful and indicating that there was a problem. This is rich. She felt able to tell him now, for the first time, because his previous verbal, emotional and physical abuse (which he was now struggling to control) had made her so afraid of him that she suppressed all her resentment about his maltreatment. In fact, making her afraid of raising her concerns was one objective of his abuse. It was his attempt to ensure that he and only his concerns determined her behaviour.

She was intended to make him the centre of her existence, to be totally preoccupied with his comfort.

This work would not have been possible without modifications in therapeutic technique, but more importantly in the paradigm for understanding men's behaviour towards women. By this I mean all men, not only violent abusers. The important therapeutic modifications are, I believe, best carried out in a group setting. There are many reasons for this, not the least of which is that it is difficult for a therapist to maintain the level of challenge required in individual sessions. However, there are other reasons for using group methods which I will address later.

Finally, I would like to make a few remarks about the profession of psychotherapy and psychoanalysis. Practitioners tend to be socially isolated, politically inactive and jealous of our privacy in a way which is not common for lay people. There is a fear of political activity, of the patient knowing too much about us. There are sound technical reasons for this, but it can also be a rationalisation of unresolved conflicts. I believe that therapists should feel free to be more active politically, and not attempt to hold to the idea that psychotherapy is a value neutral position. More than that, it seems to me that we should be attempting to change gender inequalities and take on the radical challenge to deconstruct gender differences. Politicial activism does not require placards and marches. It can also be conducted in the consulting room.

Having said all this it is now appropriate to explain what we use as a definition of abuse in a practical way and to further indicate how its isolation is removed by placing it in a social and political context.

Violent, abusive and controlling behaviour

Abusive behaviour is anything a man does which is intended to coerce his partner to do something which she would not otherwise do if she were not being made afraid by him. We ask each man, as part of his contract with the Centre, to check each type of abuse he has used in his regular contact with his partner/victim. We ask him to maintain a daily diary which analyses his abusive behaviour. If he think that he is not being abusive in any of the ways described below, then he is asked to use some time every day to analyse previous episodes of abuse. Although there is no time in the programme to go through the diary entries, there is no doubt that it can help with the process of understanding the behaviour. It is important to know that this list is not intended to be exhaustive. There may be other forms of abuse which are not included here. If so, we ask the man to add them to the list and inform us.

Physical abuse

- Slap, punch, grab, kick, choke, push, restrain, pull hair, pinch, bite, rape, use of force, threats or coercion to obtain sex.

- Use of weapons, throwing things, keeping weapons around which frighten her.
- Abuse of furniture, pets, destroying her possessions, tearing or spoiling her clothing.
- Intimidation, e.g. standing in doorway during arguments, angry or threatening gestures, use of your size to intimidate, standing over her, driving recklessly, uninvited touching, covering her mouth to stop her talking.

Psychological abuse

- Threats of violence, verbal or non-verbal, direct or indirect, self-inflicted injury, e.g. hitting your head on walls or threatening suicide.
- Harassment, e.g. uninvited visits or calls, following her, checking up on her, embarrassing her in public, not leaving when asked.
- Isolation, preventing or making it hard for her to see or talk to friends or relatives and others. Making derogatory comments about her friends.
- Yelling, swearing, being coarse, raising your voice, using angry expressions or gestures.
- Claiming the truth, being the authority. Claiming the right to define what is logical, rational, reasonable or fair in the relationship. Calling her stupid or otherwise defining her behaviour as illogical, unreasonable, irrational, etc. Logic chopping, lying, withholding information about your activities, infidelity.

Verbal abuse

- Criticism, name calling, swearing, mocking, put downs, ridicule, accusations, blaming, humiliating. Angrily waking her up from sleep.
- Interrupting, changing subjects, not listening or responding, picking up the paper when she wants to talk, twisting her words, topic stringing.

Financial abuse

- Economic harassment, getting angry with her about 'where the money goes', not allowing access to money, the car or other resources, sabotaging her attempts to work, believing you are the provider and thinking that she could not survive without you, saying that the money you earn is yours.

Emotional abuse

- Pressure tactics, rushing her to make decisions, to hurry up, walking in front of her, using guilt, sulking, threats of withholding financial support, manipulating the children.

- Using pornography, including home videos, against her wishes.
- Not helping with child care or housework, saying that you have already done a day's work. Not keeping to agreements. Abusing your power over the children, either emotionally or physically.
- Feeling stressed and tense and using this to get into a frame of mind when you blame her for everything which goes wrong: things you can't find, mess, etc. This is usually a prelude to a violent attack and you should pay particular attention to this so that you can stop before you reach flashpoint.
- Emotional withholding, not expressing your feelings or giving support, thinking your problems are more important than hers, not giving attention or compliments, not respecting her feelings, rights or opinions.
- Not taking care of yourself and refusing to learn basic life skills, cooking, etc. Abusing drugs, alcohol, not eating properly, not making friends and seeking help and support from them. Believing you have the right to define appropriate wifely and motherly behaviour and not offering your expectations to negotiation. Criticising her motherly qualities or performance. Accusing her of neglecting the children or using threats of taking them away, etc.
- Telling her that if she doesn't like it she knows what she can do, pack, leave, etc. Not acknowledging that the relationship is important to you, telling her that you don't need her or love her, etc.

It is important to say that it is not possible to draw up an exhaustive list of abusive behaviour. Whether or not an action is abusive depends entirely on its context. The major element in that context is whether or not the woman is afraid. All couples argue. In my opinion it is healthy for couples to argue, and to do so without threatening or attempting to intimidate the other, or without name calling or swearing at the other. In a caring and loving relationship swearing during an argument would be taken as an expression of intensity, not intimidation. Where a man has been abusive this is not possible.

Pro-feminism

It is apparent that our work is pro-feminist. By this I mean that we accept without reservation the analysis of male abuse which has been put forward by both victims of that abuse and the women who work with them in the refuge movement. This does not mean that we disavow psychodynamic understanding when we attempt to honour men's accounts of their behaviour. On the contrary we have a dynamically based model which is very explicit in its understanding of the unconscious roots of male abusiveness and this is a centrepiece of the groupwork programme. Rather it means that in honouring their accounts we do so with the explicit understanding that they are based on a fundamental lack of awareness of the social, economic, political and psychological position of women; that this lack of awareness is individually motivated, not only because it helps to maintain dominance and the practical benefits which this provides, but also because it keeps at bay profound anxiety about threats to the self-image. One of the basic beliefs mentioned is that male violence does not occur in isolation; that it is simply the most extreme on a continuum of abuses which individual men inflict on individual women and which have their counter-parts in structured forms of abuse within the wider society. The continuum within which we locate violence is as follows (quoted with the kind permission of David Adams).

Institutional controls

- Male monopoly of policy making institutions

    - business
    - government

- Male control of reality defining institutions

    - history
    - science
    - art
    - religion
    - psychology
    - medicine   are reinforced by:

Covert controls

- Anger
- Emotional withholding
- Conversational politics
- Body space and politics
- Sex roles
- Pornography   which are subliminal cues to:

Violence

- Rape
- Battering
- Sexual harassment
- Pornography

The Centre has frequently been accused of suffering from certainty in the way we understand men's abuse of women, and that intimate male/female relationships are much more complex than we seem to think. Most analytically inclined therapists believe that dynamically derived models, whether family, system or other theories, reflect this complexity in the methods used to deal with domestic violence. To this I can only say that it is my experience that it is far more difficult to work with violence within the model we espouse than within a dynamic model. Dynamic models offer a kind of certainty which is socially syntonic and which most people have been long prepared to accept. Notions such as 'it takes two to tango', 'there are two sides to every story' etc. are deeply embedded in the psyche. Our alternative offers uncertainty and confusion to our clients and to facilitators. To be told, explicitly or implicitly, that he is not wholly responsible for his abusive behaviour, as many of our clients have formerly been informed by doctors, psychiatrists, counsellors and therapists, is music to their ears. They are confirmed in their objectives, to change their partner's behaviour, but informed that the means they are using are not effective even though they are understandable given his description of her appalling, provocative stance. In any case, the evidence from over a decade of American research is that socially syntonic theories simply do not work in changing men's violent behaviour to women and it is argued (see Ptachek 1985) that this is because these theories are supportive of the attitudes and values from which they derive. A pro-feminist model of sexual politics, by which I mean concerned with power, is not a simple alternative. It presents a radical challenge to the basis of personal identity, its gender component. It questions gender roles and stereotypes. Our clients are continually confronted with questions about what it means to be a man and how we learn to become men. I believe that this was the source of the radicalism of early psychoanalysis. It is difficult to escape the impression that in its modern day dealings with gender issues, in practice, psychoanalysis has become a social agency for the policing of gender roles.

There is no doubt that many therapists feel a deep unease when they are confronted with a pro-feminist model of male abusiveness. I share this unease. We are frequently asked why we reduce all issues, concerning men's violence to women, to gender. Surely, we are told, class and race, to name but two, are equally important. In addition, doesn't it make sense to account for the way that women and men subjectivise their respective positions? If not, it is said, a pro-feminist model ends up as one more source of women's oppression. I know from many painful confrontations with women, who may see themselves as having feminist attitudes and values in the broadest sense, that they can find it personally insulting to be told that all men are abusive, and that it is not possible to be a man and not be abusive. Many women have the experience of being with men who do not abuse them and with whom they have equal and satisfying relationships. It is clearly the height of arrogance and undoubtedly oppressive to suggest that they are self-deluding or that they are taught to be blind to the subtle ways in which men oppress them. This poses something of a problem for the inclusive model of abusiveness which is put forward here. In the past, this criticism has been met with the assertion that men who are not actively abusive are passively abusive in that they derive benefits from other men's abuse and do nothing to confront other men's active abusiveness or sexism. We also need to be reminded, as Liz Kelly's research at North London Polytechnic's Child Abuse Studies Unit shows, that it is the experience of the majority of women that they are abused by men (Kelly *et al.* 1991). This does not obviate the necessity to know why some men are not actively abusive.

The working hypothesis

I mentioned earlier the somewhat crazy notion that at the Men's Centre abusive men are told they are responsible for all the difficulties in their relationships. Of course this is not presented in such a bald way. It is done so almost in the manner of a suggestion by a slightly crazy therapist, almost as a joke. However, it achieves something which these men have been unable to reach on their own; it creates a space for thought about their behaviour whilst at the same time allowing some leeway for denying responsibility. It is a creative, almost a play space, a transition between adult responsibility and childlike magical thinking. It allows the unthinkable to emerge.

Let me give an example of how it works in practice. The man, Alan, is an actor, aged 35. He is married to an angry and undeniably needy, dependent woman and they have one child. His background is a nightmare of abuse in his own childhood, a story which reduced me to tears. He has a fragile personality, as does she, and is frequently overwhelmed by his partner to the point where he physically attacks with great ferocity – which is more than returned by her. Almost all his violence is occasioned by her demands on him, demands which he cannot meet and which she insists on pressing. His rage with her helplessness and dependency evokes homicidal feelings in him. In the group he received a lot of support for his perceptions of her. For some weeks he regaled the group with escalating tales of the injustices of her behaviour. The group derived a lot of comfort in at last having a woman who clearly was at fault, most of them by this time having failed to create similar perceptions of their own partners in the group. However, it quickly became clear that this work was going nowhere. Alan himself was complaining that things were not getting any better. It emerged that when he was a child he had made a decision that no matter what he had to be entirely self-reliant, that he would never depend on anybody for anything – a decision which made great sense as a survival strategy in his family but which is wholly inappropriate for a healthy life. After a rather despairing silence after he complained that nothing was changing, someone asked him what he might have done to make his partner so dependent and angrily demanding. At this point Alan actually smiled a smile which I have seen many times. It is what I call the cookie jar smile – as if a child has been caught with his hand in the jar. 'I wondered when you would ask me that', he replied. He went on to recount all the ways in which he had systematically undermined her since they met. He had criticised every aspect of her behaviour and personality until he recognised that he had reduced her to a wreck who felt incapable of performing even the simplest tasks. The changes in this man in subsequent weeks and months were extraordinary as he finally accepted responsibility for the fiasco of his marriage and his wife's parlous state and gave up his abuse of her. Of course this was not without consequences. He became quite depressed and finally went into analysis to deal with his long-standing personality problems and his childhood abuse. Nothing could better illustrate the power of the working hypothesis. From a systemic point of view it also makes sense. Even though it is possible to work systemically with such couples, whatever the political problems and the implications for the innocent victim, one has to ask the question 'why bother?'. It matters not how one intervenes to change the system so long as the system changes, and surely any intervention which protects the woman from more abuse, especially guilt about being abused, is worthwhile.

6 The bubble

Part objects and no objects

I hope by now it is clear that when a man is trapped in his bubble he actually cannot see his partner at all. What he sees is more in the nature of a witch, the embodiment of all evil and all manner of sadistic impulses towards him. I would like to describe precisely what I believe to be the origins of this perception and how the object can be perceived in this way. This will return us to the question of the connections between fixation, regression and the encapsulated psychosis or bubble and abusive behaviour. Perhaps there is perhaps no better place to start than with Michael Balint's description of primary love and the reaction of a baby who is denied what Balint calls the opportunity to love in peace.

> In my view, all these processes happen within a very primitive and peculiar object relationship, fundamentally different from those commonly observed between adults. It is definitely a two person relationship in which, however, only one of the partners matters; his wishes and needs are the only ones that count and must be attended to; the other partner, though felt to be immensely powerful, matters only in so far as he is willing to gratify the first partner's needs and desires or decides to frustrate them; beyond this his personal interests, needs, desires, wishes etc., simply do not exist.
>
> (Balint 1967, p. 23)

He goes on to say (p. 70):

> if any hitch, or disharmony between subject and object occurs, the reaction to it will consist of loud and vehement symptoms suggesting processes either of a highly aggressive and destructive, or profoundly disintegrated nature, i.e. either as if the whole world, including the self, would have been smashed up, or as if the subject would have been flooded with pure and unmitigated aggressive-destructive impulses. On the other hand, if the harmony is allowed to persist without much disturbance from outside, the reaction amounts to a feeling

of tranquil, quiet well-being which is rather inconspicuous and difficult to observe.

It is important to add that Balint is describing adults who are deeply in the process of psychoanalysis (a highly technical and complex process) or an infant with his mother or primary carer. However, there are similarities with abusive men which cannot be overlooked.

Balint's description of the object – the mother or the analyst – is revealing and instructive. *She is not to have any needs wishes or desires of her own.* Anyone who wishes to talk to women who have been abused will soon discover that this is an all too common observation about their abusers. Indeed many women would say that this is all too common amongst men who do not physically abuse – that it may be one of the defining characteristics of heterosexual men. I will return to this. For the moment I wish to elaborate what is meant by the concept of part object. Perhaps it is best illustrated with everyday examples. A man who is walking along the street and who sees a woman and thinks to himself that she has a nice body part – her breast, bottom, legs etc. – is relating to a part object. This is actually material in this case in that he is relating to a physical part of her body and is oblivious to her whole person status. At that moment she consists only of her part or parts. That she may be worrying about the pain in her back or her children's education, or her job would simply not occur to him. If it did he would probably lose interest in her parts, except insofar as he might use his awareness of her inner world to gain access to those parts he values (the charm syndrome). You might complain that I am making too much of ordinary male desire and that such part awareness is healthy and common. That may be so. However, I am convinced that such part relating is a foundation stone of men's abuse of women.

Let us get closer to the heart of the matter. When a man is abusing, or when the harmony, which Balint describes, is disrupted, he sees only an object whose sole desire is to cause him pain by frustrating his desire. This is perceived as wilful and sadistic. At worst she is perceived as wanting him dead. All her other qualities as a lover, mother, friend, athlete, career woman, her inner world of complex emotions and desires simply disappear. She is a sadistic witch and nothing but a sadistic witch! As such she needs to be punished or destroyed or controlled in order to prevent the catastrophe which the man perceives is about to, or has already occurred (of course it has already occurred, but a long time ago and almost certainly not with his present victim).

His relation to the part object (or in Winnicott's terms the object as environment) is what holds the whole system of beliefs, attitudes and abusive behaviour together. One of the reasons that apparently simple incidents can start the most massive forms of abuse is because an abusive man spends so much time keeping at bay his paranoid relation to the witch part object whom he assumes wants to destroy him and whom he wants to destroy. He cannot understand why she sees him as so bad when he spends so much time and energy protecting her from his nastiness. This is mostly what he is aware of, the time spent protecting her – not the actual abuse he inflicts on her either actively by turning down her desires, denying her a voice and indicating in so many ways that he does not enjoy her company, but also passively by sulking and withdrawing. Many writers have commented on the speed and ease with which men who abuse perceive a threat in their communication with their partner/victim and then equally rapidly move to the experience of crisis. This move always happens during abusive episodes and is entirely derived from and is a function of their relation with the bad/witch part object which is split off and suppressed or repressed. His ongoing control, apart from being intended to instil fear in order to ensure the continued provision of services (frustration, pre-emption), is also equally an attempt to prevent her behaving in ways which threaten the emergence of the part object relation of which he is terrified. In *Why Men Hate Women* I expressed the view that the predisposition to the Perception of Threat derived from the abuser's unconscious guilt and anxiety about his sadistic attacks on the internal bad object. I see now that, although this guilt is not irrelevant, this was a partial view, and actually mistaken in the importance I ascribed to guilt. Implicit in my argument then was the notion that an abuser lives the whole time with the effort of keeping at bay the possibility that the internal bad object will internally overwhelm him and then, necessarily, become externalised through his attempts to provoke his partner's introjective identification. I now see that it is this fear, omnipresent and imminent, which predisposes to the perception of threat. Abusers always use phrases which indicate to their victims that such an episode is about to occur and which are intended to mitigate the threat. Most common are variations on 'don't start!'. Inevitably, this is, at some point, insufficient and the man will act abusively. It is not surprising therefore to hear many men, in their accounts of their abuse, articulating their belief that she must want 'it' to happen (i.e. they were provoked) because she knows what 'winds me up'. The threat is that she will frustrate his expectations (and they are manifold) and he will see her as sadistic and damaging.

This is the phase of perception of threat. The speed of movement from the perception of threat to the experience of crisis, when the abuser will escalate his controlling abuse usually from verbal/emotional to physical, is a function of the fracture in his ego derived from his failure to integrate the good and bad objects and the fixation at the failure to come to terms with the fundamental anxiety that the object he loves and needs to survive is also the one whom he hates and wants to destroy because she sadistically, homicidally frustrated him. Once he is confronted with the bad part object he is convinced (because he is in a split off part of his own ego – the bubble – which is incapable of construing any other way) that the part is the whole. She is all bad, all dangerous, all sadistic. He is not the perpetrator, he is the victim. The crisis is a life-threatening one and calls for extreme measures.

To return to Balint's description of the object. It is clear from this that if there is a parallel between this primary frustrating object and the witch in the abuser's bubble it matters not whether she actually frustrates him – it would be enough for her to have a need, wish or desire of her own! This confirms what I have said elsewhere. There is no such thing as a trigger to an abusive attack. All of this occurs in a non-verbal, almost pre-symbolic world. The crucial question, and it was already flagged in the discussion of attachment theory (and lest it is not clear let me spell out that we are in a privation paradigm here, not one concerned with instincts or impulses), is whether abusive men are those in whom this failure in harmony occurred at the time when it was most important that it did not. That is, during infancy. I think the answer to this must be yes it did, and for all of them. The clinical evidence certainly supports this contention. But we are then presented with more problems than we have solved. Apart from the clinical implications of this finding, we have to ask ourselves why it is that women do not abuse men. Is it that they do not suffer the same failure of primary love and the development of a basic fault, or is it that they do and we have to look elsewhere for an explanation for male abusiveness? I think we are partway to an answer here. It seems to me that a basic fault is an essential or necessary condition for men's abuse of women, but that it is not sufficient. In this way we can begin both to account for women's relative invisibility in spouse abuse statistics and go some way to explaining another vexing question for clinicians – feminist or otherwise – which is why is it that some men do not abuse? Nor, to those of you who are already thinking ahead, is it sufficient to say that the extra condition is the possession of a penis. That is certainly another necessary condition but it is not sufficient even when combined with the basic fault. Let me recap. Abusive men are developmentally fixated at a point in the emotional life when they needed to be able to use an object (usually the mother, see Winnicott 1969) in what from an adult point of view is an entirely omnipotent way, such that her needs, desires and wishes should not exist. She should simply be there like air, to draw on when needed and without resistance. The complex of needs and wants and the feelings of ineffable grief and rage, terror of fragmentation and annihilation are split off, denied and then repressed to form what I have called the bubble or, what Hopper (1992) refers to as encapsulated psychosis. When the little boy grows up he can, under certain circumstances regress, that is psychologically shrink, back to being an infant boy, but with all the physical power of an adult man to deal with the object he perceives to be his tormentor. Let us leave the theoretical mapping for a moment to return to the treatment process itself.

Living in the bubble: the private self

This seems an appropriate time to elaborate the 'bubble' in work with abusers. My experience has taught me that that an understanding of this phenomenon is essential as a basis for forming an intervention strategy with abusers.

There is a well known phenomenon in working with people who are schizoid. They often describe themselves as being trapped behind a glass screen. This is a serious and disturbing experience and graphically describes the anguished isolation which is symptomatic of this condition as the person struggles to find a way to both withdraw from and feel connected with others. It is also experienced by people who are in states of depression. One can understand this variously as a state of dissociation or derealisation. It is undoubtedly symptomatic of an extreme state of anxiety.

There is a similar state of mind which I often observe in abusive men and which I am convinced is operable every time they are abusive. However, it is not characterised by anxiety as with the schizoid person. In fact, most are unaware that they are disconnected at all, although the people with whom they relate will experience it. I have grown used to referring to this state in work with abusers as 'the bubble'. I was rather surprised when I began to use this phrase, that the men seemed to know exactly what I was referring to: 'being in the bubble' has become a catch phrase in my groupwork with abusers. *The essential quality of it is that the man has a private mental life which he never shares with others.* His everyday interactions seem normal, indeed are normal. However, alongside the cognitive processing which this requires there is another, completely unexpressed self which processes data from a frame of reference, or multiple frames of reference, which are not visible or conscious but which are very close to consciousness in certain conditions particularly in their primary relationship. One could call this a narcissistic frame of reference, and that would describe it to some extent. It undoubtedly derives from what are normally thought of as narcissistic wounds. The abuser's bubble contains values, attitudes and beliefs which are perfectionistic, arrogant, prideful, contemptuous, frustrating, mistrustful and objectifying of others. It covers a perception of a hostile world, fairly red in tooth and claw, where survival, destructiveness and competitiveness reign. All in all there is a feeling of knowing exactly what is right and wrong. Within this 'space' the man is convinced that he is self-sufficient, even self-created. In fact the bubble is an island. From within it the man can abuse and believe that he is helping the victim, because 'everyone wants to be perfect, don't they?'. Within the bubble he is a black hole of rage, frustration and emptiness.

I vividly remember one man from Morocco who was hitting his wife three or four times a week. He said with total sincerity that he had to help her to correct her mistakes and learn to be a good wife. Even the fact that she had left him did not shake his conviction. He presented to me for help in changing her without hitting her. There is a total absence of humility, uncertainty or self-doubt. This bubble is connected to the encapsulation, but is not the same thing. I like to think of it as the outer skin: a way of defending against the insanity and fragmentation of the encapsulation by keeping reality and people at a distance and not being threatened by perceptions which contradict one's cognitive structures, attitudes, beliefs values etc. There is no reality testing in the bubble, only hostility. Reality is known and anything which contradicts is ignored or discounted. The bubble is predicated on the notion that the world is a dangerous place and it has to be defended against. Perhaps its most important feature is that within this frame of reference the individual views his own needs as the most important element in any situation. Reality, and particularly his relations with significant others, will be evaluated in terms of how far they go towards meeting these needs. He will rarely, if ever, think about the relationship and what might best serve that or about his behaviour towards others. In general he interprets his own behaviour as entirely passive, as being a reaction to other's treatment of him. He does not perceive himself as an agent, always as a victim. His fundamental experience is of himself as powerless although he will resist this understanding when it is presented to him. His frame of reference determines that he will always think about others in relation to him and not himself in relation to others. It requires massive hostility to maintain this frame of reference in the face of all the evidence to the contrary.

Naturally, not everything is defended to the same extent. The most important structures within the bubble, those which will be defended to the death in some cases, are those relating to the self and to the most intimate relationships, particularly the partner. The rigidity which is commonly seen by the partners of abusive men is articulated from within the bubble. It expresses the rigidity of these cognitive structures and the threat which alternative realities represent to the abuser's integrity.

The bubble is not the sulk. The bubble is more concerned with a chronic anxiety of being influenced, which an abusive man experiences as being controlled by others. The sulk occurs within the bubble because the bubble is more of a way of being in the world. In a sense, all experience takes place within the bubble. To some extent we all live in a bubble because the bubble is constructed of the frames of meaning by which we interpret the world. We are all narcissistic and rest content that our grasp of reality, especially our definition of ourself and our immediate environment, including the people in it, is sound, even true. Survival would not be possible if the disjunction between our reality and the consensual reality were too great. We would be seen as crazy, mad or, less extremely, eccentric. The crucial factor with abusers is the dread of being open to influence by others, which is basically a schizoid or paranoid anxiety. Abusive men will use a great deal of hostility to maintain their truth in the face of evidence to the contrary. Hostility may take the form of actual aggression, including violence directed towards people who contradict it. Less energetically it may take the form of internal discounting of contradictory evidence in an ongoing internal dialogue with the self. My experience indicates that this is often fuelled by substantial contempt towards others as a defence against the pain of envy and frustration.

Treating the bubble

Let me give an example. The client, Roger, is a successful business consultant in the City of London. He had left his first wife of ten years in order to marry his then mistress, now wife, Elenor. For 15 years he had related to her in exactly the same way as to his former partner although, he says, with the exception of having affairs. His description of his treatment of Elenor eventually became known as 'putting lines on the kettle'. This referred to his practice of drawing lines on the kettle in order to prevent Elenor from boiling too much water and wasting money. In itself this does not sound so bad. However, it became a metaphor precisely because it expressed his attitudes to Elenor in every aspect of their relationship. There was not a single thing he did not wish to control. For example, he drew lines on the garage wall so that she would park the car just so. She dressed as he wished, raised the children in his preferred way, had sex in his way etc. There was not a single aspect of her life which he did not control. He had never been physically abusive towards her, although he had frightened her by shouting and smashing objects. Throughout the whole of these 15 years he had believed that he was helping her to become a better, even perfect, person because he was perfect and was teaching her to do things in his way. He never at any time thought that his behaviour was questionable or that it would have any negative consequences. He successfully persuaded first himself and then her, by abusing her and completely undermining her self-esteem, that she had no power over him because he did not need her. It almost destroyed him when he discovered she was having an affair. His response was to attempt to destroy her and her lover.

He interpreted her behaviour in the same way as he interpreted everything else, as being an attack on him. There was nothing which did not fall sway to his egocentricity, narcissism or omnipotence. He had never seriously questioned that she would want to be what he wanted, an extension of himself, or that she might have or want her own beliefs, attitudes, values and behaviour. He simply could not consider her as having an independent existence. For him, she was inside the bubble as an object under his omnipotent control. It took a long time before he was able to accept that her affair was a consequence of his treatment of her, not simply an attack on him, although it also was that. Primarily, however, it was her attempt to get some of the tenderness and affection lacking in her life, and to restore her sexual integrity. He eventually came to see that he had been masturbating inside her for the duration of their marriage.

Once, in discussing his bubble (a concept to which he had no difficulty in relating), I asked him how things got inside. His response was that he found it almost impossible to take things from anybody. It has often been said that all psychotherapy is about difficulties concerning giving and taking. This is a central issue for men who abuse their partners, particularly insofar as they almost universally experience that they are deprived by their partners, even if they are unable to articulate the nature of the deprivation. It is instructive to direct their attention to their own behaviour in relation to their partner, to encourage them to be object to her subject, to position themselves differently with respect to her desires. Invariably, these men have great difficulty in giving in ways which are important to their partners. This is always a profoundly useful exercise as most abusers are obsessed with their partner's behaviour and rarely think about their own. The motives for this are usually clear: if she can be defined as inadequate or bad in some way his abuse is justified or minimally wrong and he does not have to change his behaviour, she has to change hers (abusers are usually in sympathy with Balint's view that in order for their hatred to change to love the object will have to change). The exercise is one of the most useful ways I know of breaking into the bubble. One characteristic of being inside it is the lack of any capacity, actually I think desire, for empathising with the partner. I believe it represents a lack of motivation in that these men, even those who seem quite bubbled in a schizoid way, clearly have this capacity which they use in a perfectly functional way in everyday life. I am aware that this could be a description of sociopathy. However, these men, or at least the majority of them do not meet Clecky's diagnostic criteria for sociopathy. It is generally thought that sociopathy is not a clinical pathology, and I agree with this. In fact, depressingly, many of the qualities which Clecky defines would seem to be essential for success in the modern world. I am often led to believe that sociopathic qualities have distinct survival value.

To return to the issue of treatment. If sociopathy is not an illness, even though many sociopaths may feel very uncomfortable much of the time, then how can we talk of treatment? By whose criteria are we to make judgements? Providing the sociopath, and let us assume for the sake of argument that many abusers are sociopaths, is well adjusted to the demands of normal life we cannot intervene to change him. The fact is that sociopaths do not suffer, at least not enough for them to present for treatment. However, it is widely known that the immediate acquaintances of these people do suffer, which is precisely the case with the partners of abusers. Let me remind the reader of the 16 factors by which Clecky characterised sociopaths or what are more commonly known as antisocial personalities. They are:

- superficial charm and high intelligence
- absence of delusion and irrational thinking
- absence of neurosis or nervousness
- unreliability
- untruthfulness and insincerity
- lack of remorse and shame
- inadequately motivated antisocial behaviour
- poor judgement and failure to learn from experience
- pathological egocentricity and incapacity for love
- general impoverishment of major affective reactions
- lack of insight

- unresponsiveness to interpersonal relations
- fantastic and uninviting behaviour with drink and sometimes without
- suicide rarely carried out
- trivial, impersonal and poorly integrated sex life
- failure to follow a life plan.

These can be contrasted with the characteristics of the so-called borderline personality, a diagnosis which is becoming increasingly popular in cases of abuse (including sexual):

- impulsivity or unpredictability in areas that are potentially self-damaging (food, money, sex, gambling etc.)
- pattern of unstable and intense interpersonal relationships marked by shifts in attitude, idealisation, devaluation or manipulation
- inappropriately intense anger or lack of anger control
- identity disturbances manifested by uncertainty about identity issues (self-image, gender, goals, career, friendship, values or loyalty)
- affective instability with marked shifts from normal mood to depression, anxiety or irritability usually lasting a few hours and only rarely more than a few days
- intolerance of being alone
- physically self-damaging acts
- chronic feelings of emptiness or boredom.

Interestingly it is often remarked that the mothers of borderlines cannot tolerate separation from their children and are often borderline themselves, sharing many of the characteristics of their offspring.

Likewise, there is general agreement that the childhood of sociopathic people is generally characterised by parental cruelty and domination. This results in a mistrust of authority and the environment, and an inability to rely on others.

> There is a determination to reject all guidance…and a reduced ability to learn impulse control techniques. Protecting themselves from others, providing their own pleasure and pain, handling emotions in their own ways and being almost totally self-reliant or autonomous are all elements of their style.
>
> (Bolton and Bolton 1987, p. 66)

As I read this I am struck by how these qualities are esteemed in society at large, and particularly by men in general. Apart from the inability to learn impulse control techniques, which is not a diagnosis I have any sympathy with as I indicated earlier, these qualities are also possessed by abusers who live in the 'bubble'. In fact, they are qualities of the self inside the bubble. However, these qualities do not constitute the whole person, which the above description of sociopaths purports, seemingly, to do. When men act abusively they act as if a part of the self is the whole, in much the same way as they relate to their partners/victims as part objects. When she is seen as wholly bad, he also relates to her, that is abuses her, from a part of himself which is bad, and he has available complex cognitive structures which provide excuses and justifications for his deviant behaviour.

Let me return to the issue of treatment for sociopaths, particularly in relation to living in the bubble. The major problem with antisocial or sociopathic people is that it is very difficult for them to form meaningful relationships including with therapists. I am in agreement with Reid (1981, p. 152) that the aggressiveness of sociopaths can and has been overestimated. In connection with the bubble, the most salient fact about sociopaths is their degree of egocentricity. They are so self-concerned that other people are not treated as significant. Not that this contempt, for such it is, is conscious, or that the man would easily agree that others are so unimportant to him. In fact, he more than likely thinks that his evaluation of and respect for others is greater than the norm. He is in the habit of making the most favourable interpretations of himself, as indeed are we all. This is undoubtedly true of most, if not all, male abusers of their female partners. Bolton and Bolton (1987, p. 66) note that sociopaths also perceive the outside world as being very threatening, which I take to mean, in abusive men, anything outside the scope of their omnipotence within the bubble.

To return to the issue of treatment. Although I am sure that the majority of the thousand-plus men I have worked with during the past 11 years are not sociopathic or personality disordered, as described above, it is equally clear to me that they have many sociopathic qualities when it comes to their abusive behaviour and attitudes. I remember Jacqui Schiff (1976) telling me that the best, if not the only way to treat character disorder was to put eight or ten of them into a locked room and tell them to get on with it. I was amused by this at the time. However, most of the treatment programmes for young adult offenders, who are usually diagnosed as character disordered, rely on precisely this. If you put eight of them together, all with a high degree of hostility, something has to give. I shall return to this in the later section on groups as the treatment of choice for abusive men. It seems appropriate at this point to elaborate my theoretical understanding of male abusiveness as a psycho-social phenomenon.

7 A social psychology of male violence, helplessness, vulnerability and sexuality

I have made clear that as far as our understanding is concerned, many orthodox models for understanding male violence to women, whatever their philosophical underpinnings, are actually dangerous to women when used as a basis for clinical intervention with abusive men. The real challenge is to create a model which accounts for the social construction of gender and which also accounts for individual motivation in a way which is clinically useful. If it relies too much on social construction we are left with a system which offers little in helping individuals to which they can relate on a personal level. If it relies too much on psychodynamics it belies the truth of social learning and construction, and particularly the power dimension which is of central importance. Moreover, it offers an understanding predicated on individual psychopathology which severely constrains, indeed misleads us, in our capacity for understanding the prevalence and universality of male violence – the sheer normality of it in all its manifestations. Although many abusers may be disturbed, it is simply too widespread to be only symptomatic of pathology. The fact is that men, qua men, are unbelievably violent. Even discounting a monolithic model of maleness, and presenting historically specific analyses of masculinities, one is led to the same conclusion, that most violence is perpetrated by men, on other men and on women and that men's capacity for violence and cruelty seems limitless. This intrigues me and although it is not the central concern of this book, it is simply not possible to research the problem of male abusiveness without addressing the roots of male cruelty and male criminality.

What I will attempt to do is to articulate the model which has been developed in working with male offenders over the last thirteen years in the Men's Centre and which pulls together the disparate strands which have so far occupied this book. The title of this chapter was suggested by a comment by Saraga and Macleod (1990) in an article in *Feminist Review* in which they suggest that it is difficult for professional men to challenge or think seriously about the orthodoxy in dealing with child sexual abuse (which they define as any model which implicitly or explicitly places responsibility for abuse anywhere than on men) because we would then have to ask painful questions about the relationship between violence, helplessness, vulnerability and male sexuality. What they are addressing is the type of resistance with whose sources we are familiar from everyday therapeutic practice. To this I would only add that another huge hurdle arises from the reflexive nature of these questions and the difficulty of locating one's own desire as an object in the perceptual field when it is so clearly a (the?) major determinant of that field.

It would be hard to contradict Saraga and Macleod's analysis of this resistance. Its sources are not only personal, although they are severe enough. I believe it also reflects, and badly, on the prevailing frameworks through which we as professional carers understand the construction of our male sexuality and violence. What I want to attempt here is to do the difficult thing and articulate what seems to be otherwise so unthinkable. It has become increasingly clear to me that it is mistaken to isolate male violence, whether rape, child sexual abuse or wife battering, and to attempt to explain it from a straightforward psychodynamic perspective. Rather, what I have begun to do is to see physical violence as the extreme manifestation on a continuum of abusive controls (see p. 103). This follows the work of Liz Kelly at North London Polytechnic and pro-feminist psychologists in the USA (Adams 1988a; 1988b).

I was struck, recently, by a comment of Bowlby's (1988, p. 77ff.). He remarks, 'it seems to me that as psychoanalysts and psychotherapists we have been appallingly slow to wake up to the prevalence and far reaching consequences of violent behaviour between members of a family, and especially the violence of parents'. This illustrates precisely the difficulties Saraga and Macleod point up. Although I am taking his remark slightly out of context, in that Bowlby was also addressing the problem of traumatic abuse of children by their mothers, his following remarks justify this misprision. He goes on to present what is undoubtedly one analytic clinical orthodoxy in understanding the abuse of women by their partners. He argues that violence is the product of interaction between the partners and that women who are victims of it are invested in their own maltreatment. Some authors (Schlapobersky and Nathan 1995, whose work, in other respects, is fascinating and ground-breaking) even go so far as to diagnose 'violent couples'. The difficult question, which Bowlby does not address, is why, in the vast majority of cases, is it men who maltreat women?

Bowlby, the developer of attachment theory, believes, in common with Zulueta, that abusers become perpetrators as a result of being victims of abuse and quotes a study by Gayford (1975) which has been subsequently widely criticised, and which is not born out by my own research, for its finding that 51 per cent of batterers (defined as men who beat women with whom they have intimate relationships) had themselves been abused as children. Suffice it to say that my own findings indicate that fewer than 35 per cent of abusers have been abused, even when using a very harsh definition of abuse. In addition and far more importantly, what Bowlby, in common with most other practitioners, fails to address, is why it is, if being abused is the cause of subsequently becoming an perpetrator, that the vast majority of sexual abuse is by men on little girls? If the assumption were correct, that internalised abuse is followed by identification with the abuser, we should expect, following the 'inter-generational cycle of violence' theory (ibid., p. 94; see also Renvoise 1978), that the next generation would be dominated by massive sexual abuse of little boys by their mothers. This is not the case.

What needs to be addressed is the male near-monopoly of abusiveness, whether sexual or violent. Orthodox analytically derived models (see Bentovim *et al.* 1984) of understanding of child sexual abuse or male violence to women redefine the problem. Rather than male violence or abuse being the focus of intervention, the identified underlying causes are addressed. This is reflected in the language used by orthodox practitioners. For example, the rape of daughters by their fathers is called incest or an incestuous relationship. This implies that the daughter could give informed consent and that the responsibility is shared. Incest is a genderless crime. Men's violence to women is redefined as family violence or as a violent relationship, again genderless (for a discussion about this use of language see Scott 1988).

Apart from implicitly blaming victims for men's behaviour, the abuse is implicitly supported as a strategy for coping with the more important underlying cause until this, itself, is mitigated. The violence is not seen as being the problem. The man is not seen as being responsible for his violence and abusiveness. It is accounted for in terms of the women's addictiveness and masochism and the man's insecurity and unhappy childhood or in terms of family dynamics which suppport patriarchal definitions of roles, rights and expectations. It is not uncommon in case reports of father/daughter rape to read that the mother was depressed and unable to perform her duties as a wife and that the man therefore turned to his daughter for the satisfaction of his natural needs (Bentovim *et al.* 1984, pp.11–16). Alternatively, and no doubt unintentionally, the child is made partly responsible by the attribution of vulnerability factors which predispose her to becoming the victim of abuse (ibid., p. 8). Intentionally or otherwise, such perspectives implicitly support men's abusive behaviour. If the wife did her duty he would stop battering her, or sexually abusing his children. The woman is ultimately responsible, whether by being sexually depriving, the wife, vulnerable/ sexually provocative, the daughter, or enjoying violence.

Is it simply contentious to wonder how many therapists would maintain that banks are responsible for being robbed? How many of us would continue to work with a patient or client who continued to break any other law? This is not mere sophistry. How many therapists actually tell a male patient that they will not continue to work with him if he does not stop his abuse? How many male therapists know what women experience as abusive behaviour? Do we, like most men, retain a male frame of reference which defines women's experience?

Bowlby, like the majority of analytic practitioners, acknowledges the issue but fails to follow its clinical implications to a conclusion. The form of his acknowledgement, that analysts have failed to recognise the impact of 'family violence' on child development, may actually reinforce the very prejudices which I and Saraga and Mcleod believe encourage, at worst, and condone, at best, the phenomenon he designates 'family violence'. Not that there have been no efforts to integrate the findings of feminist research into clinical practice. A recent volume of papers (Perelberg and Miller 1991) describes the attempts of a number of family therapists to make the issues of power and gender central to therapy practice. Perelberg herself acknowledges that family and systems theory 'has not challenged the way professionals have approached the genders in the clinic. More specifically, it has not taken on board the paradoxical role which has been allocated to women, as both the professional's main ally and their main target for change' (ibid., p. 6). The reference to women as the 'main target' refers to the increasing emphasis of the state on the importance of mothering in raising 'healthy' children during the last century. One has to be aware that this process itself, the 'ideology and the idealisation of motherhood' has been the subject of searching critical feminist analysis which depicts it as profoundly oppressive to many women (see also Welldon 1993).

In the vast majority of cases, it is not 'the family' but men who are violent and abusive. Finkelhor (1986) points out that 85–90 per cent of recorded sexual abuse is inflicted by men. Straus (1991) indicates that over 99 per cent of violent abuse between heterosexual couples is by men on their female partners. This is not to deny that many women are physically and emotionally abusive to their children, but, from a feminist perspective this cannot be equated with male abusiveness. In any case, it is not simply equated, it is more often severely punished in a way that men's abusiveness is not (Edwards 1984). Women's violence is seen as more deviant than men's. It is hardly surprising that many women are abusive to children given the madonna-like expectations which men place on mothers, many of whom (Kelly 1988) are being violently abused and most of whom are being emotionally abused by the men they live with. Studies show that as many as 40 per cent of men will admit to using physical violence on their partners and that they regard it as a right if their partner is stepping out of line (Andrews 1987). This is reinforced by research into marital relationships and male attitudes which indicates that the greatest offence a man will hold against another is if he fails to exercise sufficient authority over his wife (Whitehead 1976).

If we adopt a feminist perspective and regard violence as simply the most extreme on a continuum of abusive behaviours which men use to control women (Kelly op. cit.), it is not difficult to justify an assumption that the majority of women are suffering abuse if we include the less serious abuse of psychological and emotional cruelty. It would be difficult to sustain an argument that emotionally abusive men are also the only men who are physically abusive.

Psychoanalytic and systems theories equate a woman's behaviour with the violence it is presumed to evoke. This is fundamentally a male perception. It contradicts the essence of the social and political reality for most women. Women do not have and are not allowed equal power with men. It also equates the destructive power of behaviour which men interpret as provocative (usually meaning that they do not like it) with physical violence. Intentionally or not, this provides justification for male abusiveness and locates with the woman the power to stop it. My own work with violent men shows that this is untrue. Men who are violent will always find a justification, no matter to what lengths a woman might go in adapting her behaviour – in other words submitting to men's demands for, and 'legitimated' expectations of, control and authority. Unsurprisingly, abusive men offer a similar interpretation of their behaviour, that they would not have inflicted it if their victims had done as they wanted. We used to draw up lists of 'triggers' to violence with our clients, but soon realised that this is a fruitless exercise. The list is endless and changes, even for individuals, from day to day. Our experience taught us that it is far more effective for the client if we interpret any behaviour of the woman's, which he uses to justify or excuse his behaviour, as symptomatic of prior abuse and not causative of it.

What the analytic and systems theory orthodoxy does, in its emphasis on the encapsulated world of family dynamics is to deny the historical, social, political and cultural context of abuse. Group analysts, from Foulkes on, have paid attention to the foundation matrix and its importance in articulating some fundamental group processes. However, the recognition of the matrix, whilst essential, is flawed if it fails to include the political, social and psychological powerlessness of most women and to recognise that this is socially constructed and gendered. Misogyny is enjoying a vogue at present. There seems to be an attitude abroad that 'we've heard all this before', and some sort of wholly misplaced consensus that women have achieved what they have been striving for since Mary Wollstonecraft first put pen to paper in *A Vindication of The Rights of Women* (1972). This is not the case.

Is it any longer deniable that the foundation matrix, culture itself, is sexist, patriarchal and fundamentally hostile to women? Is it still possible to believe that society is not predicated on male dominance and female inferiority and subordination? Even a cursory examination of the facts, not including women's direct experience, suggests otherwise (see the UN Report 1982). What I want to do is to address what it is about men which establishes the matrix. In other words, what is our investment in establishing and maintaining women's oppression? And what precisely are the connections, if any, between vulnerability, helplessness, violence and male sexuality?

For some time Earl Hopper has been teaching about his interest in taking a broader and deeper look at group processes. When he relates Bion's basic assumptions to Klein's development model, he suggests that dependency has no natural home in the way that fight/flight and pairing can be related to the paranoid/schizoid and depressive positions respectively. He suggests that there is a fourth basic assumption in groups which is related to the failure of dependency. This assumption, which he calls aggregation/massification, derives from a fundamental failure of primary care. Chronologically, it pre-dates the paranoid/schizoid position. He suggests that we see it most in evidence in situations where there is social breakdown (failed dependency on the state) leading to the individual's becoming subsumed in the mass (massification) in a process of political revolution. He posits the existence of a universal encapsulated psychosis (what I have earlier called the 'bubble') containing a mixture of primary dread of annihilation, fission and fragmentation, grief and rage (to which I would add overwhelming frustration and emptiness). These are the feelings which are defended against, and to some extent acted out in revolutionary uprisings. He cites the French Revolution and the rise of Hitler as examples of such massification. Aggregation, with which massification oscillates, is seen in groups which disintegrate or in which each individual feels utterly alone and totally different. He has recently published his views about the encapsulated psychosis and its history (Hopper 1991).

I do not want to take up here the issue of whether there is in fact a fourth assumption based on a pre-paranoid/schizoid developmental position. Rather, I want to address what seems to me to be obvious about this description. I believe from my own work with violent and abusive men, that there is a universal encapsulated psychosis – a psychotic bubble. However, it seems to me that its development and expression is entirely different as between male and female. Although not explicitly, Dr Hopper's own examples seem to support this.

Although I believe that the frustration, rage and aggression which are central to the encapsulation are equally powerful in men and women, I will argue that the vicissitudes of these powerful effects are profoundly different and that the determining factor in this is gender. I would make it clear that I believe women to be as capable of violence as are men, but that the social and cultural pressures which shape gender identity preclude this as a form of behaviour for women. Women do not start revolutions nor were they culpable in the rise of Hitler and the development of the final solution. The fate of the *sans-culottes* during the French Revolution is interesting in this regard. There is little doubt that they were extremely violent and randomly homicidal until the male-dominated Assembly decided they had had enough of female assertiveness and equality and passed a series of laws designed to ensure that women rediscovered their rightful place in the home (see Tomlin 1974, *The Life and Death of Mary Wollstonecraft*). Female infants do not escape the experience which Hopper designates as failed dependency, but their fate is rather different from that of the man's. At its bluntest, men are provided with, in fact they construct, an object on whom to transfer this failure, the feminine m-other, and, as Chasseguet-Smirgel (1976) says, possess a penis with which they may then escape her and, I would add, the encapsulation which has become attached to her.

It seems to me that an understanding of the contents of this capsule is crucial if we are to fully appreciate the nature of the foundation matrix as it is experienced by women and also to enable us to appreciate the fundamental links between the variables identified by Saraga and Macleod. I should like to illustrate my argument by reference to some work of a client in an anti-abuse programme.

Andrew is a professional man in his early fifties. He has a long history of abuse of women in and out of marriage although this abusiveness has been largely socially syntonic and he has avoided any contact with the police or statutory agencies, mostly by good luck. This is not usual for our clients. Largely as a result of his behaviour he has been twice divorced and eventually self-referred to a psychiatrist. He was apparently diagnosed as schizophrenic, although there was no evidence for this in his history or presentation. He has many schizoid features which are evident when he is pressed about his abusive behaviour, but this is par for the course. As we have seen, denial, projection and splitting are the norm in relation to violent behaviour and impulses. The vast majority of our clients show similar schizoid features when confronted, but are neither disturbed nor unusually depressed. Without doubt the people with whom they are intimate are very distressed, but our clients are not suffering from personality disorders that render them dysfunctional in most areas of their lives. This is crucial for further understanding. We know that up to 40 per cent of men hit their wives and see nothing inappropriate in this. In fact many women accept it and expect it. If this violence is contextualised as only the most extreme of a continuum of controls which men use in maintaining what we see as our rightful authority over women, the proportion of men who may be defined as abusive increases dramatically.

During his early work in the programme, Andrew had made it clear that he felt his abuse was justified. His accounts of his relationships with women were scattered with references to 'castrating bitches'. Again, this is not uncommon. It is the rule rather than the exception for violent abusers to experience themselves as victims of women rather than as perpetrators of abuse. In fact, my belief is that most men feel this way about our relationships. This is the case even with relatively liberated men whose abusiveness may not extend further than always holding onto the remote TV control and deciding which show to watch, or the one-car family where the man always has the car keys. The victimisation is precipitated by a woman's failure to service what he regards as his rightful expectations of her. What became increasingly clear with Andrew was that he did indeed feel very frightened of women, and at no time more so than when they behaved in ways which he felt challenged, or represented a challenge to his authority, control and dominance in the relationship. His emphasis, in common with all other men we work with, was on the extreme fear or the, usually undifferentiated, peril of the moment when his control or authority was challenged. This peril was quite ineffable. It always resulted in an attack of verbal or emotional abuse or, more usually, physical violence. He was completely unaware of what triggered these attacks of peril although it was obvious to other members of the group.

At other times during his life Andrew was and acted 'normal'. Although he had some problems with work, he was in most respects a respectable and productive member of society. Even his abusiveness was slight compared with many of the men we work with, most of whom never get anywhere near a psychiatrist because, unlike Andrew, they do not question their abusiveness and do not identify it as a problem. Paradoxically, Andrew's contradictory sensitivity to women had resulted in his being diagnosed schizophrenic, a traumatising experience for him. As a matter of interest, any competent therapist would have little hesitation in diagnosing most of our clients as potentially borderline, or otherwise personality disordered, if he or she questioned them closely about their behaviour with women. The fact is that they are not. However, fewer than 5 per cent of men who are violent to women (including convicted rapists) suffer from any diagnosable pathology. (See Kelly 1989 for a discussion of this; see also Finkelhor 1986.)

What then is it that evokes such extreme peril in men that it can lead to physical violence against women? As I have already stated, the peril undoubtedly arises when the man's authority or control is challenged or when he is made aware that he is not in control. For men, the polarity is control/authority versus helplessness/vulnerability. In other words he is made to feel helpless and vulnerable. For most men we work with, this peril is of a life-threatening event. As we shall see, I believe that this derives from the connection between helplessness and the encapsulated psychosis.

At that moment, the man experiences such confusion that he is actually unable to differentiate his feelings. Most insist, at least during the early phase of the programme, that they do not feel hatred or even anger prior to the violent attack on their partner. All he is aware of is his profound vulnerability and that his life is under threat. What is the nature of this threat? As will be clear, I believe it derives from the natural link between the separate, frustrating object and the absent or abandoning and therefore persecuting object. The threat or challenge to a man's control evokes the original experience of what Hopper calls failed dependency and what I prefer to call failed symbiosis (what Benjamin (1990) would call a failure in 'rapprochement').

Here then we have two of Saraga and Macleod's variables, vulnerability and helplessness, evoked by threats to a man's assumed or actual control of a woman whom society gives the right to control or dominate, including the right to use violence. This 'right' is an essential aspect of the foundation matrix which is not taken into account in psychoanalytic models. It is the fundamental patriarchial assumption of women's inferiority and submissiveness and men's superiority and the right to dominate and control women. Nor should we forget, as E. and R. Dobash point out (1980) that the marriage licence is, de jure, a licence to abuse. Violence against women is, within certain limits, socially condoned and encouraged. Some recent judgements against men who have killed their wives might even lead one to question whether there are any unacceptable limits to violence inflicted on women within the 'privacy' of marriage. In one case a man who had battered his 23 year old wife and small son to death was set free on the grounds that the severity of his guilt had caused him enough suffering.

This analysis raises more questions. What is the connection between vulnerability/helplessness and the man's peril? What is the connection between peril and violence? Finally, how do these relate to male sexuality? The first of these question brings me back to Hopper's hypothesis of an encapsulated psychosis containing the foundation of a fourth basic assumption. He pinpoints its origins in the experience of failed dependency. I take issue with him on this point. The experience which he designates as failed dependency is universal and, to repeat, genderless. The infant, however, is not aware of its dependency. It is apparent only to the adult observer. The moment when the infant becomes only too painfully aware of the primary carer's separateness (universally constructed as female m-other) is the moment when what we as adults experience as dependency arises. Unresolved feelings of dependency, like desire itself, contain the seeds of their own failure. The object always contains its own loss. The shadow of the lost object sits on the shoulder of the present object; as Mitchell expresses it 'desire persists as an effect of primordial absence' (Mitchell and Rose 1982, p. 6).

The traditional, Freudian view of ego development is that the ego is formed by the introjection of the absent object. The encapsulated psychosis is like a primitive ego which is largely body-oriented – it seems unlikely that there is sufficient ego functioning to deserve the name. Kleinian and other object relations theorists see the ego as being formed by the introjection of the present and good enough primary carer (breast, mother). Mitchell, again, expresses it thus: 'Freud's subject is constituted by filling the interstices where something is missing: one hallucinated, has delusions, tells stories. Klein's person becomes himself or herself by taking in what is present' (Mitchell 1986, p. 395). The encapsulated psychosis is formed by the absent object.

I agree with Dr Hopper's description of the contents of the encapsulation, and interestingly it is very close to Mitchell's description of what patients experience when they fall into the gap between signifier and signified. Essentially, it is a gap of non-meaning: 'all the patient can do is bear witness; a horror that is about absence but which can be filled with phantasmagoria. The emptiness of chaos made carnate, a plethora of unorganised feelings and objects' (ibid., pp. 392–3). By contrast, the present object comes to contain the organising principle of meaning. I visualise it as a containing structure for the encapsulation.

For Lacanians, gender becomes the way of organising meaning. The phallus symbolises what it attempts to deny: the gap, the absence, and ultimately the bedrock of masculinity, castration. Castration anxiety stands in for the terror of the fundamentally ruptured subject. The real terror is not of losing something but of falling into that place in which there is nothing to lose – a well of frustration, rage, terror and emptiness.

This chaos made carnate (what Jones called aphanisis) is the helplessness and vulnerability. The peril is not simply loss of life, but loss of self. The anxiety gets structured in many ways during the boy's development. Ultimately these constructions collapse into one or another form of fantasy of deprivation by the primary object: a metaphor for absence and abandonment. The chaos (the unconscious) is without structure but not without content. The self is structured on the gap. It originates in the awareness of presence and absence. The entry into language, the symbolic order, concretises the fundamental rupture. The self contains no-self in the same way that desire is symbolic of its own failure.

What then of violence and male sexuality? The encapsulated psychosis contains ineffable fear, rage and frustration. I have said that this becomes structured in relation to fantasies of deprivation by the primary, feminine object. The hatred of women (and its mild Oedipal derivative, normal contempt for women) as the source of the rupture is inevitable.

The deprivation itself (the rupture) and the resulting dependency, are real enough. However, there is no innate fantasy of a good enough, or indeed any other kind, of breast. What there is, what the child is born into, is a culture which is founded firmly and essentially on gender and more particularly, gender inequality. Is it questionable to assert that emotional, physical and psychological deprivation is associated with mothering as a gender based activity performed by women? Sadly, in my view, psychoanalytic thought mirrors and indeed contributes to the construction of this reality in its drift away from the Oedipus complex. It is inevitable, for the vast heterosexual majority, that frustration will come to be associated with the absent female other. This frustration evokes the threat of being overwhelmed by the encapsulated psychosis. I believe this is the source of men's motivation for controlling women with whatever means are necessary to pre-empt frustration. Socially legitimate expectations of rightful control and authority over women as the property of men, bolstered by and bolstering men's (society's) normal contempt for them provides the justification for violence as a means of control. The underlying encapsulated hatred provides the motivation to use it to ensure that the man is not cast into the rupture evoked by the separate and ultimately therefore, infinitely and ineffably frustrating other. One of the consequences of men's abusive behaviour is the forcible projection of our own chaos into the victim. The Battered Woman's Syndrome (Walker 1979) attests to this.

Men's control of women not uncommonly includes the use of violence and in many more cases, threats of violence. Unconsciously, deprivation is construed as a sadistic attack. The semipermeable membrane of the encapsulation is a world of sadomasochistic objects. The primary object, woman (and the inheritors of the transference – wives, girlfriends) assumes its sadistic qualities when she behaves in ways which frustrate the man/child's socially constructed, socially legitimised expectations of servicing and authority. The introjection of this primary sadomasochism forges the links between being hurt and inflicting hurt. When my clients are inflicting pain they are unaware of it. Their violence is consciously associated with peril and terror and, as Andrew and others have expressed it, 'the need to get rid of the most unbearable tension'.

To recap, we now have three of Saraga and Macleod's variables: vulnerability, helplessness and violence. What remains is to attempt to connect these with male sexuality.

Freud first drew attention to auto-erotism as a means of providing oneself with comfort in face of the absent or frustrating object. Little boys inevitably discover the pleasures of an erect penis and its implied triumph over the frustrating or traumatising object. His acceptance of the Law ensures that his triumph is secure so long as woman remains in her place. Further, his sexuality is indelibly associated with hostility towards and triumph over, the castrated woman (see Stoller 1986 for further discussion of this). She is at one and the same time, venerated as the object who he needs to complete him (she caused the rupture by depriving him of what she possesses and still retains) and hated as the source of so much pain. The erect penis contains the opportunity, in fantasy, of healing the rupture through orgasm inside the object. That it is inevitably associated also with the persecuting, absent and frustrating object is assured by the emergence of genitally sexualised desire in the context of incestuous fantasies concerning the constructed cause of the rupture, m-other.

The erection contains the urge to batter through, to penetrate the object and take what is denied – possession. It brooks no frustration. Unconsciously, it attaches to itself the encapsulated destructive urge to attack the cause of the failed, primary symbiosis. That the erection is a perennially available escape route from pain, intolerable or otherwise, can be attested to by any therapist who routinely works with her patients' masturbatory practices and fantasies. I do not want here to discuss the man's fantasy of his penis as an instrument of healing. Suffice to say I am aware that this, also, is invariably present. What is of interest is that men commonly use sexuality – masturbatory, chase and conquer, flirtatious or otherwise – as a means of empowerment in the face of feelings of helplessness, vulnerability and anxiety and these are derived from the primary rupture in the self. The masculine encapsulated psychosis lies at the root of aggressive male sexuality and violence towards women. I am often aware, in my work with men, that they act like 18 month old boys in their relations with their partners. In terms of analytic metaphors, they all seem to be fixated in the separation/individuation phase in which they want to stray from the mother and explore the world but with the reassurance that when they return she will still be there providing the secure base which Bowlby describes so well. However, I believe it is mistaken to see the problems of their abusiveness as deriving from a fixation at this stage even though the separation/individuation issues are prominent. In fact it seems to be the separation issues rather than individuation issues which are uppermost in the minds of my patients. To my mind anxieties concerning individuation are more primary and occur earlier and the conflicts around separation are used to defend against these more primitive anxieties which are at the core of the encapsulation. With increased mobility the child is provided with the opportunity to expressively act out in a way which was not possible earlier. This acting out continues into adult life because the underlying encapsulation is not resolved and individuation in relation to the mother has not been fully achieved. As well as men's widely known capacity for sexualising all frustration through masturbatory fantasy, I believe this process is also at the root of most perversion.

There is nothing on the other side of the other – fetish/woman. Woman is constructed as containing all men need to complete the self – she is other than male/man. She cannot live up to this. Men need to dominate in order to ensure that women are available as this object of fantasy – sexually in particular. Men have no choice but to define and shape female sexuality. When she fails to be controlled, either by asserting her independence or frustrating men's expectations, the man is in danger of falling into the gap, the point of non-existence. The peril results directly from frustrated expectations because they evoke the encapsulated psychosis, the threat of no-self, no organising principle, the principle of the absent object which is the origin of the encapsulation. He is drawn to his frustration as a moth to a flame – he will always find a justification for inflicting it on a woman. Woman has failed her destiny, to be other for man. This peril is associated with tallion sadistic and homicidal rage directed at the historically constructed cause, the feminine. When she fails to be controlled he becomes violent because he cannot tolerate seeing the emptiness on his other side. The phallus, which assumes its importance from its absence on a woman, is the symbol of domination and the erect penis is its instrument. The Oedipus complex structures the erection as the instrument of male domination, and the only potential for intimacy through the eroticisation of dominance in heterosexuality. Woman has, is, no-thing.

Although the penis has particular significance as the instrument of desire and domination, derived from its absence on a woman, I think it would be a mistake to be blinded by this myth into thinking that this is what needs, especially, to be explained. To put it into context one has to look again at the origins of the ruptured self in the failure of the primary symbiosis. Although the encapsulation varies in intensity and severity according to the variables so well described by Klein, its presence is inevitable. The dependency which it creates is also inevitable as the child, and later the man, attempts to restore the lost paradise.

The psychosis is repressed, and meaning, which suddenly becomes so imperative, begins to be organised around the central concept of gender, without which there is no subject. The foundation matrix, to which sexual differentiation and patriarchal values are fundamental, offers role stereotypes consonant with a definition of women which are consonant with a definition of them as passive objects of male needs and desires. Woman's fundamental role is to service man, sexually and otherwise, to ensure that he does not fall into the rupture. As Chasseguet-Smirgel points out, the penis, hence sexuality, is a man's escape from the failed symbiosis (the terrifying primary maternal object), and the phallus symbolises it. The foundation matrix provides legal, medical, political, moral and philosophical structures and discourses which articulate, support and reinforce this definition.

In outline, this arrangement mirrors the original symbiosis. It is constructed and reproduced through the quintessentially female role of mother. It is for this reason that feminist thinkers urge a major realignment of childrearing practices towards shared parenting, although Segal (1987) correctly points out that this would require nothing less than the dismantling of present means of production and economic organisation. The major difference between the original symbiosis and its adult inheritor is that instead of the primary object (mother) being in charge, control is invested in a tyranical male child/adult who has permission to use violence to ensure that the encapsulated psychosis is not evoked by a woman's refusal to live up to expectations.

An uncontrolled woman is the ultimate frustration, the knowledge that there is no other. Male violence is an attempt to make woman fit the impossible expectations of gender differentiation and preserve the myth of earthly paradise. It is also, in the familiar way of these things, a punishment for her inability to do so, a reality of which men are all too well aware. Male sexuality as it is presently constructed is more about the sexualisation of loss and absence than phallic triumph.

This chapter cannot end without at least a nod towards the fate of the psychosis in little girls and women. However, the terrain is much less secure in this regard. I am mainly influenced by analytic thinkers such as Nancy Chodorow and in particular by modern feminists who place great stress on the value of the concept of the Stockholm syndrome as a framework for understanding 'female masochism'. They, in common with Luce Irigaray and others (see Bograd and Yllo 1988), would deconstruct the Freudian notions of passive-masochistic-castrated-female as being consequential of male power: that is as secondary not primary. In this their ideas are similar to those expressed by their predecessors (Horney, Deutsch, Lampl-de-Groot) during the great female sexuality debate during the late 1920s and early 1930s. The essence is that little girls are taught to accept male power and authority and their own subordinate status. This inevitably leads to envy. The pressures on little girls and women to eschew aggression and violence are intense. This is graphically illustrated by the excessive social disapprobation heaped on women who act out of role. Studies of the sentences given to battered women who murder their husbands and who use the provocation defence, compared with husbands who murder their wives led Jeremy Horder (1992), fellow in law at Worcester College, Oxford, to assert that the provocation defence is a device devised by men for the benefit of men. Four times as many men as women kill their partners or former partners. Three out of four women who kill their partners have been battered, though this applies to hardly any of the men who kill their partners. Of the men who plead provocation 30 per cent are found guilty of manslaughter. By contrast just over half the women succeed in pleading provocation. 'One must ask', says Dr Horder, 'whether the doctrine of provocation, under the cover of an alleged compassion for human infirmity, simply reinforces the condition in which men are perceived and perceive themselves as natural aggressors and in particular as women's natural aggressors. Unfortunately, the answer to that question is yes' (ibid.).

Psychodynamically, the girl's indentification with the mother, which the boy has to eschew in order to attain his masculinity (Greenson 1968), coupled with these social pressures as mediated through her mother's role as a model in relation to her father, act to ensure that she turns her violence and hatred inwards. Finally, however much her husband may evoke feelings of deprivation, frustration and anxiety, he is not an 'appropriate victim of violence'. To the extent that she has learned well, she will instead feel guilt because the relationship is failing, a failure for which she is taught she is ultimately responsible as the source of nurturance in the private domain.

8   Working with men who are helpless, vulnerable and violent

It seems to be time to try to pull together these different strands of thought. I have repeatedly described the hypothesis of a universal encapsulated psychosis – the bubble – underlying the violent behaviour of wife batterers. I attempted to account for the ubiquity of the abuse of women by men and, by implication, not only those in intimate relation to their victims. I was critical of traditional analytic models of understanding such behaviour and stated my belief that such models can not only be misleading but implicitly dangerous for women. What I now propose to do is to describe how we work with abusive men from the understanding of male psychology and behaviour that we have reached.

There are a number of fundamental beliefs which follow from our understanding. These beliefs form a basis from which we can understand abusiveness and intervene to change individual men's behaviour without the necessity of instigating the deep and fundamental changes in character structure which can be brought about by intensive psychoanalytical work.

1   *Men have power and authority over women, both de facto and de jure. Men believe they have a natural right to this power and authority and to be in control of women and to use any means necessary to assert these rights.*

2   *Men are completely responsible for their abusive behaviour.*
    In practice what this means is that violence and other forms of abuse cannot be justified or excused by reference to the behaviour of the victim. We have learned in our work that batterers like nothing more than to talk about what their victim did that made them batter her. They all present as if they were the victims. I am not suggesting that this does not represent their subjective reality, but it is completely out of touch with what actually happens. Describing her behaviour is actually an account of his justifications as well as a way of attempting to receive support and reinforcement for his denial. I made the point earlier that when our expectations are frustrated we all feel like victims. Abusers actually use these feelings as a justification for their behaviour, which is about guilt avoidance, and in order to obviate the necessity for self-examination. Experience shows that it is possible to help a batterer stop battering

without his ever needing to talk about his victim's behaviour. However, it is difficult to prevent this kind of acting in, and it is necessary to allow a little, not only because the information is valuable but simply to develop enough goodwill to be able to confront his underlying attitudes and beliefs about women.

3   *Violent abuse does not occur in isolation, it is the most extreme in a system of abuses which are aimed at undermining and dominating the woman. Private abuse is underpinned by institutional abuse at every level of society.*

When a man physically abuses a woman it is usually the end of a long process of escalation. Lenore Walker (1978) identified a three-stage process in a battering. It begins with a rise in tension which is accompanied by verbal abuse and then the attack takes place. This is followed by a period of calm and even apparently loving behaviour. This calm period then changes as the tension escalates. In my experience of working with abusive men, the rise in tension is a period when a host of other forms of abuse may be used. In my work it is apparent that the rise in tension is caused by his increasing resentment that he has to be nice to get his own way, and more importantly to behave as if he is now concerned about his partner's concerns and relinquish some of his demands. This is a challenge to his authority. At the same time, it may be that his partner is developing increasing confidence to resist his demands in the mistaken belief, which his behaviour is designed to instil, that he may have changed and she is now safe from attack. This period will vary not only between men, but also from one attack to another for the same man. It usually ends when the man begins to increase his demands and it may be that what determines the length of the period is his tolerance for frustration and the lengths to which the woman goes to adapt. Eventually he finds a demand to which she could not respond or adapt and he will attack. It seems necessary that in order for a man to stop physical abuse he must also learn about his cycle and give up the other forms of abuse which precede the physical attack.

4   *Abusive behaviour is not usually symptomatic of psychopathology. It is purposive or instrumental violence and is an extreme expression of normal male behaviour towards women. It is predicated on the assumption of the male's right to dominate and to do whatever is necessary to assure the submission of women.*

Cathie (1987), gives as good an account as is available of the orthodox way of working with abusive men. He goes to some lengths to demonstrate that battering men suffer from various forms of infantile deprivation and inadequate attachment experience with the mother which lead to inordinate fears of abandonment. He displays great sensitivity in showing how traditional dynamic models can help to elucidate why a particular man might batter his partner. He unthinkingly follows the

Freudian/Darwinian frustration-aggression hypothesis and makes no reference to the strong sociological and anthropological evidence for the social construction, not only of feelings but also of anger expression. He is obviously not alone in subscribing to this hypothesis, but it must be said that there is no indelible/innate link between feeling angry and acting violently. He also asserts that batterers share a difficulty in that they have failed to develop what he regards as the innate masculine principle,having been raised in a home with an absent or a hostile father. He quotes a paper by Glasser (1982) as saying

> When the self is threatened in any way – loss of identity through inner confusion or through domination by the object, a blow to self-esteem, an insult or humiliation, a loss of emotional supplies – aggression will be a prominent component of an overall response and, other things being equal, violent action will occur aimed at negating the source of assault on the self.

To all these assertions, that battering is a symptom of failed attachment, fears of abandonment, a threat to the self or frustration I would ask only two questions. Why is it that it is very nearly always women who get battered and men who do the battering? Do women not suffer from frustration, failed attachment, fears of abandonment, absent and hostile fathers and threats to the self? I think that these questions have relevance even within an analytic understanding based on the recognition of the boy's different task in dis-identifying with the mother during his resolution of the Oedipus complex. In fact I think that the analytic model makes these questions more relevant, given that the Oedipus complex describes the cultural construction of gender identity. There is no doubt that Glasser is correct in his understanding, but he fails to recognise that violence is culturally constructed and that he is reflecting the way things are and not, as he implies, *the way they are meant to be by nature.*

In attempting to refute the anti-sexist feminist understanding of male abusiveness which, Cathie says, is that 'responsibility for the violence lies entirely with the men. Their battering behaviour is only an extreme form of normal masculine behaviour and is related to society's patriarchal structure and men's expectations that they should be dominant' he ends by doing what seems to me the exact opposite by affirming the existence of an innate masculine principle which, if frustrated, will end in violence. He makes a plea for men being helped to find a source of strength within them that will make battering redundant. This is precisely the opposite of what I would advise. Our belief is that men have too much power. Work with batterers should be aimed at helping them to come to terms with not being in control and feeling comfortable with powerlessness. Women should be empowered by work with batterers. I am very much in sympathy with Cathie's aims in his paper. I agree with him that many men feel confused and uncertain about their role in these times when so many of the old certainties are being swept away. Perhaps the question 'what does it mean to be a man?' has never been more relevant. I do not believe that an appeal to psychobiology and the concept of innate masculinity, however disguised in Jungian symbolism, will provide us with an answer. This seems to be simply a backlash against feminism and a rallying call to the disaffected troops.

As far as pathology is concerned, our own research supports the findings of the Bolton and Bolton (1987) and Finkelhor (1986) reviews. Apart from personality disorders, fewer than 5 per cent of our clients could be diagnosed as suffering from any form of pathology. The 'cycle of abuse' theory (Renvoise 1978) is also not sustained by our findings at the Men's Centre. As an inadequately funded agency, we have to charge most of our clients and consequently have a high proportion of professional middle class men. As I mentioned earlier, no more than 35 per cent of our client group have either been abused or are the children of abusing fathers or mothers. It may be possible to substantially increase this figure if one broadened the definition of abuse to include failures in attunement or maternal empathy and/or powerlessness, sufficient to achieve the status of victim. Actually this may be true (see Miller 1991) but as we have seen we are still left with the problem of why it is usually boys who identify with the aggressor. In addition, these figures contradict the view that low socio-economic status is a determinant of abusive behaviour. This view seems more to reflect the closer connections between statutory agencies and lower socio-economic groups and subsequent higher visibility and reporting.

These, then are the fundamental axioms from which we work with abusive men. Clearly, this is not a value neutral position. We are firmly convinced that in working with abusiveness, whether criminal or otherwise, neutrality is neither possible nor desirable. When working with men who abuse women and children, the issues involved are such that professionals will have their own strongly held attitudes and beliefs. We believe it is necessary to articulate the message that abusive behaviour is wrong and should be stopped. This is what our work aims to achieve – to stop the abuse.

Apart from some individual counselling to prepare clients, or to hold them until a place is available, all the work of the Centre is conducted in groups. Once a week for a minimum of 26 weeks a group of between six and ten men meets for two hours with two facilitators and usually one trainee. Although it is not unique, the nature of our work is unusual in that our client group is, on the whole, resistant and unmotivated. The vast majority are mandated to attend the Centre. Only a small minority are statutorily mandated, the rest are socially mandated by pressure from family, friends or, more usually, the victim who has either left the home or is threatening to do so.

The subjectivisation of abuse

There is another important point to be made before describing our work. The focus of the Centre's work is abusive behaviour. This means precisely what it says. Although it may be true that our clients have suffered from one or indeed many forms of abuse as children, or even, more rarely, that they may be diagnosably neurotic, we do not believe that these are the problems of which their violence is simply symptomatic. This is a crucial point. Many of our clients are insecure, suffer from low self-esteem, or are depressed. We do not believe, and experience shows this to be true, that the abuser needs to feel more secure, increase his self-esteem or relieve his depression before he decides to stop being abusive and violent to his partner or to other women in his power. There are many people who suffer from these problems and are not abusive. It is more than likely that he suffers in the way he does because he is abusive rather than the other way around. Equally, there are many women who suffer so and do not abuse men. Neither do we accept that abusiveness is caused by substance abuse. The world is full of women who abuse substances and do not behave violently, and there are many men who are not violent when they are under the influence of toxic substances or are violent only on some occasions when they are under the influence of substances.

Not that these other problems are ignored. We, like our clients, are interested in how they subjectivise their violence. It is always possible to erect psychodynamic hypotheses which seem to connect their violence to childhood trauma or present difficulties of one sort or another. In addition, and naturally, our clients are keen to present themselves in the best possible light as well as maintaining a consistent self-image. As often as not this invariably involves presenting themselves as victims, either of their childhood, their victims, uncontrollable impulses or toxic substances. The fundamental point remains that we are seeking behaviour change. Invariably, our clients believe that a change in their behaviour can only occur if their victim changes her behaviour towards them. Although we address these other issues, particularly substance abuse, from the outset, we believe that they can and will to a certain extent be detached from their abusiveness by our programme. To the extent that they remain a problem in other areas of the man's life we hope that our clients will take the opportunity to look at these issues after they have renounced abusiveness.

I made the point earlier that our client group is unmotivated and resistant. This has an important bearing on our work. Cathie, in his article, refers obliquely to this and to the difficulty in developing a working relationship with abusers, particularly when they have been abandoned by their partners, their primary attachment objects. He reasons that the origins for this resistance lie in the depth of the wound. His case studies certainly support this contention for the men described. However, it is my experience that these are the exceptions and that the *manifestation* of such deep unresolved dependencies is not the norm in men who batter.

For the kind of men he describes, I have no doubt that some form of deep psychotherapy may be the most effective form of intervention to deal with this dependency problem now that it has emerged. It is not the most effective intervention to help them with their violence, *which Cathie does not identify as the problem*. It may be that he was dealing with a biased sample, in that all of his clients had been left by their victims and were in the safety of the refuge. The majority of the men with whom we work are not in this position. Many have been left by their victims, but of these only a small minority manifest distress similar to Cathie's clients. In the majority, anger and rage, which he also reports, is the manifest response. The sense of outrage is strong and this goes to the heart of my disagreement with Cathie and the psychodynamic model either as an exclusive model for understanding or as a basis for intervening to stop the abuse. The issue for these men, the origins of the resistance, is that they believe they have a right to punish their partners if they do not obey the man's natural authority. They do not believe that the police or social workers, magistrates or other women have a right to interfere in the privacy and secrecy of their relationships within the home. As one of our clients said 'There's only room for one boss in my house!'. As far as a batterer is concerned he is the boss and he is outraged that anyone should think they have the right to interfere with his authority. When he presents to a therapist or counsellor his only motivation is to get his partner (his possession) to come home. He will do anything to achieve this end. It is mistaken to believe that the majority are motivated to stop abusiveness, although they will try to convince the counsellor that this is the intention.

In her book *The Charm Syndrome* Sandra Horley, the Director of Chiswick Refuge, describes the apparent contradiction that many batterers are extremely charming when they first meet a prospective partner. I experience this charm almost every time I first meet such men and am no longer surprised by it. Horley's understanding of the charm of batterers is in accordance with ours, although we did not expect it in our contact with them (see Jukes 1993). It took us some time after beginning this work to realise that our fears for our personal safety were, on the whole, unfounded. We had all had fantasies about being attacked and made plans about what to do in such circumstances. However, we now know that batterers are not, in general, a threat to men. Of course there are exceptions to this and we always take elementary precautions before arranging consulations. As in forensic psychiatry we are limited in the extent to which it is possible to predict the propensity to violence of a particular individual. The only guideline to future behaviour is past behaviour. In all our experience of working with batterers, we have received many threats of violence but never been attacked.

Denial, honesty and honouring abusers' accounts

In case this sounds complacent I should add that a fundamental feature of our work is that we never believe what a client tells us about his violence.

Ray Wyre tells us (1989) that he does not give his clients the opportunity to lie. Rather than asking them whether they commit certain practices, whether criminal or otherwise, he asks what seem to be outrageous leading questions. For example, if he wants to know how often they fantasise about children with accompanying masturbation, he will ask 'Do you masturbate to fantasies of children more than five (n) times a day?'. He presents compelling evidence for this break with standard counselling and therapeutic practice. It is clear that there are many similarities between child abusers and batterers and in fact the anecdotal evidence is that many abusers are dual status (Herman 1981).

As I read the above paragraph, I feel rather guilty about such a frank admission of behaviour which runs contrary to everything I have been taught is good therapeutic practice. Of course therapists are used to suspending belief with their patients, but it is not usually from distrust. Rather it is based on experience that what patients understand of their own behaviour and motivation often is superficial at worst and mistaken at best. This does not mean that we discount subconscious or unconscious motivation in our client's behaviour or that there are no similarities between our distrust and the therapeutic suspension of belief and the tolerance of uncertainty. The origins of our distrust of batterers is that all batterers, including those rare ones who really want to stop, is that they all use denial to an extent which has to be seen to be believed. My experience is that psychotherapy will not be effective in dealing with this denial, firstly because only one account of the reality of the client's relationship is available and secondly because *therapeutic training does not equip us to perceive it*. As therapists we are trained to understand the way individuals subjectivise their experience rather than understand their social reality. The motivations for this denial are complex although fundamentally it is employed to avoid massive anxiety connected with conflict and as such it is standard therapeutic material. Our technique for dealing with it is standard therapeutic confrontation although ours tends to be rather more intense. It needs to be said that time is of the essence in work with abusers. We take great care not to use our clients' victims as subjects in a therapeutic research programme; the risks to their safety are too great.

Stopping abusive behaviour

So far I have outlined the basic assumptions of the Centre and our model of denial and briefly discussed our pro-feminist orientation. It remains to describe how we actually work with abusers.

The most important aim of our work is to stop the man's physical, including sexual, violence. The vast majority of our clients are mandated to attend the Centre, very few are willing participants. The agenda varies, but usually they see their attendance as showing willing to their partner in the hope that she will return or cease her threats to leave. At the moment we do not have a situation where magistrates will order attendance at the Centre, although many strongly recommend it. Approximately 80 per cent of our clients are self-referred although only about one in four will make the first contact. Usually it is the victim who does so at the perpetrator's behest. This data is interesting and revealing in that apart from expressing the perpetrator's anxiety it also reveals his belief that his abusiveness is, at least in part, his partner's/victim's problem and that she should take responsibility for finding a solution to it.

When a man has finally contacted us and we have assessed the extent of his problem he will be asked to sign a contract with the Centre in which he agrees to abjure the use of abusive behaviour during his attendance at a programme.

No matter what the reason, excuse or justification he comes with, including being out of control, during nearly thirteen years of running programmes we have had very few incidents of contract breaking involving violence. It needs to be said that we do not simply ask him to agree to stop, but also provide him with an alternative to abusive behaviour. This is called 'Time Out' and is a simple anger management technique. Although anger management is important, we make it clear to him that we are not interested in simply helping him to control his anger for the rest of his life. We inform him of our belief that *anger is another way men control women, not a cause of violence*, and that we would like to help him to stop feeling so angry. We explain that we think of anger as the result of frustrated expectations and that as men we have many expectations of women which are not always known to us, but which have an important influence on our relationships with women. We contract to help make his expectations explicit so that he can re-examine them in a new light and learn new ways to meet them or to change them where it seems appropriate. During this process he will learn that his violence and other forms of abuse are instrumental. Men usually discover that they make decisions at every moment when they are abusing: decisions to stand up, to shout, to make intimidating gestures, to strike, to close his fist or slap, to hit in the face or arm or body. Another important insight is that there is no automatic connection between anger or rage and acting violently. This becomes clear when we ask our clients to note how often they feel similar anger or rage outside the home and do not attack. This underlines that they have attitudes and beliefs about violence towards female partners which allow them to use violence to achieve their ends. Crucially, when asked to account for their non-violence outside the home, most report that they control their behaviour because they know that it would have severe consequences whereas they believe they can get away with it at home. This is not to suggest that getting away with it is a cause of violence, but simply that knowing they can act with impunity removes a major inhibition.

It is true that many abusers, or simply men, have great difficulty in differentiating feelings. As they analyse their behaviour in the group they see that they go through a whole range of emotions during abusive episodes. One of our tasks is to help them to tolerate and contain these emotions in order that they can think about them and find other ways of expressing them. If we are successful in doing so, many of our clients become depressed as they give up acting out. This is a difficult period and can lead to real risks of suicide and suicidal behaviour. There is also a risk of homicidal behaviour during this period with feelings of intense resentment towards their partner for 'getting them into this mess' and doing nothing to relieve the pain. The other men in the group can provide crucial support at this time. We actively encourage this whilst ensuring that any contact outside the group is discussed. Male bonding behaviour can be based on sexist attitudes and beliefs of a sort which underpin male violence and extra-group contact is discouraged. Some researchers believe that there are significant differences between batterers and that there may be a set of discrete personality profiles. In particular Dutton (1994) quoting Ganley (1989) and Sonkin *et al.* (1985) believes that during treatment self-referred men turn their anger inward and court-referred men turn it outward. Clearly the former may be more at risk of depression and suicide whereas the latter are at risk of homicide. I cannot say that my own impressions confirm this although further research is obviously required.

Each man in a group is required to analyse at least one of his major attacks on his partner. We ask him to systematically examine other methods used to achieve or maintain control of his partner which are outlined in a checklist. Each man maintains a daily diary of his contact with his partner designed to analyse his abusive and controlling behaviour. Often a man who is successfully using self-control during the honeymoon period of the programme will report that there is nothing to record in his diary. We remind him that he has a long history of abusiveness and that he should use his diary to analyse this. Although there is no time to work with the material this provides, it is a crucial element in the programme and resistance to it is regularly confronted.

Groups also provide the opportunity to begin articulating early childhood trauma. This can only be a beginning but all our clients are given appropriate referrals to continue therapeutic work after completing a programme. We inhibit this sort of work early in the programmes because we believe that it colludes with various forms of justification for abusiveness and to that extent it reinforces the behaviour. Only after a client has gone through the four stages of our denial model will we not actively intervene to prevent his dealing with his own pain.

Intimacy

In the marital therapy literature there is a great deal of attention paid to what is the most common form of marital relationship which presents for treatment or help. It is most often referred to as the Pursuing Wife and

Distancer Husband syndrome. This syndrome is characterised by the wife's need for intimacy and the husband running away from it, whether emotionally, sexually or otherwise. Historically, the woman has ended up being the focus of much of the work in these situations simply because she is the most active during treatment and is the one who often presents as having a problem, many of the men saying that they are quite happy with the way things are if only she wouldn't get so angry with him. The danger of this is that the woman's need for intimacy may end up being pathologised or defined as neurotic and she will be persuaded that she ought to back off and give him the chance to come forward to her. In fact, this is what many of these women have done for many years without success and their anger and reproaches reflect this failure on the man's part. Many of the men with whom I work become abusive when their partners refuse to cease their attempts to become intimate and reproach the man angrily for his failure to give her what she wants. I do believe the need for intimacy is gender constructed although that is not my concern here. The cycle is depressingly familiar. The woman asks for more, the man seemingly misunderstands, the woman gets tearful and angry and the man feels guilty, threatens her and/or withdraws angrily. The woman feels even more hurt as this is repeated and her reproaches intensify. Often the cycle ends when he physically abuses her and she ceases her demands for a while.

Paradoxically, many abusive men are rather passive in their relationships and it is precisely this passivity which is the source of most of their partner's difficulties. More precisely, what I am referring to is emotional passivity, although physical passivity can be a problem too. It is often difficult for such Distancer men to see that this problem, although it is about fear of closeness, is also centrally about control. It is not so much that they are incapable of intimacy although this is often true and is a very difficult, sometimes intractable, problem suffered by many men, not only abusers. It is often not that they cannot tolerate intimacy but are only prepared to tolerate it on their terms, in the way they want and when they want. It may well be, of course, that many of these men, as little boys, did indeed have to cope with premature demands for intimacy from their mothers and developed a basic fault founded on their mother's narcissistic preoccupation where there could have been a maternal preoccupation. Could it be that Freud was correct when he hypothesised that little boys universally represent for their mothers the penis for which they have always longed, or is this male wish-fulfilling fantasy? Either way, it remains the case that abusive men do not accept that women have the right to make demands in a relationship. Their role is to service male needs, demands and expectations.

This leads me to the central issue I want to address in this section: how men cope with women's anger. In the cycle described above, the woman will eventually become angry with her partner's continued frustration of her needs so that eventually these can become demands, or angry needs. In these circumstances the man will report to me, and to many marital therapists that the reason he cannot respond to his partner's needs is that she is so angry when she makes them clear and this evokes, not tenderness or love, but resentment and spite. Such a man will frequently say that if only she would stop making angry demands he would be able to give her what she needs. This is patently untrue. Although he will undoubtedly be able to give more to her, and more often, it will always be on his terms; he will always be in control of the intimacy in the relationship – either way she ends up adapting to and being controlled by him. Nevertheless, the majority of men who make this claim are sincere. It has often been so long since the man gave anything spontaneously and since he was not angry or resentful that he has come to believe his rationalisations and justifications for continually turning her down, whether sexually or emotionally. (This reminds me of that wonderful joke from the film *Bananas* by Woody Allen when he is being rejected by his girlfriend. When he asks her 'why?', she says he is immature. 'But how?', asks Allen, bewildered. 'Sexually, emotionally and intellectually', she replies. 'Yeah, but what other ways?', replies Allen.)

In these circumstances it is important to confront the man with this understanding, this reframing of the situation which places his rejection of her at the centre of the explanation for her anger. This may require some energy in dealing with his resistance to assuming responsibility for the situation and giving up a long established habit of projecting it onto her with his blaming. As it succeeds his treatment will focus on his learning some important skills. The first is in coping with her anger. Even if he should begin to behave differently by becoming more emotionally active and taking initiatives in defining problems in the relationship, she is not, in my experience, going to stop being angry, either immediately about his past treatment of her or in the relationship generally. I believe that taking the initiative, giving up passivity in relation to women, is one of the most difficult things for men to learn. I cannot count the number of times that partners of my passive male clients have told me that he seems to be quite happy whatever is going on in the relationship. He seems not to care that it is not intimate or that it is cold or distant or practical. His belief, which I have heard stated many times, is that he is simply doing everything he can to preserve a non-conflicted harmonious relationship (shades of Balint here) and he can't understand why she isn't happy with things the way they are. This adds insult to injury as far as she is concerned. Actually, it is not true that the man is careless about the absence of intimacy. He may well be in a state of repressed despair, because he wants and needs intimacy but cannot cope with the contradiction between this and needing to be in control of its parameters and the relationship. Often my clients cope with this conflict by being in total denial and as frequently by having affairs or flirtatious relationships ('my wife doesn't understand me'). The second set of skills concern the establishment and maintenance of intimacy and techniques for dealing creatively with conflict – assuming he has already learned that conflict is inevitable and does not need to split in order to deal with his anxiety (see Jukes 1993).

Reality

Perhaps the first thing we need to teach our clients is that there is no such thing as reality. This is profoundly important for abusers to know. They are convinced that they know what is real, in particular what is real for their victims. The most common, and poignant example of this is when she tells him that he hurt her and he replies 'no, I didn't'. I imagine that there are few readers who have not used such a reply at some time in their lives. Abusive men have the greatest difficulty in according equal status to their partner's perceptions or experiences, for all the reasons with which we are now familiar. However, such a reply is frankly crazy. You cannot simply deny another's reality, however painful or guilt-inducing it is, and still remain in communication with them. As far as I know, the first rule of communication is that you have to acknowledge the other's existence as a different, separate person with a unique grasp of reality. Of course you may think that their reality is crazy, or not consensually valid, in the bushes, off the wall or whatever, but before it can be negotiated it must first be acknowledged. Abusive men do not do this.

It is crucial for abusive men to learn that one does not control the object, that she is a subject and may actually leave or fall out of love at any time. Abusers need to learn that what keeps relationships together, prior to her suffering from the battered women's syndrome and Learned Helplessness (Walker 1978) when she will probably suffer any amount of abuse, is tenderness and love, even though there are difficulties. The resolution of difficulties in a non-abusive way is only possible if partners are truly equal and each accords the other the respect of listening and attempting to understand rather than change or discount, whether by minimising or other techniques, their reality.

The underlying pain and fear of fragmentation in the encapsulation are defended against with the rage which fuels the basic mistrust. The rage is a product of accumulated resentments about non-negotiable and frustrated expectations deriving from a basic failure of dependency. As I pointed out in an earlier chapter, these expectations are inevitable. They arise during that period when we assume the beginning or the birth of the subject in the separation and individuation phase from the primary object, the object universally constructed as feminine mother. In the treatment of this rage (which we could call narcissistic), cognitive and behavioural strategies are essential and in short-term intervention are probably the only ones which are efficacious with any degree of consistency and reliability. The treatment focus is not the rage qua rage, but its continued replication by the client or patient. Hydraulic models, which see the patient as a container of pent-up, archaic affects which require ventilation, have little place in the immediate treatment of abusers. As Freud (1937) was to say of the theory of the Birth Trauma and the abreaction/ventilation treatment based on this as proposed by the analytic defector Otto Rank,

> probably it has not accomplished more than would be done if the men of a fire brigade, summoned to deal with a house set on fire by an upset oil-lamp, merely removed the lamp from the room in which the conflagration had broken out. Much less time would certainly be spent in so doing than in extinguishing the whole fire.

This is not to say that such pent-up and repressed effects do not exist; we can probably all attest to that. Rather it is that the way these states of arousal are socially constructed, by a process of differentiation, naming and behavioural elaboration, is the prime concern. Powerful affects provide a justification for being abusive, or any other form of deviant behaviour including, often, murder because they are culturally constructed as out of control experiences, e.g. passion. This rage provides the motive power for abuse which punishes for past and present failure and therefore attempts to establish control and future adaptation through fear of the consequences of failure.

As I have mentioned earlier, abusive men are particularly predisposed to perceive threat where none exists and to go from that perception to the rapid experience of crisis. The perception of threat, which is evidenced by phrases such as 'she goes on; she nags; she won't stop' is that if the man listens he will have to yield to a definition of himself which simply contradicts his self-image and threatens to rupture the bubble and swamp him with the helplessness etc. in the encapsulation. This is a source of massive anxiety and guilt because he also knows that he is deceiving himself. Another major source of the threat is that being in control of a woman is a primary source of his maleness. The threat of not being in control is that he will be attacked and destroyed by the phallic woman (although some authors, e.g. Welldon 1993, believe that the fundamental anxiety is of being devoured by the woman). In fact this destruction is castration, because if he is not in control, in his mind she must be. He cannot conceive of a relationship in which someone is not in control, in which dominance and submission are not the basis of the relationship. It should be questioned whether, in fact, women believe the same thing, but simply make the assumption of submission. Personally I do not believe women do make this assumption that if the man is not in control then she has to be. I believe they have a better integrated idea of partnership and yielding than men do, because this is part of the learning of femininity and femaleness.

Given that maleness involves the feeling of being in control, especially of a woman, a man rightly perceives a threat every time she behaves in ways which challenge his control, either of her or his immediate environment. The threat is real; it is not imaginary as some writers imply (Bolton 1989). The move from the perception of threat to the experience of crisis is rapid simply because unconsciously the threat is a massive crisis. Of course, what I am describing here is what passes for normal male paranoia. If she is in control he is castrated. His primary gender identity is undermined at the phallic level and his primary perception of the witch is evoked. When she is in control she is assumed to want to sadistically control him, i.e. by castrating him – the phallic anxiety – and by annihilating/eating him – the oral cannabalistic anxiety. He wants to control how he is seen and experienced by his partner and will not (he thinks cannot) tolerate a perception which is different from his own. This also applies to other non-personal issues like politics, money and so on, all of which he needs to control. It is rare in my experience for such issues to be framed in this way in groups for abusers, although they will use words which graphically communicate such anxieties, such as fears of being overwhelmed, smothered etc.

Treating narcissistic rage has been problematic for psychotherapists for many years. In treating abusers it is important to reframe emotions, to shift the frame of reference. One way of doing so is to inform the abuser client that emotions are behaviour like any other action, and that they are instrumental; they enable other behaviours without responsibility; they widen the behavioural choices for responding to particular situations. This approach is obviously educational and psychodynamic therapists may argue that it is not therapeutic, that what is really required is the working through of the emotions in a secure transference relationship where the emotions can be metabolised and mitigated. Attractive though this is, it is a questionable assumption. It is important to learn that we need not be passive in the experience of emotion, that emotions are behaviour. That it makes as much if not more sense to assume we have them in order to legitimise behaving in ways which might be otherwise unacceptable. This is much more in keeping with psychodynamics also in that it sees people as agents even where there is no conscious awareness of motive. I realise that there is the cultural difficulty of legitimising this idea when compassion for human weakness is so much a part of our culture; at least for men, as witness Horder's research into the treatment of women who murder their husbands (Horder 1992).

It is important to help abusers come to terms with the basic issue which is that they have a need to punish and cause pain to their partners. This desire, apart from its controlling aims, has its origins in the desire for revenge for the primary wound. Helping him accept this is the only way to help him examine that part of himself which is so different from his conscious self or self-concept. This other part of him is emotive and seemingly governed by irrational primary processes, whereas actually it is just as rational as the conscious self. The difference is that it operates from a different set of values, attitudes and beliefs about men and women than the conscious self. Without the acknowledgement of this desire the abuser will stay in denial of responsibility even if not of behaviour.

A very important issue during this phase of the work, which is actually the second stage after getting behavioural disclosure and working with the main forms of his denial, is to let the man know that he is not a bad person, but that his behaviour is nasty and bad. Depression, confusion, ambivalence and the risk of serious acting out during this period are high and the risk of suicide is a serious one. It is at this stage that important thinking processes are interposed between the desire to attack and its acting out. There are no miracle interventions, just patient, steady analytic work with thought and verbalisation being the medium of change. It may involve going over a particular attack a few times and each time a new insight or piece of information may emerge. However, even if not, the man is having the invaluable experience of thinking about the previously unthinkable. His capacity for reality testing and his tolerance of psychic pain and the 'unbearable tension' of frustration is being enlarged. Abusers have a very low tolerance for any form of psychic pain and the only way to increase this tolerance is to evoke it and hold it. In fact this could be said to be the main therapeutic aim of programmes for abusers. With the development of tolerance for psychic pain will come self-control and the inhibition of abusive behaviour. In this respect the treatment of batterers is the same as that for any forensic patients. I will say more of this in the section on group work in Chapter 9.

Male sexuality and dominance

It is important to stress that every effort is made to get our clients to disclose their use of pornography and the nature of their masturbatory fantasies. It is only in this way that we can access their abusive and controlling sexual behaviour and determine the extent of the risk they represent to the sexual integrity of their partner.

The last chapter emphasised the connection between dominance/power and male sexual desire. Along with many feminists I am convinced that heterosexuality is constructed around the eroticisation of dominance and submission, that it is essentially sadomasochistic. I have reluctantly reached this conclusion after thousands of hours analysing men's masturbatory fantasies and their use of pornography. It seems that Freud's analysis of the difficulty, for men, of integrating sexuality with affection is as true as ever. However, this view does not go unchallenged, even, perhaps especially, by feminists. Lynne Segal, in particular, is critical of what she sees as this monolithic view of male sexuality and stresses what she interprets as most men's fear of women, their experience of impotence and sexual anxiety and their desire to be passive. However, I believe she betrays her own confusion in that after her strong critique of the trans-historical, monolithic perspective (Segal 1990, pp. 207–16) she goes on 'before we can rest upon the joyful shores where positive meanings connect to sexuality, we have to wade through the swamp in which men's porno-graphic fantasy and actual sexual violence suffuse our consciousness of sex' (ibid., p. 217).

The fundamental problematic of psychoanalysis, the construction of gender, was taken up seriously in feminist theorising with the advent of *Red Rag*, the feminist journal which emphasised the role of the family in gender reproduction. This was picked up and developed, first by Chodorow (1977) and Dinnerstein (1976). More recently, however, with the publication of Adrienne Rich's 1980 essay on the invisibility of lesbianism, concern has shifted to the compulsory nature of heterosexuality, to use her term, and to its status as the fundamental political institution. There has been, and is, a heated debate within feminism and psychoanalysis about the nature of heterosexuality. Radical thinkers, and they tend to be lesbian separatists such as Jeffreys (1990), believe that it is sadomasochistic. It seems to me that psychoanalytic therapy has drifted away from the fundamental problematic of gender, particularly with the emphasis in the past 40 years on the power of the mother and the importance of attachment. It is not difficult to argue that this is sexist in its reinforcement of gender role stereotypes. Perhaps the difficulty is that the apogee of analytic success is a resolved Oedipus complex, at least in the man, and the acceptance, for men and women, of our anatomical destiny as it is presently and historically constructed. For the man this involves the development of normal contempt for the castrated woman and this is actually the point at which we engage with the men in our programmes. To the extent that this metaphor mirrors reality it clearly represents a major limitation of what we can achieve with abusive men and no doubt this is one of the reasons that homosexuality is now such a problem in psychoanalysis. My experience, however, is that although contempt for women is 'normal' in men, it does not resist analysis to its underlying envy and frustration. Heterosexuality is a different matter. We can engage with conscious attitudes and beliefs about men and women and achieve substantial gains in raising awareness, but the unconscious roots of desire seem intractable. Psychoanalysis may attempt to deconstruct them but they are left untouched in our clients. One of the difficulties is that we do not have any alternative to offer them. Homosexuality, after the early heady hopes of gay liberation, now seems more stratified into alternative dominance/submission arrangements than is heterosexuality.

In spite of that, our work challenges many of our long cherished notions of maleness and femaleness as we struggle with our clients to evolve new ways of relating with women which offer the possibility of mutual satisfaction without the shame of subordination or the guilt and rage of oppression.

Ambivalence

I want to end this chapter with a discussion of ambivalence. It is a word I have used often and it seems appropriate to centralise it by placing special consideration of it at the end of this clinical chapter.

The patient, Roger, is a young man in his early thirties, a careworker, married with one young child. His wife is an immigrant of Latin origin. He first presented in a threatening and paranoid state and initially caused a lot of alarm in the group with his level of violent agitation and inaccessibility. Even allowing for this it became clear that his wife is clearly quite disturbed. She constantly criticises him, physically attacks him and is otherwise very unpleasant. I should say that in the face of such descriptions it can be difficult to stay with the working hypothesis. However, he was not denying his own violence, which was considerable. Nor did he deny that he always initiated the physical violence. She, however, defends herself with vigour, sometimes giving more than she gets. He had married her on the rebound from another relationship and has suffered severe doubts about his feelings for his wife since the day they met. Since they married he has often told her that he does not love her and never has.

When he first presented for treatment he was certain that she was the problem in the marriage, her lability and general level of aggression being what he most talked about. He was still very much in love with the woman who had rejected him before his marriage although he had not been in contact with her for seven years. He agreed that he idealised her. Week after week he would consume the group with horrific tales of his wife's behaviour including her attacks on him with lethal weapons. He had called in the police on many occasions when she seemed uncontrollable. What caused constant surprise was that when the group began to reflect to him their perceptions of her he would defend her vigorously and state that he loved her and that the group had the wrong idea of her. The group placed great pressure on him to leave the relationship for the sake of his child and the health of himself and his wife. He steadfastly resisted this suggestion. He told how they had an active and intimate sexual relationship and that at times there was much tenderness between them. He was quite able to see that his lability, the constant change in his affections towards her, without any apparent precipitator, was responsible for her mood swings and her frustration. Over the months it became clear that whenever there were times of intimacy he would do something which would spoil this and lead to another major row with violence as an inevitable outcome. To his despair he began to recognise that he could not tolerate being loved and that in spite of the pain of it he preferred the times of great stress and confusion when they were at odds with each other.

Roger came from a dysfunctional family. His father was very violent to his mother. His mother had been very violent to all the children. His father, unusually, was not violent to the children. Roger, however, was very afraid of him and hated him. It was some time before he saw that these feelings were a defence against his fear and hatred of his mother, with whom he had identified and whom he had until then idealised and seen, quite rightly, as a victim of his father's threatening and violent behaviour. His dis-identification from his father was intense. As this began to dawn on him, Roger became increasingly confused and depressed as he saw how he provoked his wife into behaving violently in order to create the conditions he required to experience his hatred of her, as a mother substitute. During this work he made an early decision to abjure any violence towards her and stuck to this religiously. He read assiduously about women's experience of violence from men and began to feel empathy for his wife and his mother as a man rather than from his earlier identification with his mother. He discovered feelings of affection for his father which had been deeply repressed and which had been unrequited during his childhood. Roger had split his hating and loving feelings for his mother, maintaining a conscious idealisation, which required physical distance to sustain (hence the lost ideal partner), and repressing his hatred for her. His defence of his wife in the group when his presentation of her was mirrored to him, initially evoked great anxiety. His personality was held together by his identification with his mother, his father was not an alternative. He had never reached the depressive position and struggled with paranoid conflicts in a largely hostile universe.

It should come as no surprise that Roger had intense conflicts about his sexual orientation. He was not yet ambivalent. He failed to experience that the woman he loved and hated were the same. Of course he recognised this intellectually, but emotional insight is a different order of event. The confrontation in the group threatened him with the possibility of integration and the onset of debilitating depression. Clinically, the work at this point was the same for him as it would be for a patient in analysis or therapy: to help him to experience his ambivalence and develop the capacity to hold and contain it along with the anxiety and depression this entails. For much of his time in the programme he felt quite crazy. His provocation of his wife escalated until it became clear that there was a real risk she would actually kill him. Analysis of this in the group led to Roger articulating his deep confusion about who was really crazy, him or his wife. If she did attack him it proved it was her and that he was sane. He eventually saw that this was in fact what he was attempting to prove and that it derived from a deep confusion in his childhood about what sense to make of his mother's physical violence. He had eventually begun to use what Fairbairn (1952) called the moral defence of the traumatised victim. He had concluded that he must be bad because this at least offered the chance of redemption if he could change. If he had concluded that his mother was bad or mad there would be no hope. This sticking plaster for his ego had, however, become increasingly difficult to hold to. He could not continue to consciously deny his mother's violent rages against his siblings, and particularly during his adolescence it required superhuman effort to hold this structure together. If his wife/mother were mad than he, Roger, was sane. On the other hand if his wife/mother were mad he would, he believed, disintegrate.

I cannot claim that Roger's treatment has been a success. It is ongoing. These issues are only slowly giving way. However, he is no longer violent to his wife and his provocative behaviour is greatly lessened. Her attacks on him have reduced substantially and no longer involve lethal weapons. Roger exemplifies some of the issues which most abusers need to go through. His rather borderline personality gave him access to material which more defended men have great difficulty with. He is unusual in having clear memories of a mother who he thought was trying to kill him and who exemplifies all the qualities of the phallic/witch mother of the male unconscious. She is there for us all in unconscious fantasy, even if she was not remotely like Roger's mother.

9 Groupwork

The majority of the work undertaken at the Centre, and in my private practice, is in groups. Often, however, this is combined with individual sessions when crisis threatens or at the beginning of treatment when anxiety may be too severe to allow constructive work in a group setting. This is not the place to go into a detailed examination or give an elaborate account of groups. The literature on groups is extensive and anyone wishing to work with abusers in a group setting should familiarise themselves with it. Of particular value are the works of Foulkes and Anthony (see the Bibliography), the developers of group analysis, and other members of the Institute of Group Analysis in London.

Although as a group analyst I have great faith in the efficacy of groups for mitigating even quite severe pathology, I believe they have particular relevance for abusers providing the group is homogenous and also providing that certain changes are made in the way the group is conducted and in particular in the way that treatment is contextualised. Homogeneity is important. I have experimented with placing substantiated abusers in mixed open groups, and I have also supervised groups where they were present. My experience is that the presence of an abuser, who has presented for treatment of his abusive behaviour, can be so threatening to women in mixed groups that it interferes with their capacity for using the group effectively to meet their own therapeutic needs and with the benefits to the man himself. It has to be said that this is not always the case, but I know of no way of predicting beforehand whether it will be so with a particular man and a particular group. It is also very difficult to use any psycho-educational methods with abusers in generic groups, as this would run contrary to the usual methods employed in such groups. In abuse groups, the conductors take far more responsibility for the level of activity than is the norm in open analytic groups. In the circumstances it has not seemed to me to be worthwhile to pursue the experiment although I have placed men in heterogeneous, mixed gender groups after they have completed anti-abuse treatment. This has seemed to be particularly effective.

Before I outline why homogeneity is especially important and apparently efficacious I want to say something about the particular strengths in the approach of the Men's Centre which I believe are worth addressing. One has to say something about the state of mind of men when they first present for treatment in order to fully understand why dedicated treatment seems the most effective. The vast majority only present after many years of active abusiveness. In the beginning they did not feel particularly anxious or upset about their behaviour, indeed did not regard it as a long-term problem. It is only after the slow realisation that they abuse in many different circumstances and/or when they are threatened with abandonment by their victim that they present for help. They will have made many promises over the years that they will change and they will have blamed everything except themselves. Often they genuinely feel that they can change with a little help from their partner and they will have been provided with all the support she can muster under the circumstances. Finally, in a state of high anxiety, often depressed because their relationship is in such a parlous state, and desperately confused about why they continue to behave in destructive ways they (or their partner as is usually the case) approach the Centre. As often as not they will not have mentioned to anyone what they have been doing. They usually feel very isolated, knowing that what they do is shameful yet not feeling shame, genuine guilt (by which I mean guilt which would lead to a real change) or remorse. If these feelings are there, they are usually undifferentiated and lost in the turmoil of their emotional and intellectual confusion.

They are often slightly paranoid when they first arrive. They expect admonishment or at least reproach. They get neither. I have often seen that in agencies which work with abusers these men are seen as being different, as alien and the support in the agency for such work is less than it would be for other agency clients. The origins of this are not difficult to discern. However, it can have a negative impact on the treatment or change process, frequently affecting attendance and motivation of both staff and clients.

After being asked for their account of what is going on, during which they usually present in ways outlined earlier, they are soon presented with the violent, abusive and controlling behaviour checklist (see Appendix 1) and asked to check off any behaviour which they themselves have inflicted on their victims. They are not asked if they have shouted at, threatened or beaten, etc., their partner, but how often.

My impression is that although this causes anxiety and defensiveness, it is a source of enormous relief to the man. It may seem paradoxical but I believe it offers him his first experience of legitimacy since he began his abusive behaviour. One of the corollaries of being abusive is a profound feeling of illegitimacy, and necessarily, of alienation. However unpalatable it may also be, the man is given his first experience of being with someone who wants, and in some respects already seems, to understand what he is doing and why. Importantly, he no longer needs to dissemble. Important parts of him which have never been given a voice are suddenly welcomed. He is encouraged to disclose the most unacceptable desires and fantasies of violence and sadism. He is also given to understand that with appropriate effort he may be able to change. In a sense he is invited back into humanity. Also, implicitly, if his behaviour has a cause or causes, if it is accessible to understanding then it is not mad – it falls within human limits of ways of behaving, feeling and thinking.

> I believe there is something about the radical nature of the checklist that is engaging and compelling, perhaps even hope-generating, even at the same time as it is forbidding. What sounds and looks like a stick is also from their perspective a carrot. Their denial, as well as being an instrument for sanctioning misbehaviour is also a burden that weighs heavily on their shoulders and the very radical nature of the contract plus the conviction of its necessity draws them in by offering a definitive challenge to their denial. The contract offers them social legitimacy but psychological freedom as well.
>
> (Dr N.R. Aldus personal communication)

What of the particular value of groupwork? At this point it is important to state my position regarding what is commonly called anger management training. Such training for abusive men is usually provided in groups. It is a structured form of re-education which aims to help men to find non-destructive ways of handling their angry and abusive feelings. Such programmes have proliferated in the UK, particularly in programmes provided by the Probation Service for court-referred abusers. The literature on anger management is wide and I do not intend to review it here. I have no doubt that such techniques have a place in the early stages of treatment with abusers, but as far as I am concerned the overall strategy is the equivalent of soul murder if such techniques are not used by clinicians who are also psychodynamically trained. If a man believes that he is always going to have to struggle with the levels of frustration, rage and anger, the anguish and fragmentation which underlie abusiveness and that the best he can hope for is self-control how could he not experience despair? I believe much more than that is achievable, even within time and resource limited programmes which are governed by 'what works' with offenders. I believe that analytic groupwork conducted within an explicit socio-cultural and political perspective, can both stop the abuse and also mitigate other problems which abusers present such as post-traumatic stress disorder, borderline personality symptoms and even personality disorder.

I cannot here give an exhaustive account of the factors which are curative in groups. However, it is worth restating those which Yalom outlines in his seminal work *The Theory and Practice of Group Psychotherapy* (1985; adapted by Lionel Kreeger 1989).

- Instillation of hope. This is crucial to all psychotherapies but is most explicit in faith healing and Alcoholics Anonymous.

- Universality. Many patients enter therapy feeling that their problems are unique and that no one feels as bad as they do. The discovery that this is not so is often a great source of relief.
- Imparting of information. Patients give each other advice and information. Therapists often give didactic instruction.
- Altruism. It is a source of self-esteem to patients to discover that they can be of help to others and that their destructiveness can be creative when put to the service of the group. They discover that they can offer support, reassurance and insight to others.
- The corrective recapitulation of the primary family group. Early family conflicts can be reworked in the group. The constant challenging of rigid roles or stereotyped behaviour can correct early unresolved conflicts.
- Development of socialising technique. People can learn social skills in a group in their interactions with others. They can develop empathy and responsiveness and their judgementalism can be mitigated in relation to self and others.
- Imitative behaviour. Identification with others, including the conductors, can be a powerful process.
- Interpersonal learning. This is of three kinds:

  a   the correction of interpersonal distortions;
  b   corrective emotional experience through the opportunity to interact with others more deeply and honestly and the development of reality testing and the recognition of inappropriate behaviour;
  c   the group as social microcosm. Each member's interpersonal style will eventually appear in the group. Self-observation, feedback, acceptance of personal responsibility and increased motivation for change leads to an adaptive spiral both in and out of the group, resulting in increased self-esteem and individual autonomy. Abusers will always act out their abuse in relation to the group as a whole (particularly in relation to boundaries such as attendance and timekeeping) as well as towards other members.

- Group cohesiveness. Members gain approval and ultimately improve by participating maximally in the group tasks of: acceptance of patient role; self-disclosure; honesty; non-defensiveness; interest in and acceptance of others; support of the group; personal improvement.

   In cohesive groups, members are more able to express hostility towards each other and to the conductor other.
- Catharsis. The free expression of feelings is very important to the group.
- Existential factors: responsibility; basic isolation; contingency; recognition of mortality; capriciousness of existence.

Yalom did not include these existential factors in his first edition of the book in 1970 and was never happy with the term 'existential factors', although the entire category was ranked highly by patients in terms of therapeutic outcome.

It is not possible to construct an absolute hierarchy of therapeutic factors as they are influenced by the type of group, the stage of therapy, extra-group forces and by individual differences.

Foulkes, the founder and developer of Group Analysis, stated what he thought to be the basic rule of group therapy:

> The group members 'collectively constitute the norm from which, individually they deviate'.

This is a profound statement and one which is born out in therapeutic practice even with abusive men. It is remarkable to hear one man who abuses informing another that he understands his behaviour and that he also does the same thing and then to hear them jointly explore their motivations and alternative ways of behaving. Even where it is clear that each of them transgresses in the same way, they are capable of developing ethical norms and standards which are not only socially constructive but which will mitigate their destructiveness and their abusive feelings. It seems to me that this occurs because groups offer to individuals the opportunity to use their interpersonal destructiveness in a creative and ultimately constructive way.

In addition to the list of factors which Yalom gave as therapeutic in groups, Foulkes mentions two not given by Yalom. I believe these are more likely to operate in groups conducted on psychoanalytic principles. It is worth quoting him at some length (Foulkes 1964: pp. 33–4):

> The patient's realisation that other people have similar morbid ideas, anxieties or impulses, acts as a potent therapeutic agent, in particular relieving anxiety and guilt. That other people suffer as well, or even more, acts as a relief; that others break down or show insufficient will-power to tackle difficulties makes for resolution to do better. It is easier to see the other person's problems than one's own. Repression and the repressed, for instance, can be recognised when pointed out to others. This acts, however, at the same time as an analytic agent in one's own person. The discussion, interpretation or analysis of such material is, therefore effective in a number of people at the same time, even if they merely listen to it. A good deal of therapeutic effect, in particular also relief of anxiety and guilt feelings, is therefore brought about in the position of projection. Apart from counteracting narcissism, forces of identification and contrast are at work here. This whole set of factors we feel inclined to distinguish by giving them a special name, for which we propose 'mirror reaction'.
>
> The loosening and stimulating effects in a group are in parts also of a specific nature. Many more themes are touched upon and it is easier to talk about them when they have been brought up by others. Something similar takes place on a deeper level so that even deep unconscious

material is expressed more readily and more fully. It is as if the collective unconscious acts as *a condenser*.

So, to Yalom's factors we can add (a) the Mirror reaction and (b) condenser phenomena.

I believe that all the therapeutic factors mentioned above are operable in groups for abusers. Of course there are differences from mixed open groups. The most obvious and important is that there are no women present. This presents certain problems for group members as well as for conductors. They mostly derive from the search for the 'missing woman in the group'. She is very present in her absence! Homophobia is very high and the latent homosexuality is acted out in a variety of ways – male bonding being a particularly difficult one in the context of the group's objectives as such bonding is usually predicated on the denigration of women. Highly structured abuse groups do not have to confront these problems or the anxieties which they engender. Structure is often a defence against these anxieties, and no more so than in abusers groups. Another set of problems concerns competitiveness, which is usually at a very high level. This can be a defence against homosexuality, and my experience is that this issue cannot be avoided in male groups. It is important to address the issue of men's affection for each other, especially in abusers groups. Almost all abusive men have difficulty in relating to other men with affection. They hold to hyper-masculine attitudes and beliefs in defence against their vulnerability and helplessness and the implied femininity. Intimacy between group members, which is essential for therapeutic work, necessitates a capacity to hold affectionate feelings for each other without undue homosexual anxiety. This can often be achieved quite simply by uncoupling affection between men from genital sexuality – something which they have usually found impossible. Let me give an example of the way in which group process is used.

It concerns a group for men who are violent to their female partners. It is a one year group with nine members being conducted experimentally on group analytic principles. The events I will describe occurred after five months. For some weeks I had noticed that a small group of four or five men continued talking outside my consulting rooms after the group. Attendance was unusually high, with a full group for five weeks except for one man who missed one session (a full group is an unusual event in a group of abusers). The group had been talking fairly continuously about sexuality during this period. There was a lot of laughter in the groups often at the expense of women for their stupidity or naivety. One told a story about how his wife had found him making love to another woman and he had managed to convince her that she had imagined it. 'They will believe what they want to believe,' he said. This caused enormous amusement in the group, although the anxiety was clear. Promiscuity was a prominent theme and there seemed to be a lot of energy put into asserting how masculine each was. Assertions that women like to be chased and conquered, indeed dominated, are innately passive, want strong men, are only interested in the home etc. and that men are hunters and biologically programmed to chase women were made with great conviction. At one point one of the members disclosed that he felt he had never been able to make love to his wife but only to have sex with her, that he had never been able to be affectionate during their sexual relationship. The group discussed this for a while with some men agreeing that they felt the same. At some point one of the men shouted in a joking voice 'for Christ's sake, don't fuck me, make love to me!'.

This particular session was excited, almost manic. It was fairly easy to construe, within a traditional frame, that this group was going through a phase of inclusiveness and that members were beginning to feel intimate with each other. This had raised intense unconscious homophobic anxiety against which the male bonding was instituted as both defence and expression. Locating the woman in a men's group is always problematic. Previously she had been firmly located outside the group, although efforts had been made to locate her in various men in the group, usually me, as well as the group itself, as was evidenced by the various ways in which these men abused it. I subsequently learned that after this particular session one of the men had said to another that he had 'a couple lined up for Friday' and did the other want to join him? (couple being in this context, 'birds' as he subsequently put it. I should say that members are discouraged from meeting for any purpose outside the group and that if they do so it should be brought into the group). This process continued until I made a mild interpretation about the group's fears of being intimate and their uncertainty about the sexual boundaries of male intimacy. Whether or not this was a correct interpretation (whatever that is!) it had a surprising effect. The group rounded on me with open hostility and vehemently denied any homosexual anxieties. It would have been easy to interpret this hostility as a defence against the anxiety but I did not do so. Thinking about it later I reviewed the histories of all the men in the group (of nine) and was surprised to rediscover that they all, without exception, had grown up with absent and authoritarian, mostly abusive fathers. I was aware of my affection for the men in this group and indeed this counter-transference had been one of the factors leading to the homophobia interpretation. However, I began to understand that this was a misreading of the situation. Of course there was intense homosexual anxiety – in that respect the interpretation had been correct. Where I believe I was wrong was in colluding with the social conflation of a need to be intimate with men, and experience the love of another man as both brother and father, for being like them – as identification – with needing to be loved by the father as the mother. One construction (an unreconstructed one) is that the group was in fact being denigrated and attacked as a mother and that I was the father whom they were testing out. Equally it could be said that their hostility to my intervention could represent their seeing me as the denigrated contemptible female. The 'normal contempt' they were expressing for women is part of every man's makeup and reflects their dis-identification with the mother as well as their envy and their socially reinforced need to endorse the big Difference (a man is always a man and a woman is always a woman) deriving from the identification with the tyrannical father. An identification informed by their need to be loved by him as a son, a love frustrated because of the father's homophobia. The alternative would be to be unable to separate from mother. The identification necessitates privileging the big male/female Difference and active suppression of all those parts of the self which are similar to the feminine m/other. The woman has to be 'not me', 'out there' and denigrated in order for men to be close. I cannot count how many times I have heard men say that they have become what they never wanted to be – just like dad. Central to all this is the need to control the level of intimacy with women, just like dad, and also because intimacy evokes the earlier encapsulated fears connected with being engulfed and destroyed by her. All western cultures provide ready to hand models for achieving this.

Of course they were experiencing homosexual anxieties but these were a product of a culture which conflates homosexual love based on object choice with love based on identification and in which the notion of sameness and difference is exclusive and rigid. I think the therapeutic task in this situation is to help them with their need to be intimate but to deconstruct the notion that this is only possible if they denigrate women as they had experienced their own fathers' doing – to deconstruct, in action, their notion of the Difference as they were stereotypically expressing it and to help them contact their denied identification with the mother and their fears of their femininity. Abusive behaviour does not cease without this. When this bonding behaviour has occurred subsequently I have simply said that they seem to be unable to be close without expressing contempt for women. This seems to have created a space for reflection and has allowed for the expression of divergent points of view from the less hyper-masculine men in the group.

I do not believe any of this would have been possible in a structured group. Not that much of the same material could not be worked over in such a way, but any insight provided would be intellectual only, and lasting change follows from emotional insight. This can only be gained from the quality of emotional involvement which derives from allowing the process to unfold without interference.

Many of the problems which have been the central concern of this book are resolvable in groups. However, their resolution requires that the conductor provide the minimum of structure and simply pays attention to the group process. A high level of structure will militate against these problems becoming manifest in the group, which may be well if the group is simply psycho-educational. However, if one is seeking a deeper and more lasting change it is necessary to set a safe context within which the affective states underlying abusiveness can be accessed and modified. Life in the bubble needs to be seen and heard. Given the opportunity, most abusive men will grasp it with enthusiasm. Structure in groups will always militate against this, and my impression, from having experimented with both structured, semi-structured and unstructured groups is that minimum structure provides the optimum conditions for such change. It is important to emphasise that we set a context which is apparent from a reading of the various appendices to this book. The contract, the diary, the Time Out instructions, etc., leave group members in no doubt about the frame of reference for the work they have to do. This is reinforced by the recommendation to read books and watch films which address the issue of men's abuse of women.

David Adams, the founder of the Emerge programme in Boston Massachusetts, has given a good description of the processes which occur in semi-structured groups conducted on group analytic lines (Adams 1988a). He draws attention to the way that dissonance and anxiety is created as the group develops. The beginning of conscious conflict about abusive behaviour, and the accompanying depression, is the harbinger of real change as the man begins to develop some psychic muscle to contain and think about his feelings and states of mind rather than simply act out by inflicting them on the women in his life. I have no doubt that manifest depression is essential if real change is to occur. Process oriented groups can both initiate the processes which lead to depression and contain it when it occurs in a way which no other therapeutic milieu can provide.

10 Conclusions

I realise that, in spite of my best intentions, I have not succeeded in presenting a view of masculinity that will be very palatable to most men. John Rowan, in a review of *Why Men Hate Women* for the journal *Achilles Heel*, accused me of spreading despair in the way I held up a mirror to the worst of men's qualities. I have no quarrel with that. Any reservations I have about its veracity, at least in the way it reflects our relationships with women, are confounded by the feedback I receive from ordinary women, living with ordinary men who never physically abuse them. Overwhelmingly, that confirms the picture painted here. However, I am not despairing of men's capacity for change and the possibility of creative heterosexuality, nor of the contribution that forms of treatment based on psychoanalytic thinking can contribute to that process. I have seen far too many examples of successful reparation to believe otherwise.

At its root, men's abuse of women, and our need to have power and control over them, both individually and collectively, is a simple frustration pre-emption strategy. The intensity and severity of that abuse varies enormously according to three variables: the intensity of the original frustration, which I stress is universal to men; the models of masculinity available to the developing infant and young male; and, finally, the extent of culturally approved and legitimised violence in the culture in which he is raised, especially in relation to women. Any treatment programme must address all these sources of men's abuse, as well as the many other factors already mentioned. I might go further, and may well do so in later work, and assert that most forms of criminal behaviour are related to these three factors, with frustration, as it is understood here, being the primary motivation. Precisely what it is that leads one man to ambition and achievement, another to crime, another to despair and illness and yet another to addiction will no doubt continue to exercise clinicians and policy makers for many years.

Shortly after its publication in 1994, I was involved in a public debate at the Institute of Contemporary Arts in London about the impact of *Why Men Hate Women*. In that debate I was quite roundly criticised for writing a text that, in the reading of one contributor, would he taken up by the anti-male feminists, particularly in America, and used to further widen the division between the sexes at a time when we needed texts which could bring us closer together. One point, which I also thought was well made, was that in addition to the value of beginning a discourse about men's hatred for women, we also need texts which address the problem of how to develop a basis for creative heterosexual relationships. For a number of reasons – that I am heterosexual, and because I was not feeling particularly well that evening – I heard myself being quite defensive, saying that there was another book that needed to be written, and that my rather banal thought was that it would probably be about how to preserve love in relationships in a post-modern feminist world. Later, I was thinking about this particular discussion and I realised that my defensiveness was unnecessary. If the discussion occurs again I will make the point that I hold no brief for furthering or promoting heterosexuality, that it seems to be doing quite well on its own – at least in survivalist terms – and that in any case I fail to see why it is assumed that this position can lay claim to the moral high ground. I will make the simple point, which seemingly needs constant repetition, that by all accounts heterosexuality does not seem to be very good for a great many people, not including gays and lesbians. I am not worried if my work is used in the way that some men fear. That is partly its purpose. The charge seems to me to mirror the anxiety of abusive men when they are confronted with the consequences of their behaviour. He, the abusive man, will frequently attack his partner for threatening the relationship if they make too much (for the man that is) of his abusive behaviour by, for example, constantly reminding him of it, going to a refuge or telling family or friends of his abuse. It seems to me to be a plea that women should collude with men's denial of our destructive behaviour towards women. That if only we did not discuss it, somehow it would go away. The point is not that I am against addressing how men can be creative in heterosexual or any relationships but that there is no moral imperative to do so. Sexuality may be natural and innate, but heterosexuality is no more natural than riding a bicycle. I realise that this may sound nihilistic, given that the whole world is organised around heterosexuality, but it is not, or should not be the role of psychotherapists to support social or political institutions. Our role is to question the taken-for-granted world, to deconstruct it and reframe it. We are not agents of the state dedicated to upholding its institutions and routing out deviance, but agents of disorder who should be encouraging a greater measure of tolerance for what we think of as abnormality, particularly in sexuality. It is not that I believe we should act as agents of anarchy, but that if our work is effective it would challenge rigidity in individuals and institutions and extend the boundaries of the normal. I realise that it is easier to say this than to do it because psychotherapy is a meritocracy, and its practitioners, if we wish to be included and successful, are subject to the same social pressures as members of any profession.

Recently, it seems to have become fashionable to opine that men are going through a time of great confusion and doubt about what it means to be a man – a 'crisis of masculinity' as it is being called. I am quite bewildered by this. I do not experience myself as being in a masculine crisis, nor does it seem that men's concerns have changed, at least in the way they have been presented in my consulting room over the last twenty-five years. Interestingly enough, most of this concerned debate is from women, and quite powerful ones at that – women who have probably contributed more to the attempt to deconstruct masculinity than have men. I commented on this to a well known psychologist, looking to discuss it. He laughed. 'What masculinity?' he replied. 'There's no such thing.'

From within the complex discourses that define these things, I know that he is right. However, to the man in the street this is crazy talk. He knows that he is a man and that he is masculine, however fuzzy he is around the edges and whatever his sexual orientation. As we have seen, the elements which go to make up this gender identity are complex, but they certainly have a lot to do with the notion of being different from 'female' and 'femininity'. There is no doubt that the way men think about masculinity has been under critical scrutiny for some time, and from a number of directions. First, feminist discourses about femininity, female subordination and male abusiveness, control and power. Second, the world-wide campaigns for gay rights and, not least, the wholesale restructuring in the Western world of post-industrial economies, which has led to the transfer of many traditionally 'manual' jobs to developing and the establishment of service-based economies offering traditional female occupations. This has certainly led many men to question their attitudes and beliefs about what it means to be a man, and for many men to take on roles inside and outside the home that were previously seen as the exclusive domain of women. But does this add up to a masculinity crisis? It is certainly being talked up, but the evidence is impressionistic, anecdotal and thin. It seems mostly to derive from the anguish of male partners of successful and powerful female journalists. There is no decline in rape, murder of women, battery or domestic abuse, nor has there been any appreciable increase in the average of female earnings in relation to males in the last twenty years. In fact, if we include local wars, more women are being raped and murdered than ever before. If there is a crisis it is that men are being increasingly forced to look for ways of dealing with our frustration which do not include inflicting it upon women. To describe it otherwise would be equivalent to describing a criminal crisis in response to effective policing. My anxiety about the so-called 'masculinity crisis' is that it may he the thin end of the wedge, providing the intellectual and moral framework for a reassertion of traditional masculinity. There are already worrying signs of a backlash against the gains of feminism.

Finally, I would like to add a plea to policy makers and particularly those government departments concerned with criminal policy and the treatment of offenders. It is virtually impossible to raise funding for the treatment of batterers outside the statutory system. This means that many men are denied treatment even when they are motivated to accept it. I believe that the abuser should pay, but often even very low cost treatment is beyond the means of many men who require it. Self-help groups are of little use in the treatment of serious abuse. It requires highly trained clinicians to effectively steer a path between the complex psychodynamics of men who abuse. This requires funding. The issue cannot be ducked. Clearly it is a priority to fund places of safety for women who are being abused and to encourage a rapid and effective policing response that includes the arrest and charging of the worst offenders. However, we should not be misled into thinking that this does anything to deal with the causes of what is an appalling social problem whose sequelae cost the state billions in welfare for victims, and later psychological and behavioural problems for those who witnessed or were subjected to such behaviour in their family of origin. Treatment centres for men should not compete for the same funds. Battering is a crime and funding should come from those agencies whose responsibilities cover criminal behaviour and its treatment. I am convinced that treatment for offenders is cost-effective and, particularly in groups, it can be provided cheaply and relatively quickly providing there is the political will to do so. Treatment, however, is not the final solution. That can only come from a change in the way we construct gender, and that is the outcome of a complex series of interlocking social, economic and political discourses arid practices. There are encouraging signs of such a change, and discouraging signs of a backlash against it.

I do not believe it is time to relax a grip that has been so hard to establish and which still, at least in relation to the themes of this work, is tenuous.

Appendix 1

Violent, abusive and controlling behaviour checklist

We ask you, as part of your contract with the Centre, to check each type of abuse you have used in your regular contact with your partner/victim. Using the procedure detailed in the 'Time Out' document you should maintain a daily diary which analyses your abusive behaviour. If you think that you are not being abusive in any of the ways described below, then you should use your daily diary time to analyse previous episodes of abuse. Although there will not be time to go through your diary entries in the group programme, you will be asked to present it occasionally so that we can help you with the process of understanding your behaviour. It is important to know that this list is not intended to be exhaustive. You may be using other forms of abuse which are not included here. If so, add them to the list and inform the Centre staff. This will help us to help you and increase our effectiveness with other men.

Physical abuse

- Slap, punch, grab, kick, choke, push, restrain, pull hair, pinch, bite, rape, use of force, threats or coercion to obtain sex.
- Use of weapons, throwing things, keeping weapons around which frighten her.
- Abuse of furniture, pets, destroying her possessions, tearing or spoiling her clothing.
- Intimidation, e.g. standing in doorway during arguments, angry or threatening gestures, use of your size to intimidate, standing over her, driving recklessly, uninvited touching, covering her mouth to stop her talking.

Psychological abuse

- Threats of violence, verbal or non-verbal, direct or indirect, self-inflicted injury, e.g. hitting your head on walls or threatening suicide.
- Harassment, e.g. uninvited visits or calls, following her, checking up on her, embarrassing her in public, not leaving when asked.

- Isolation, preventing or making it hard for her to see or talk to friends or relatives and others.
- Making derogatory comments about her friends.
- Yelling, swearing, being coarse, raising your voice, using angry expressions or gestures.
- Claiming the truth, being the authority. Claiming the right to define what is logical, rational, reasonable or fair in the relationship. Calling her stupid or otherwise defining her behaviour as illogical, unreasonable, irrational, etc. Logic chopping, lying, withholding information about your activities, infidelity.

Verbal abuse

- Criticism, name calling, swearing, mocking, put-downs, ridicule, accusations, blaming, humiliating. Angrily waking her up from sleep.
- Interrupting, changing subjects, not listening or responding, picking up the paper when she wants to talk, twisting her words, topic stringing.

Financial abuse

- Economic harassment, getting angry with her about 'where the money goes', not allowing access to money, the car or other resources, sabotaging her attempts to work, believing you are the provider and thinking that she could not survive without you, saying that the money you earn is yours.

Emotional abuse

- Pressure tactics, rushing her to make decisions, to hurry up, walking in front of her, using guilt, sulking, threats of withholding financial support, manipulating the kids.
- Using pornography, including home videos, against her wishes.
- Not helping with childcare or housework, saying that you have already done a day's work. Not keeping to agreements. Abusing your power over the children, either emotionally or physically.
- Feeling stressed and tense and using this to get into a frame of mind when you blame her for everything which goes wrong: things you can't find, mess, etc. This is usually a prelude to a violent attack and you should pay particular attention to this so that you can stop before you reach flashpoint.
- Emotional withholding, not expressing your feelings or giving support, thinking your problems are more important than hers, not giving attention or compliments, not respecting her feelings, rights or opinions.
- Not taking care of yourself and refusing to learn basic life skills, cooking, etc. Abusing drugs, alcohol, not eating properly, not making

friends and seeking help and support from them. Believing you have the right to define appropriate wifely and motherly behaviour and not offering your expectations to negotiation. Criticising her motherly qualities or performance. Accusing her of neglecting the children or using threats of taking the kids away etc.

- Telling her that if she doesn't like it she knows what she can do, pack, leave, etc. Not acknowledging that the relationship is important to you, telling her that you don't need her or love her etc.

Appendix 2
Basic group contract

1   **Confidentiality**   The group is confidential. There are two exceptions to this and it is important that you understand these exceptions when you sign this contract. The first is if the staff think that a group member is in a state of mind where he might be a serious risk to himself or to others. In those circumstances staff will act to protect the group member and his family. The second is that the staff undertake to give any information to the group members' partner which will help her to assess how safe she is. Our programmes are designed to help men to stop from being abusive in order to make women safe. We believe that it is necessary that she has information about her partner's behaviour in the programme in order that she does not have to rely on his assessment of the threat he represents. We are willing to talk with group members' partners at any time we are available, and to offer our opinion of his progress in the programme.

2   **Fees**   All group members must pay for attendance as agreed with the Centre. Fees are payable monthly in advance.

3   **Safety**   During the group, members will be working with some frightening feelings and behaviour. It is essential that feelings are expressed in ways that make group members feels safe. Nobody will be asked to participate in anything which makes them feel unsafe and group members must be prepared to take joint responsibility for this.

4   **Support**   As far as safety outside the group is concerned, all members have made a 'Time Out' contract and are expected to keep to this agreement. Members are not under pressure to give details about themselves to each other but the Centre hopes that you will soon feel safe enough to make safety plans which will include giving each other support in times of crisis.

5   **Withdrawing**   Being a member of a group, particularly for the first time, can be an anxiety provoking experience. There will be times when you will want to stop attending. It is important to understand that a decision to stop attending is the same as deciding to continue abusing your partner. It is important to discuss your anxieties in the group and to understand them rather than simply acting on them. If you feel you

don't want to come, telephone the Centre. If you cannot make a meeting for whatever reason, it is important that you inform someone in the group so that we know you are not breaking your contract to attend. It is impossible to guarantee that completion of the programme will stop you being violent or abusive. We can say, however, that not finishing the programme is more likely to result in your going on being violent and abusive. *Your contract is to finish the programme.*

6   **Control**   During your time in the group we will be looking at your abusive or violent behaviour towards your partner. As you already know from your initial consultation, the Centre believes that violence is only one form of abuse that men use in order to try to frighten women in order to get control of them and force them to meet men's expectations. We will be asking you to look at all the ways you try to coerce your partner to do what you want her to do or to get your own way. One of the main aims of the group is to help you to control yourself in positive ways which do not involve controlling your partner.

CONTRACT BETWEEN .... AND THE MEN'S CENTRE

I agree to end all physical, mental and sexual violence towards my partner

....

This includes verbal and non-verbal threats.

I will not engage in abuse of alcohol or drugs whilst attending the Centre.

I undertake to attend a counselling programme for the treatment of drug or alcohol abuse if the Centre thinks it appropriate.

I will genuinely work, in and out of the group, on ways to stop controlling my partner.

I will honestly report to the group any violent actions, threats of violence, or violent impulses towards my partner or others.

I will keep a diary record of my feelings and behaviour each day and use this to report back to the programme. The diary will concern itself with my feelings, behaviour, beliefs and attitudes, and not those of my partner.

I agree to attend a full programme of at least 24 weeks and to attend for longer if the Centre staff recommend. This will be determined by my progress through the programme and my position on the denial continuum.

I undertake to pay the fees for the programme as agreed with the Centre.

I agree to pass on accurate details of the Centre and its work to my partner.

If the Centre staff believe that my partner is in any possible danger from my behaviour, I agree to their informing my partner without first seeking my permission.

SIGNED.. DATE............................

Appendix 3
The daily diary

How to keep the daily diary

The following contains the information necessary for the effective use of your diary. The diary is one of the tools that we expect you to use all through the programme in order

1   to help you become more aware of your violent behaviour and feelings
2   to develop your ability to understand the intentions and beliefs that support your abusive and controlling behaviour
3   to develop new, alternative and non-violent, non-controlling behaviour which is respectful of your partner

   We recommend that you use your diary regularly, ideally every day or as often as you communicate with your partner (including telephone calls) and you end up having some sort of disagreement or argument, but *especially* every time you

   HAVE THOUGHTS OR FEELINGS TELLING YOU THAT YOU WANT OR ARE ABOUT TO ACT IN A WAY THAT IS CONTROLLING, ABUSIVE OR VIOLENT

or

   YOU DIDN'T STOP YOURSELF AND ACTED VIOLENTLY OR ABU-SIVELY AND ATTEMPTED TO CONTROL HER

In either of these two cases you must then take a 'Time Out' and during that hour you are away use the guidelines which follow to write about *your* behaviour thoughts and feelings in your diary. It is important that you spend time thinking about each of the six points below in order to learn as much as you can about your abusive behaviour and become responsible for it.

1   **My actions**

   a   Describe your behaviour from the beginning of the incident to the
       end. Note your escalations.
       Use the Checklist if you are not sure that what you did was abusive.
       Be specific about what you did. How much force did you use? How
       many times? How loud or threatening were you? Notice how much
       you want to minimise what you really did.
   b   Describe your pattern of abuse.
       Remind yourself of how similar this particular incident is to previ-
       ous incidents when you were abusive. Describe the similarities.

2   **My intentions**

   a   Examine the functions of your abuse.
       Ask yourself: what do I do this violence/abuse for? What service, ad-
       vantage, benefit, attention, deference, obedience, compliance do I
       want from her for my own gratification? Notice how these were your
       intentions from the beginning of the incident and how your abusive
       behaviours were intended to force her into submission.
   b   Connect your intentions with your beliefs.
       What do you believe a wife/partner/mother/lover should have done
       or said instead of what she said or did? What do you think your
       rights are in relation to her? What should she have deferred to in or-
       der to be the kind of wife/lover that you believe she should be?
       Right *now*, what are you convinced you are better at than her, or
       know more about than her?

3   **My feelings**

   a   Think about all the feelings you have had since the beginning of this
       incident (this could be for months about this particular thing).
   b   Link your feelings to your beliefs.
       Here you should connect what you identified as your beliefs in 2b
       with the feelings you have. Write sentences such as: 'I feel…because
       I think she should [act or say]…instead of…[what she does or says].'
         Notice how your feelings follow on from what you believe her
       proper behaviour should be and how your abusive behaviour is the
       means you choose to get what you believe is right and to get her to
       be the way you want.

4   **Denying and minimising**

   a   Identify your method of denial. Minimising what you did (it was
       only a small push, a slap, it only happened once, etc.); not remem-
       bering what you did or said; blaming her or the alcohol or the drugs
       or your insecurity or childhood or difficulties at work, bad temper,

etc., are all ways you can deny the reality and seriousness of your violent or controlling behaviour.

As you reflect on this incident make a note of all the ways you convince yourself that you did not do what you know you did and that you are not abusive.

b   Note down how you use your belief that she is the one with the problem to support your denial that your abusiveness is your problem. As long as you do this you will attempt to coerce her into doing what you want by making her believe that she is not trying hard enough. Also, as long as you continue to deny your abusiveness you will not change.

5   **The effects of your abuse**

a   On your partner.
You will know from what you have heard in the programme that abuse has many short-and long-term effects on women, from depression to helplessness, fear and mistrust. Write down what you think your partner is experiencing as a result of this incident.

b   On you.
You are guilty of a criminal offence. You might feel depressed and guilty. Your abusiveness may cause you to drink or take drugs. You may feel lonely and ashamed of your behaviour. You are probably incapable of giving support or love and tenderness to anyone around you.

c   On your children.

d   On the relationship.
You should by now have realised that it is impossible to hold any sort of conversation or discussion with your partner which is not influenced by her fear and distrust of you caused by your abusiveness. Every moment you spend with her is affected in this way. She is now living with a terrorist.

6   **Identify alternative behaviour**

a   Think back over this incident and ask yourself what you could have done that was non-abusive at every step of your escalation. How could you have shown respect for her?

b   Write sentences beginning with 'It would be better if...' and write what you plan to do next time that will be non-abusive.

c   Make plans that will help you to use one of these alternative behaviours next time you have the experience of perceiving a threat which you want to escalate into a crisis. You should develop a plan which helps you to take responsibility for all your feelings and actions. You are not passive in the experience of emotions; they are things you do to enable you to act in certain ways.

Appendix 4
The Time Out

The most basic alternative to being violent: 'Time Out'

One hour to reflect on your abusive behaviour

The following gives a description of what we mean by 'taking a Time Out'. The Time Out is part of your overall plan to take responsibility for your abusive behaviour and feelings and is a basic but extremely important alternative to your usual violent and abusive behaviour. It is not a long term solution to your problem, but it provides you with a means of self-control rather than controlling your partner, and it may always be a part of your Responsibility Plan.

When to use a Time Out

Time Out is based on a simple fact: when you are not with your partner, you cannot hurt her. You have therefore contracted with the Men's Centre to use Time Out every time you realise you want to have an argument. Typical examples are conflicts you have with her over parenting, money, relatives, friends, sex, who is right and any other disagreement you have or invent and when you recognise your usual

1   bodily signals: finger pointing, closed fists, tension in the stomach/shoulders/neck, raising your voice/shouting, pacing the room, etc.
2   emotional signals: feeling trapped, angry, confused, etc.
3   mental signals: negative thinking about your partner where you tell yourelf that you are right in acting the way you are because she deserves it; where you use degrading names about her like bitch, cunt, whore, etc.; where you distort and twist what she is saying

As soon as you recognise any of these signs or others which are not mentioned but which are familiar to you, do not wait until you get worse; tell your partner, *'I am getting very tense and aggressive and I don't want to be abusive or violent, so I need to take a Time Out'*.

What is a Time Out?

After telling your partner, you calmly leave the home for exactly one hour, not for 50 or 90 minutes. During that time you should be doing the following:

1   Calm yourself down.
    Don't drink alcohol or take any drugs. Don't drive. During this first part of the Time Out, for about 20 minutes, it is your responsibility to calm yourself down, to control your own behaviour, not to think of better ways of controlling your partner's. You might want to do something physical, such as going for a walk or a jog which may reduce the physical build-up of tension. You might want to do something else such as medi-tate or read Men's Centre material about the programme, ring a friend who cares about you and your partner. Whatever you do, make sure it is something which calms you down.

2   Examine your behaviour.
    During the second part of the hour, when you have calmed down, we want you to write down your thoughts about your behaviour, not your partner's. Use the Violent and Controlling Behaviour Checklist to re-mind yourself of what abusive behaviour is and write down what *you* did, thought and said that was intended to control your partner. Think about your beliefs about her and your expectations of her and the rela-tionship, and what you believe you have a right to in this particular incident which you were not getting and which led to your feeling abu-sive. Think about alternatives to your abusive behaviour and what you are going to do when you go back to discuss the issue with your partner without using coercion or threats.

3   Returning home.
    Before you return it is a good idea to phone and let your partner know that you have calmed down and that you will be back at the end of the hour. When you return let her know that you are back. If she wants to discuss the situation with you do so in a non-abusive and non-blaming way. This is the occasion for you to let her know what were your thoughts and feelings about *your* abusive behaviour during your Time Out. This is not so that you can tell her how to change her behaviour to prevent you feeling or being abusive. If during the discussion you begin to feel abusive tell her so and take another Time Out. If your partner doesn't want to talk about it then, ask if there is a time when you can both be available to talk and if she is not prepared to do so, then leave her alone until she suggests she wants to.

Informing your partner about Time Out

It is very important to talk about the Time Out procedure with your partner well ahead of the time you will need to use it, and at a time when you are not feeling abusive or acting abusively. We are aware that Time Out can be used abusively to withdraw from a genuine discussion, instigated by your partner, about her genuine concerns and feelings. However, discuss this document with her when you are calm and when she has agreed to discuss it. If she does not want to do so, do not coerce her or threaten her. Ultimately your abusiveness is your responsibility and even sharing this document with her can be a way of asking her to share some of this. It is important that your partner knows how Time Out works so that she can know if you begin to use it abusively by storming out in the middle of an argument pretending that you are taking a Time Out when all you are doing is discounting her needs and concerns. Do not ask your partner to tell you when you need to take a Time Out. It is your responsibility to know when you are being abusive and to recognise this. Do not tell your partner that she needs to take a Time Out. Time Out is not an excuse to go to the pub or stay out late; these are forms of control and are abusive.

Note

Time Out information adapted from *Men Stopping Violence*, Atlanta (USA) and from B. Hart, *Safety For Women*, PCADV, Harrisburg (USA).

Appendix 5
Information for the partners/wives of violent/abusive men

What is the Men's Centre?

The Men's Centre exists to help men stop their violent behaviour towards their partners. The primary goal of the programme is to help each man accept total responsibility for his violence and to stop it. We believe there is no place for violence in any relationship and that it is never justified. Many of our clients approach us after they have been arrested, or after their partners have left them, threatened to leave, taken out an injunction for non-molestation or started divorce proceedings because of their violent behaviour; some men might be under court orders to attend the programme and others are referred by various professional agencies. All our clients have one thing in common: they are violent, abusive and controlling towards their partners.

What is violence or abuse against women?

We are concerned with all physical and mental abuse to which women are subjected by men with whom they live or have lived; husband, partner, boyfriend, lover, brother, father or other relative. Physical abuse and violence includes rape or any forced or unwanted sex, being hit, punched, kicked, pinched, slapped, having your hair pulled or your throat squeezed, being pushed around, etc. Mental and emotional abuse describes being constantly criticised or humiliated, being told you are useless or stupid or called degrading names, being deprived of your freedom to go out, money, or the right to see friends. Abuse also includes threats of violence such as shouting, banging or breaking objects around you, and any other means of intimidating or controlling behaviour on his part which keeps you too frightened to move or protest.

Who is responsible for the violence?

He is. Always. On every single occasion. You may have heard people say that a woman being battered or abused must provoke it or ask for it in some way. This is not true. Although there may be some disagreement or argument and even if there are shared problems in a relationship, there is never any justification for the attacks. Blaming the woman has been and continues to be a convenient way for the man to avoid responsibility. However much he says he was out of control, he is making a conscious decision to be violent; it follows that he could also choose to behave non-violently and to control his own behaviour instead of controlling you.

Is he emotionally or mentally sick?

No. Many men from all walks of life are abusive and violent towards their partners. Only a tiny percentage suffer from any diagnosable and serious emotional or mental illness.

What about marriage guidance or couples counselling?

It is not a solution if he is still being physically violent towards you. You cannot communicate freely and openly with someone that you are afraid of and a marriage counsellor can never take away that fear so long as the violence continues. By coming to our programme your partner learns that his violence is not a reaction to your actions but rather a response to his feelings and frustrations and, more importantly, it is his attempt to control you.

Do alcohol or drugs make him violent?

No. Some men inflict the worst violence when they lower their inhibitions with drink or drugs, but it is more than likely that they do this in order to be violent. It is not a cause of abuse, but is itself abusive. It makes it easier for them to disclaim responsibility for their behaviour and becomes just another excuse like stress or money problems or a bad childhood or an uncontrollable temper. If your partner abuses drink or drugs then he has two problems for which he must learn to take responsibility. Our programme will help him to see how his drink or drug problem fits into his pattern of violence or abuse but it is important for you to know that even if he does sort out these problems he is not going to stop abusing you unless he also gets help to give up using violence to get his own way.

What if he is sorry?

Many men who abuse their partners are sorry about it afterwards. Some women are willing to forgive and forget at this point, only to be abused again when his guilt evaporates and turns to resentment against her. Men use apologies (and flowers etc.) as further tools to manipulate their partners and to prevent them from leaving. Once he had achieved his goal of making you believe what a nice guy he is and that he will never do it again he is likely to resume his abusiveness and his control over you. It takes more than apologies and promises to end violent and controlling behaviour; he must make a commitment to stop his violence, accept total responsibility for it and take action to fulfil that promise.

Can he change?

Yes, he can but it won't be easy for him. Admitting he needs help and counselling is a big and important step, but it is only the first. After that he will need the motivation and commitment to change his attitudes, beliefs and expectations and learn new ones which help him behave respectfully towards you.

What help is offered at the Men's Centre?

The staff at the centre are there to offer him individual consultations and a counselling group. This group will last for between 24 and 30 weeks, once a week for two hours. Each man has to contract to attend the whole course. Each course is staffed by two trained facilitators whose aim is to help participants to gain insight into their motives and beliefs that underpin and support their abusive and violent behaviour, to challenge their denial, justifications and excuses and to teach them new ways of behaving. Our primary aim is to stop them behaving abusively.

The group programme

Besides the common goal of ending his violent, abusive and controlling behaviour, each man will make particular contracts which reflect some of his own difficulties. Each will have to learn to negotiate his needs with respect for his partner, to communicate differently and to handle disagreements without being controlling or abusive. During each session the men will report on their behaviour during the previous week and share difficulties with each other. They will look at how and why they control and attack their partners, at their assumptions and expectations of women and at how growing up as men has affected their attitudes towards women.

Should I leave if he is violent again?

Maybe you should leave before he is violent again. Your first consideration, and ours, is for your own physical safety and support. His being in our programme is no guarantee that he will change and is not a substitute for using your own judgement about how safe you are.

How do I know if he has changed?

There is no simple answer to this question. Only you can tell based on your own perceptions of your partner and your own sense of safety. However, there are some questions you can ask yourself which might help you decide whether he has changed enough for you to feel safe and secure with him:

- Has he stopped being violent or threatening towards you and others?
- Does he still make you afraid when you are with him?
- Is he able to be angry without being verbally or physically abusive?
- Are you able to be angry with him without his becoming threatening?
- Are you able to make decisions about your own life without fear of being punished?
- Is he able to hear and respect what you are saying even though he may not agree?
- Can he negotiate with you without being attacking or controlling?
- Can he respect your right to say no or to disagree with him?
- Is he able to express feelings other than anger?
- Does he still blame you for his anger, frustrations and violence?
- Has he shown genuine remorse for his past abuse of you?
- Is he able to tolerate your anger about his past abuse without getting defensive or aggressive?

Is there any help available for me?

You may want support from other women who understand your situation and have experienced the same sense of isolation, craziness, self-doubt, despair and depression that you may be feeling, with whom it would be possible to talk without being blamed or judged. It is a good idea to contact these groups even if you do not believe you will need them; remember that you partner's participation in one of our programmes cannot guarantee your safety.

You are also welcome to contact us at any time during the programme, whether to check on something your partner has told you or to find out further information about the service we offer. We would be pleased to hear from you in the strictest confidence. We would not inform your partner you have contacted us unless you tell us to do so.

Note

This guidance was prepared from an original written by Anne Dickson.

Bibliography

Adams, D. 1988a. 'Stages of Anti-sexist Awareness in Change for Abusive Men.' In: L. Dichstein and C. Nadelson (eds) *Family Violence*. Washington DC: Appi Press.

Adams, D. 1988b. 'Treatment Models of Men Who Batter. A pro-feminist Analysis.' In: M. Bograd and K. Yllo (eds) *Feminist Perspectives on Wife Abuse*. Sage.

Allen, C. 1991. *Women and Men Who Sexually Abuse Children: a comparative analysis*. Vermont: The Safer Society Press.

Andrews, D. 1987. 'Normal Violence in Families', *Family Violence Conference*. New York: New Hampshire.

Arbuthnot, J., Gordon, D.A. and Jurkovic, G. 1987. 'Personality.' In: H.C. Quay (ed.) *Handbook of Juvenile Delinquency*. New York: John Wiley.

Archer, J. 1994. *Male Violence*. Routledge.

Archer, J. and Browne, K. 1989. *Human Aggression – Naturalistic Approaches*. Routledge.

Bachman, R. 1994. *Violence Against Women: a National Crime Survey Report*. US Bureau of Justice Statistics.

Baker, A. and Duncan, S.P. 1985. 'Child Sexual Abuse: a study of prevalence in Great Britain'. *Child Abuse and Neglect*, Vol. 9, No. 4: 457–67.

Balint, M. 1967. *The Basic Fault*. London: Tavistock.

Bandura, A. 1973. *Aggression: A Social Learning Analysis*. Englewood Cliffs, NJ: Prentice Hall.

Bandura, A. 1977. *Social Learning Theory*. Englewood Cliffs, NJ: Prentice Hall.

Baron, L., Straus, M.A. and Jaffe, D. 1988. 'Legitimate Violence, Violent Attitudes, and Rape: A Test of Cultural Spillover Theory.' In: R.A. Prentky and V.L. Quinsey (eds) *Human Sexual Aggression: Current Perspectives*. New York Academy of Sciences.

Ben-David, S. 1993. 'Two Facets of Male Violence: the public and the domestic domains', *Journal of Family Violence*, Vol. 8, No. 4: 345–59.

Benjamin, J. 1990. *The Bonds of Love*. Virago.

Benjamin. J. 1995. 'Sameness and Difference: toward an "over-inclusive" theory of gender development.' In: A. Elliott and S. Frosh (eds) *Psychoanalysis in Contexts*. London: Routledge.

Bentovim, A. *et al.* 1984. *Child Sexual Abuse Within the Family*. CIBA Foundation. Tavistock. Routledge.

Berkowitz, L. 1969. 'The Frustration Aggression Hypothesis Revisited.' In: L. Berkowitz (ed.) *Roots of Aggression: A Re-examination of the Frustration Aggression Hypothesis*. New York: Atherton Press.

Berkowitz, L. 1989. 'Frustration Aggression Hypothesis: examination and re-formulation', *Psychological Bulletin*, 106.

Berrein, F. *et al.* 'Child Abuse Prevalence in Russian Urban Population: a preliminary report', *Child Abuse and Neglect*, Vol. 9, No.1: 3–16.

Bion, W. 1961. *Experiences in Groups*. London: Tavistock.

Bograd, M. and Yllo, K. (eds) 1988. *Feminist Perspectives on Wife Abuse*. Sage.

Bolton, F. G. and Bolton, S. R. 1987. *Working With Violent Families*. Sage.

Bowlby, J. 1969. *Attachment and Loss. Vol. 1 Attachment*. London: Hogarth Press.

Bowlby, J. 1973. *Attachment and Loss. Vol. 2. Separation: Anxiety and Anger*. London: Hogarth Press.

Bowlby, J. 1980. *Attachment and Loss. Vol. 3. Loss, Sadness and Depression*. London: Hogarth Press.

Bowlby, J. 1988. *A Secure Base*. Routledge.

Briggs, C.M. and Cutright, P. 1994. 'Structural and cultural determinants of child homicide: a cross-national analysis', *Violence and Victims*, Vol. 9, No. 1: 3–16.

British Crime Survey. 1992. London: HMSO.

Brown, P. and van der Hart, O. 1992. 'Abreaction Re-evaluated', *Dissociation*, Vol. V, No. 3

Buchelle, B. 1995. *International Journal of Group Psychotherapy*, 275–85.

Cathie, S. 1987. 'What Does it Mean to be a Man?', *Free Associations*, Vol. 8.

Chasseguet-Smirgel, J. 1976. 'Freud and Female Sexuality', *International Journal of Psychoanalysis*, 57.

Chodorow, N. 1977. *The Reproduction of Mothering*. University of California Press, Berkeley.

Clecky, H. 1964. *The Mask of Sanity*. St. Louis, MO: C.V. Mosby.

Cockburn, J. 1990. *Sexual Abuse*. Quoted in Monograph. Birmingham: Gracewell Clinic.

Coleman, V. 1994. 'Lesbian battering: the relationship between personality and the perpetration of violence', *Violence and Victims*, Vol. 9, No. 2: 139–52.

Colrain, J. and Steele, K. 1991. 'Treatment protocols for spontaneous abreactive memory work'. Paper presented at 3rd International Conference on Multiple Personality Changes. In: P. Brown and O. van der Hart, 1992, 'Abreaction Re-evaluated', *Dissociation*, Vol. V, No. 3.

Creighton, S. and Russell, N. 1995. *Voices From Childhood*. London: NSPCC.

Criminal Statistics 1993. *England and Wales Supplementary Tables. Vol. 2. Proceedings in the Crown Court*. London. Govt. Statistical Service.

Criminal Statistics 1994. *England and Wales*. London: HMSO.

Criminal Statistics 1994. *England and Wales Supplementary Tables. Vol. 1. Proceedings in the Magistrates Court*. London: Govt. Statistical Service.

Daly, K. 1994. *Gender Crime and Punishment*. New Haven: Yale University Press.

De Paul, J., Milner, J. and Mugica, P. 1994. 'Childhood Maltreatment, Childhood Social Support and Child Abuse in a Basque Sample', *Child Abuse and Neglect*, Vol. 19, No. 8:907–20.

Dickstein, L. and Nadelson, C. (eds) 1989. *Family Violence: Emerging Issues of National Crisis*. Washington: American Psychiatric Press.

Dinnerstein, D. 1976. *The Mermaid and the Minotaur*. New York: Harper and Row.

Dobash, E. and Dobash, R. 1980. *Violence Against Wives: A Case Against the Patriarchy*. Open Books.

Dobash, R., Dobash E., Wilson, M. and Daly, M. 1992. 'The Myth of Sexual

Symmetry in Marital Violence', *Social Problems*, Vol. 39, No. 1: 71–91.

Dodge, K.A. 1980. 'Social Cognition and Children's Aggressive Behaviour', *Child Development*, 51: 162–70.

Dodge, K.A. 1991. 'The Structure and Function of Reactive and Proactive Aggression', In: D.J. Pepler and K. Rubin (eds) *The Development and Treatment of Childhood Aggression*. Hillsdale, NJ: Lawrence Erlbaum.

Dodge, K.A., Bates, J.E. and Pettit, G.S. 1990. 'Mechanisms in the Cycle of Violence', *Science*, 250: 1678–83.

Dutton, D.G. and Starzomski, A.L. 1994. 'Psychological Differences Between Court Referred and Self-referred Wife Assaulters', *Criminal Justice and Behaviour*, Vol. 21, No. 2, June.

Edwards, S. 1984. *Women on Trial*. University of Manchester Press.

Egeland, B. and Sroufe, L.A. 1981. 'Attachment and Early Maltreatment', *Child Development*, 52.

Eron, L.D. 1987. 'The Development of Aggressive Behaviour from the Perspective of a Developing Behaviourism', *American Psychologist*, 42.

Fairbairn, W.R.D. 1952. *Psychoanalytic Studies of the Personality*. London: Tavistock.

Farrington, D.P. 1991. 'Childhood Aggression or Adult Violence: early precursors and later life outcomes.' In: D.J. Pepler and K. Rubin (eds) *The Development and Treatment of Childhood Aggression*. Hillsdale, NJ: Lawrence Erlbaum.

Finkelhor, D. 1986. *A Sourcebook on Child Sexual Abuse*. Beverly Hills: Sage.

Foulkes, S.H. 1964. *Therapeutic Group Analysis*. George Allen and Unwin.

Foulkes, S.H. 1975. *Group Analytic Psychotherapy Methods and Principles*. Gordon and Breach.

Foulkes, S.H. and Anthony, E.J. 1984. *Group Psychotherapy. The Psychoanalytic Approach*. Maresfield Library Karnac.

Freud, S. 1893. *Studies on Hysteria*. SE. II.

Freud, S. 1914. *On Narcissism: An Introduction. S.E. 14 of The Complete Works*. London: Hogarth Press.

Freud, S. 1917. *Mourning and Melancholia. S.E. 14 of The Complete Works*. pp. 237–58 London: Hogarth Press.

Freud, S. 1920. *Beyond The Pleasure Principle. S.E. 18 of The Complete Works*. London: Hogarth Press.

Freud, S. 1926. *Inhibitions Symptoms and Anxiety. S.E. 20 of The Complete Works*. London: Hogarth Press.

Freud, S. 1930. *Civilisation and its Discontents. S.E. 21 of The Complete Works*. London: Hogarth Press.

Freud, S. 1937. *Analysis Terminable and Interminable. S.E. 23 of The Complete Works*. London: Hogarth Press.

Frosh, S. 1994. *Sexual Difference. Masculinity and Psychoanalysis*. Routledge

Gayford, J.J. 1975. 'Wife Battering: a preliminary study of 100 cases', *British Medical Journal*, 1 (5951).

Gelles, R.J. 1974. *The Violent Home: A Study of Physical Aggression Between Husbands and Wives*. Beverly Hills: Sage.

Gelles, R.J. 1982. 'Applying Research on Family Violence to Clinical Practice', *Journal of Marriage and Family*, 44:(1), 9–20.

Gelles, R.J. and Lancaster, J.B. 1987. *Child Abuse and Neglect: Biosocial Dimensions*. New York: Aldine De Gruyter.

Gillam, B. 1994. *The Facts about Child Abuse*. London: Cassell.

Glasser, M. 1982. *Working With Violent Patients at the Portman Clinic*, Harvest 28.

Goode, W.J. 1971. 'Force and Violence in the Family', *Journal of Marriage and the Family*, 33: 624–36.

Gottman, J. 1979. *Marital Interaction: Empirical Instigations*. San Diego, CA: Academic Press.

Gottman, J. and Krokoff, L.J. 1989. 'Marital Interaction and Satisfaction: a longitudinal view', *Journal of Consulting and Clinical Psychology*, 57: 47–52.

Greenson, R.R. 1968. 'Disidentifying From Mother: Its Special Importance for the Boy.' In: *Explorations in Psychoanalysis*. 1978. IUP.

Guntrip, H. 1973. 'Personality Structure and Human Interaction', *International Psychoanalytic Library*, No. 56. London: The Hogarth Press.

Hanmer, J. 1978. 'Violence and the Social Control of Women'. In: Littlejohn *et al*. *Power and the State*. London: Croom Helm.

Hanmer, J. and Maynard, M. (eds) 1987. *Women Violence and Social Control*. Macmillan.

Herman, J. 1981. *Father/Daughter Incest*. London: Harvard University Press.

Hoffman, K., Demo, D. and Edwards J. 1994. 'Physical Wife Abuse in a Non-western Society: an integrated theoretical approach', *Journal of Marriage and the Family*, Vol. 56, No. 1: 131–46.

Hopper, E. 1991. 'The Encapsulated Psychosis', *International Journal of Psycho-analysis*, 72.

Hopper, E. 1998. *A Fourth Basic Assumption*. Foulkes Annual Lecture. The Institute of Group Analysis.

Horder, J. 1992. *The Guardian*, 29 July.

Horley, S. 1991. *The Charm Syndrome*. Macmillan.

Horsfall, J. 1994. *The Presence of the Past*. Allen and Unwin.

Irigaray, L. 1985. *This Sex Which Is Not One*. New York: Cornell.

Island, D. and Letellier, P. 1991. *Men Who Beat Men Who Love Them. Battered gay men and domestic violence*. New York: Harrington Park Press.

Jason, J. *et al*. 1982. 'Epidemiological Differences between Sexual and Physical Child Abuse', *Journal of the American Medical Association*. In: B. Gillham, *The Facts About Child Abuse*. London: Cassell.

Jeffreys, S. 1990. *Anticlimax*. The Women's Press.

Jones, E. 1927. 'The Early Development of Female Sexuality'. In: *Papers on Psycho-analysis. 1977*. Maresfield Reprints.

Jukes, A. 1993a. *Why Men Hate Women*. Free Association Books.

Jukes, A. 1993b. *Violence, Helplessness, Vulnerability and Male Sexuality*. Free Associations 29.

Jukes, A. 1994. *Working With Men Who are Helpless, Vulnerable and Violent*. Free Associations 31.

Kalmuss, D. 1984. 'The Intergenerational Transmission of Marital Aggression', *Journal of Marriage and the Family*, 47: 11–19.

Kaplan, A. G. 1988. 'How Normal is Normal Development? Some connections between adult development and the roots of abuse and victimisation'. In: M. B. Straus (ed.) *Abuse and Victimisation across the Life Span*. Baltimore, London: The Johns Hopkins University Press.

Kelly, E., Regan, L. and Burton, S. 1991. 'An Exploratory Study of Sexual Abuse in a Sample of 16–21 year olds'. Polytechnic of North London, Child Abuse Studies Unit.

Kelly, L. 1988. *The Continuum of Male Violence*. In: Hanmer and Maynard, 1987.

Kelly, L. 1989. *Surviving Sexual Violence*. Cambridge. Polity.

Kernberg, O. 1986. 'Factors in the Treatment of Narcissistic Personalities'. In: A Morrison (ed.) *Essential Papers on Narcissism*. New York: N.Y.U. Press.

Klein, M. 1975. *Envy and Gratitude and Other Works, 1946–1963*. Hogarth Press and Institute of Psychoanalysis.

Kreeger, L. 1989. 'Introductory Course in Group Analysis', Unpublished Paper. The Institute of Group Analysis.

Kristeva, J. 1979. 'Women's Time'. In: T. Moi, 1986, *The Kristeva Reader*. Oxford: Blackwell Publishers.

Kruttschnitt, C. 1993. 'Violence By and Against Women; a comparative and cross-national analysis', *Violence and Victims*, Vol. 8, No. 3: 253–70.

Lacan, J. 1964. 'Guiding Remarks for a Congress on Feminine Sexuality.' In: J. Mitchell and J. Rose (eds) 1982 *Feminine Sexuality*. London: Macmillan.

Laplanche, J. and Pontalis, J.-B. 1980. 'The Language of Psycho-Analysis', *International Psychoanalytical Library*, No. 94. London: The Hogarth Press and the Institute of Psychoanalysis.

Lorenz, K. 1966. *On Aggression*. Methuen.

McGibbon, A., Kelly, L. and Cooper, L. 1989. *What Support?* Pamphlet pub. by Hammersmith and Fulham Council and Polytechnic of North London.

Macguire, M. 1994. *Passion, Power and Psychotherapy*. Routledge.

Main, M. and Solomon, J. 1986. 'Discovery of a New Insecure-disorganised-disoriented Attachment Pattern.' In: T. B. Brazelton and M. Yogman (eds) *Affective Development in Infancy*. Norwood: Ablex.

Main, M. and Solomon, J. 1990. 'Procedures for Identifying Infants as Disorganised-disoriented during the Ainsworth Strange Situation.' In: M. Greenberg, D. Cicchetti and E.M. Cummings (eds) *Attachment in the Pre-school Years. Theory, Research and Intervention*. Chicago University Press.

Main, M., Tomasini, L. and Tolan, W. 1979. 'Differences Among Mothers of Infants Judged to Differ in Security', *Developmental Psychology*, 15.

Malan, D. 1979. *Individual Psychotherapy and the Science of Psychodynamics*. Butterworth Heinemann.

Markman, H., Stanley, S. and Blumberg, S.L. 1994. *Fighting for Your Marriage*. San Francisco, CA: Jossey-Bass.

Marrone, M. 1998. *Attachment and Interaction*. London: JKP.

Marshall, L. 1992. 'The Severity of Violence Against Men Scales', *Journal of Family Violence*, Vol. 7, No. 3: 189–203.

Mayhew, P., Maung, A. N. and Mirrlees-Black, C. 1993. *The 1992 British Crime Survey: A Home Office Research and Planning Unit Report*. London: HMSO.

Miller, A. 1991. *For Your Own Good: The Roots of Violence in Child Rearing*. Virago.

Mitchell, J. 1986. 'The Question of Femininity and the Theory of Psychoanalysis.' In: G. Kohon (ed.) *The British School of Psychoanalysis: The Independent Tradition*. Free Association Books.

Mitchell, J. and Rose, J. 1982. *Feminine Sexuality: Jacques Lacan and the Ecole Freudienne*. Macmillan.

Moberley, E. 1987. *Psychogenesis*. London: Tavistock.

Monohan, J. and Steadman, J.J. 1983. 'Crime and Mental Disorder: An Epidemiological Approach.' In: N. Morris and M. H. Tonry (eds) *Crime and Justice: An Annual Review of Research*. University of Chicago Press.

Mooney, J. 1993. *The Hidden Figure. Domestic Violence in North London.* Middlesex University Centre for Criminology, Islington Council.

Morton, T. 1987. 'Childhood Aggression in the Context of Family Interaction.' In: D.H. Crowell, I.M. Evans and C.R. O'Connell (eds) *Childhood Aggression and Violence: Sources of Influence, Prevention and Control.* New York: Plenum Press.

Ndiaye, B.W. and Rodley, N. 1994. *International Human Rights Monitor*, Vol. 11, Nos. 2–3.

New York State Office for Prevention of Domestic Violence. 1993. *Domestic Violence Data Sheet*, August. Albany.

Pagelow, M.D. 1984. 'Factors Affecting Women's Decisions to Leave Violent Relationships', *Journal of Family Issues*, 2: 397–41.

Parkes, C.M. 1986. *Bereavement: Studies of Grief in Adult Life.* London: Tavistock.

Patterson, G.R. 1982. *Coercive Family Process.* Eugene, OR: Castalia Press.

Patterson, G.R. and Dishion, T.J. 1985. 'Contributions of Family and Peers to Delinquency', *Criminology*, 23.

Patterson, G.R., DeBaryshe, B.D. and Ramsey, E. 1989. 'A Developmental Perspective on Antisocial Behaviour', *American Psychologist*, 44.

Patterson, G.R. Capaldi, D. and Bank, L. 1991. 'An Early Starter Model for Predicting Delinquency.' In: D. J. Pepler and K. Rubin (eds) *The Development and Treatment of Childhood Aggression.* Hillsdale, NJ: Lawrence Erlbaum.

Perelberg, R.J. and Miller, A.C. (eds) 1991. *Gender and Power in Families.* London: Routledge.

Peterson, J.A. 1991. 'Hypnotic Techniques Recommended to Assist in Associating the Dissociation: Abreaction.' In: P. Brown and O. van der Hart, 1992, 'Abreaction Re-evaluated', *Dissociation*, Vol. V, No. 3.

Ptachek, J. 1985. 'Wifebeaters' Accounts of Their Violence: Loss of Control as Excuse and as Subjective Experience', Unpublished M.A. Thesis. University of New Hampshire.

Redl, F. and Toch, H. 1979. 'The Psychoanalytic Perspective.' In: H. Toch (ed.) *Psychology of Crime and Criminal Justice*, New York: Holt Rinehart and Winston.

Redl, F. and Wineman, D. 1951. *Children Who Hate. The Disorganisation and Breakdown of Behaviour Controls.* New York: The Free Press.

Redl, F. and Wineman, D. 1952. *Controls From Within: Techniques for the Treatment of the Aggressive Child.* New York: The Free Press.

Reid, W.H. 1981. 'The Antisocial Personality and Related Syndromes.' In: J.R. Lion (ed.) *Personality Disorders: Diagnosis and Management.* Baltimore: Williams and Wilkins.

Renvoise, J. 1978. *The Web of Violence. A Study of Family Violence.* Penguin.

Rich, A. 1980. 'Compulsory Heterosexuality and Lesbian Existence', *Signs*, 5 (4).

Rosen, R.D. 1977. *Psychobabble.* Wildwood House.

Roy, M. (ed.) 1977. *Battered Women: A Psychological Study of Domestic Violence.* New York: Van Nostrand Reinhold.

Russell, D. 1982. *Rape in Marriage.* New York: Macmillan.

Russell, D. 1986. *Secret Trauma: Incest in the Lives of Girls and Women.* New York: Basic Books.

Saraga, E. and Macleod, M. 1990. 'Challenging the Orthodoxy. Towards a Feminist Theory and Practice', *Feminist Review*, Vol. 28.

Schafer, R. 1976. *A New Language for Psychoanalysis.* New Haven: Yale University Press.

Schecter, S. 1982. *Women and Male Violence. The Visions and Struggles of the Battered Women's Movement.* Boston, MA: South End Press.

Schiff, J. 1976. *All My Children.* New York: Basic Books.

Schlapobersky, J. and Nathan, G. 1995. 'Couples Groups'. Monograph. The Institute of Group Analysis.

Scott, A. 1988. 'Feminism and the Seductiveness of the The Real Event', *Feminist Review*, 28.

Scott, M.B. and Lyman, S.M. 1968. 'Accounts', *American Sociological Review*, 33 (1).

Segal, L. 1987. *Is the Future Female?* Virago.

Segal, L. 1990. *Slow Motion: Changing Masculinities, Changing Men.* Virago.

Segal, U. 1995. 'Child Abuse by the Middle Class? A Study of Professionals in India', *Child Abuse and Neglect*, Vol. 19, No. 2: 217–31.

Seidler, V. 1994. *Unreasonable Men.* Routledge.

So Kim Tang, C. 1994. 'Prevalence of Spouse Aggression in Hong Kong', *Journal of Family Violence*, Vol. 9, No. 4. 347–56.

Stark, E. and Flitcraft, A. 1988a. 'Violence Among Intimates: An Epidemiological Review.' In: Haslett *et al. Handbook on Family Violence.* New York: Plenum Press.

Stark, E. and Flitcraft, A. 1988b. 'Women and Children at Risk: a feminist perspective on child abuse', *International Journal of Health Services*, Vol. 18, pp. 197–208.

Stoller, R.J. 1968. *Sex and Gender. The Development of Masculinity and Femininity.* Maresfield Reprints [1984].

Stoller, R.J. 1986. *Sexual Excitement: Dynamics of Erotic Life.* Maresfield Reprints.

Storr, A. 1968. *Human Aggression.* Harmondsworth: Penguin.

Straus, M.B. 1991. 'Discipline and Deviance: physical punishment of children and violence and other crime in adulthood', *Social Problems*, 38.

Straus, M. and Gelles, R. 1990. *Physical Violence in American Families: Risk Factors and Adaptations to Violence in 8,145 Families.* New Brunswick: Transaction Publishers.

Taylor, S. P. and Leonard, K. E. 1989. 'Alcohol and Physical Aggression.' In: G. G. Russell and E. I. Donnerstein, *Aggression: Theoretical and Empirical Reviews* Vol. 2. New York: Academic Press.

Toch, H. 1969. *Violent Men.* Chicago: Aldine.

Tomlin, C. 1974. *The Life and Death of Mary Wollstonecraft.* London: Weidenfeld and Nicolson.

United Nations. 1982. *Women: A World Report.* New York: United Nations.

Walker, L.E. 1978. 'Battered Women and Learned Helplessness', *Victimology*, 2: 525–34.

Walker, L.E. 1979. *The Battered Woman.* New York: Harper Colophon.

Weiss, B., Dodge, K.A., Bates, J.E. and Pettit, G.S. 1992. 'Some Consequences of Early Harsh Discipline: aggressiveness and a maladaptive social information processing style', *Child Development*, 63: 1321–35.

Welldon, E. 1993. *Mother Madonna Whore.* Free Association Books.

Whitehead, A. 1976. 'Sexual antagonism in Hertfordshire'. In: D. Leonard Barker and S. Allen (eds) *Dependence and Exploitation in Work and Marriage.* London: Longman.

Wilson, E. 1983. *What Is To Be Done About Male Violence Towards Women?* Harmondsworth: Penguin.

Wilson, M. and Daly, M. 1992. 'Who Kills in Spouse Killings? On the exceptional sex ratio of spousal homicides in the United States', *Criminology*, No. 30: 189–215.

Wilson, M. and Daly, M. 1993a. 'An Evolutionary psychological perspective on male sexual proprietariness and violence', *Violence and Victims*, Vol. 8, No. 3: 271–94.

Wilson, M. and Daly, M. 1993b. 'Spousal Homicide and Estrangement', *Violence and Victims*, Vol. 8, No. 1: 3–16.

Winnicott. D.W. 1965. *The Maturational Processes and the Facilitating Environment.* Hogarth Press and The Institute of Psychoanalysis.

Winnicott, D.W. 1969. 'The Use of an Object', *International Journal of Psychoanalysis*, 50: 711–16.

Wolfers, O. 1992. 'Same Abuse, Different Parent', *Social Work Today*, Vol. 23, No. 26. 13–14.

Wollstonecraft, M. 1792. *A Vindication of The Rights of Women.* Harmondsworth: Penguin [1975].

Wyre, R. 1988a. *Men, Women and Rape.* Oxford: Perry.

Wyre, R. 1988b. *Working With Sexual Abuse.* Oxford: Perry.

Wyre, R. 1989. *A Handbook for Working with Sexual Abusers.* Gracewell Clinic.

Yalom, E. 1985. *The Theory and Practice of Group Psychotherapy.* New York: Basic Books. Adapted by Lionel Kreeger, 1989.

Yoshihama, A. and Sorenson, S. 1994. 'Physical, Sexual, and Emotional Abuse by Male Intimates: experiences of women in Japan', *Violence and Victims*, Vol. 9, No. 1. 63–77.

Zulueta, F. De 1993. *From Pain To Violence. The Traumatic Roots of Destructiveness.* London: Whurr.

Index